*Jay Miller*

# Tsimshian Culture:
# A Light through the Ages

University of Nebraska Press
Lincoln and London

∞

First Bison Books printing: 2000
Most recent printing indicated
by the last digit below:
10  9  8  7  6  5  4  3  2  1
Library of Congress
Cataloging-in-
Publication Data
Miller, Jay, 1947–
Tsimshian culture: a
light through the
ages / Jay Miller.
p.   cm. Includes
bibliographical
references and index.
ISBN 0-8032-3192-X
(cl.: alk. paper)
ISBN 0-8032-8266-4
(pa.: alk. paper)
1. Tsimshian Indians.   I. Title.
E99.T8M55   1997
970.004'974 — dc20
96-35895
CIP

To Hartley Bay School
the Memory of
Daphne (Clifton) Robinson Anderson
and the Tsimshian
Past, Present, Future, Eternal

# Contents

# Illustrations

# Preface

For over two decades I have been trying to understand the intricacies of the Tsimshian, one of the most fascinating nations of Native America. This book is the result. It should have been written eight years ago, but I was lost for too long in a bureaucratic maze.

Now, with more time for reflection, the result is much more comprehensive than I had initially intended, hopefully to the better. While details of this remarkable culture have had to be segmented to study some of its facets, the ultimate goal was to present a sense of the elegance, integrity, and beauty which was and is Tsimshian culture.

From the outset, I must make clear that, throughout this book, "Tsimshian" is used as an all-encompassing term for the four divisions: Coast, Southern, Gitksan, and Nishga. Currently, this is an unpopular conjoining in the very real political world of modern northern British Columbia. Nonetheless, shared region and culture, which is my goal, takes precedence over the emphasis on differences which characterize present relations among these First Nations. In addition to their common homeland at Temlaxham, the modalities of the culture, to be fully understood, must be examined in terms of the various expressions found among these four groupings. As Norman Tait, famous Nisga'a artist, has remarked for the art, "I use the label 'Tsimshian' to describe the style that I wanted to learn about because it included all three—Tsimshian, Gitksan and Nisga'a—in one category" (Jensen 1992:9). Since the Southern

Tsimshian were until recently included with the Coast, Tait's statement nicely encompasses all.

Indeed, while my intention is to present an overview of Tsimshian culture in space and time, my personal experience relates most strongly to the Southern Tsimshian, particularly at Hartley Bay and, to a lesser extent, at Klemtu. My bias, therefore, is toward communities with stronger links to the spiritually powerful peoples to the south.

Many people have helped me to understand the complexities of Tsimshian culture. In particular, at Hartley Bay, these were Chief John and Helen Clifton; Ernest, Lynne, Cameron, and Jodie Hill; Ernest and Margie Hill Sr.; and Mildred Wilson. At Klemtu, my teachers were Violet and the late Peter Neasloss, Chief Tom Brown, and others.

One of the joys of working with Tsimshian has been the quality of one's colleagues, in particular John and Luceen Dunn, Susan Marsden, Marjorie Halpin, Margaret Seguin, Carol Sheehan, Bill Holm, Robin Wright, Viola Garfield, Amelia Susman Schultz, Jonathan Dean, Pamela Amoss, Jean Mulder, Marie-Lucie Tarpent, Bruce Rigsby, Dale Kinkade, Jay Powell, Vickie Jensen, Guy Gibeau, Vi and Don Hilbert, Chris Roth, and Stanley Newman.

Within my own family, I thank Marilyn Richen, Ann Schuh, Bob and Christine Keyes-Back, Tom and Donna Steinburn, Nancy Griffin, Louise Long, and, especially, Monday Night.

An initial draft of this manuscript benefited from my use of it as the text for the Simon Fraser University Native Language Teacher Program in Prince Rupert early in 1993. Among my students, these especially have my gratitude for clarifying and expanding my thinking: Cameron and Eva-Ann Hill, Nadine Robinson, Mel Tait, Maureen Yeltatzie, Beatrice Skog, Isabelle Hill, Pansy Collison, Deborah Schmakeit, Marilyn Bryant, Karla Gamble, and Shani Heal. Mary Tomlinson, Mercedes de la Nuez, and Thomas Perry helped me smooth out complications with Canadian bureaucracy.

# Orthography

Like other languages of the Pacific Northwest, Tsimshianic has a complex series of sounds that are written in a practical orthography developed by John Dunn (1978, 1979a, 1995) and taught in native schools.

In Tsimshianic, the vowels, pronounced short or long, are *a, e, i, o, u;* and the consonants, sometimes further specialized, are *b, d, dz, g, h, k, l, ł, m, n, p, s, t, ts, w, x, y.*

The sound of *s* can be said as either "s" or "sh"; *dz* is like that in the English word "adze"; *ts* is like that at the end of "hats"; and *ł* (called "barred *l*") is like the middle of "clay" or the Welsh name "Llewellyn," said out of the sides of the lips with the tip of the tongue against the front of the roof of the mouth. Gitksan write this last sound as *hl.*

The specialized consonants are:

'    called glottalized because the throat gate is closed to say these sounds, such as *k', p', t',* and *ts'*. As a distinct sound, it is the pause in the middle of "uh'oh." Sometimes written as ʔ, Tlingits spell it as "." using a period.

_    underlined to indicate a sound is pronounced further back in the throat, such as *g* (called "back *g*"), or *k̲* (called "back *k*" or "*q*"). Interior and Southern Tsimshianic have more of these backed sounds.

¨    doubled-dotted to indicate a sound is pronounced with the lips unrounded, such as *ü* (called "double-dotted *u*"), or *ẅ* (called "doubled-dotted *w*").

By convention, beings who served as crest and spirit animals have capitalized names, while the ordinary species do not. Thus, Orca Blackfish, Eagle, and Raven refer to supernaturals, while orca killer whale, eagle, and raven are the animals themselves.

At the end of 1996 intertribal agreements-in-principle standardized many spellings of Tsimshianic words, too late to be incorporated in this text. The most current spellings do appear in the index: *halaayt* (rather than *halait*), *kluusms* (*klusms*), *spaksuut* (*spaksut*), and *p'teex* (*ptex*).

*Tsimshian Culture*

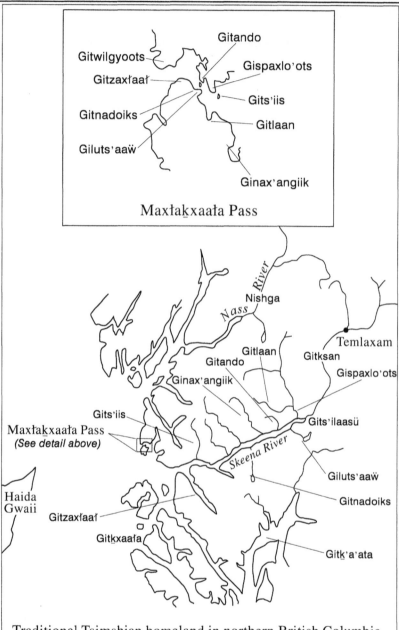

**Maxłakxaała Pass**

Inset labels: Gitwilgyoots, Gitando, Gispaxlo'ots, Gitzaxłaał, Gits'iis, Gitnadoiks, Gitlaan, Giluts'aaẅ, Ginax'angiik

Main map labels: Nass River, Nishga, Temlaxam, Gitlaan, Gitando, Gitksan, Gispaxlo'ots, Ginax'angiik, Gits'iis, Gits'ilaasü, Maxłakxaała Pass (See detail above), Skeena River, Giluts'aaẅ, Haida Gwaii, Gitnadoiks, Gitzaxłaał, Gitkxaała, Gitk'a'ata

**Traditional Tsimshian homeland in northern British Columbia.**

Main map shows location of summer economic homelands along tributaries of the Skeena River, and the inset shows their winter locations along Maxłakxaała ("saltwater passage"). The Gitwilgyoots shared their homeland, the southern end of the Tsimshian Peninsula, with other tribes from the northern side of the Skeena, while tribes from the south branches wintered on Digby Island.

# Introduction

Because Tsimshian culture appeals both to the intellect and the senses, it has been difficult to sort out its various expressive branches. For thousands of years this nation has remained a vital and regional force on the north Pacific coast, yet prior considerations of its genius have been too fragmented, disjointed, and piecemeal to provide a full appreciation of its wholeness. By dividing the culture into topics like technology, economics, polity, kinship, religion, and language, Tsimshian integrity has been lost to scholarship, though not to the people themselves. Further, by looking only at one aspect—such as the potlatch, ecology, or historical change—the vitality of this on-going system has been rendered lifeless. Of course, all of these topics, and more, will be presented in the following pages, yet my ultimate intent is to show them existing as facets of an overall culture, a system providing order and meaning of and for the Tsimshian.

Strange circumstances led me to the Tsimshian. As an undergraduate at the University of New Mexico, Bruce Rigsby often lectured about his fieldwork on the Gitksan language, which, with Nishga, comprises the interior speech community of Tsimshianic. My friends John and Luceen Dunn, then graduate students, spent a year living on the coast, and John's dissertation was concerned with theoretical aspects of the phonology of Coast Tsimshian. John taught me in particular about details of grammar, texts, and kinship, revealing the fourfold crest division as a set of semi-moieties. This advance in our understanding of Tsimshian culture allowed more meaningful comparison with their neighbors.

*Moiety* means "half" and both Tlingit and Haida divide their worlds into moieties. The Tsimshian have four major crests—Blackfish (Killerwhale, Orca), Raven, Eagle, and Wolf—which once seemed to belong to a different scheme of organization. Now, however, scholars recognize that each aboriginal Tsimshian town actually had moieties, often Blackfish-Wolf and Raven-Eagle, but later relocations to European outposts obscured this arrangement.

John Dunn's more recent works, including his grammar (1979a), dictionary (1978), and poetic translations continue to provide basic information for both natives and scholars interested in Tsimshian traditions.

Of the hundreds of Tsimshian texts in print or manuscript, a few of the most significant for understanding the culture have been included in this volume because they continue to be used to express the vitality of this lifeway. Again and again, when a detail is under discussion, elders recount a saga to explain why things are so or how they got to be as they are. While the texts may not be exactly as a Tsimshian would know them, because linguistic and geographical features, at native request, often are deleted, an epic is presented to amplify the previous discussion of some aspect of the society or culture.[1]

After I had finished my own dissertation on the Pueblos, I taught at the University of Washington, where I met Viola Garfield and Amelia Susman—both of whom had studied with Franz Boas, the founder of Northwest Coast studies, worked with William Beynon, native scholar and Gitlaan Wolf chief at Port Simpson (cf. Halpin 1978), and delved deeply into Tsimshian society and language.

Viola Garfield had taught fourth grade at New Metlakatla to earn money for her own college expenses and became curious about the Tsimshian kinship system of matrilineality, that is, descent through mothers with leadership passing from mother's brother to sister's son (maternal uncle to nephew). Crests (inherited art forms), houses, and moieties were all traced through the mother among the Tsimshians, Haidas, and Tlingits. As with Lewis Henry Morgan, whose fascination with Iroquois matrilineality led him to become "father" of kinship studies, Garfield became an anthropologist. In particular, she contributed to our understanding of the economic importance of slavery and the political changes whereby the Coast Tsimshian developed a class of royalty and a high chief.

Claude Lévi-Strauss was all the rage in the 1970s. He had gained considerable attention for his analysis of the logic of mythology (mytho-logic) by concentrating on versions of the sacred history (*adawx*) of Asdiwal. While Tsimshian have said that Lévi-Strauss's analysis was "too complicated," it served to regenerate an interest in Tsimshian research among a new group of scholars, both natives and others.

Having read the interpretations of Lévi-Strauss and his critics, and the primary data of Marius Barbeau (largely provided by William Beynon), Boas, and Garfield, I was ready to undertake my own research. Through the efforts of John Dunn, I was invited to join him on a visit to Hartley Bay, where I was made most welcome.[2] My initial interest, growing out of my research among the Delaware and other tribes in Oklahoma (Miller 1979), was in the interrelations of language and culture, particularly in terms of symbol systems.

During that trip John continued his pursuit of a fourth Tsimshian language and was rewarded by working with a speaker of what has come to be called "Southern Tsimshian." In quest of ethnographic details about its context, I visited Klemtu for several weeks and learned about the relations between the Tsimshian and the Wakashan to the south, along with the bicultural borders of the Tsimshian homeland. Since both Xaixais (Haihais, Northern Kwakiutlan Wakashans) and Tsimshianic-speaking Gitisu live in Klemtu, I got a sense of the cultural dynamics that have characterized the coast for centuries. Throughout the region, the cultural hub of the Bella Bella, known to the Tsimshian as the *wütsdaa,* was significant for the dissemination of the secret orders, elite shamans, and priesthoods that constituted membership in the privileged ranks of royalty. Great shamans of the Tsimshian went to Bella Bella to become confirmed in privileged positions.

Throughout my research in the Americas, it has been just this kind of sensitivity to context and connections that fieldwork has provided. Before, during, and after time in the field, I immersed myself in the published and unpublished accounts of a nation, in this case the Tsimshian, then discussed my sense of these materials with informed elders and others. Because my overall goal was a comprehensive statement about each culture—sensitive both to contemporary, reflective, hidden agenda usages of the cultural framework and to continuities with past traditions—visits to the community were more to watch, interact (although hours of manual labor, plunging fishing boats, and open seas are not my forte), question, and discuss the hows and whys of my emerging focus and model for the culture whole, grounded in some aspect that is an all-inclusive public aspect of belief and behavior (J. Miller 1983a, 1983b, 1984a, 1984c).

During the early 1970s, a congenial group of scholars became involved in Tsimshian studies. Marjorie Halpin produced a superb dissertation on the

Tsimshian crest system (1973) by immersing herself in the copious notes sent by William Beynon to Marius Barbeau at the Canadian National Museum in Ottawa (cf. Cove 1985). Wilson Duff (1961, 1964a) had already mined these sources and laid the foundation for her research. Halpin showed how Tsimshian crests were different from others on the coast in that each of the four had a vertical dimension of rank. While the Tlingits, Haidas, Tsimshians, and some northern Kwakiutlans shared the same crests as discrete categories of difference, sometimes called "pseudo-species," only the Tsimshian added an internal ranking that distinguished each crest in terms of factors of prestige and pedigree.

The decade of the 1970s was an exciting time because there were people to talk to about ideas and theories, a fund of archival sources to explore, and a willingness among the Tsimshian themselves to encourage our efforts in the hope of gaining materials to use in their schools. Twice, the assembled Tsimshianists met in Hartley Bay to present papers to each other and to interested Tsimshian (Seguin 1984b).

George MacDonald was literally grounding much of these efforts through his excavations of sites in Prince Rupert harbor, long the winter home of all the Coast Tsimshian tribes. The findings of his crews showed that the Tsimshian had existed in their homeland in identifiable form for thousands of years (Inglis and MacDonald 1979; Matson and Coupland 1995).

About ten thousand years ago, obsidian was being traded from Mount Edziza, north of the Stikine River, throughout northern British Columbia and the Alaskan panhandle. By five thousand years ago, there were established towns and trails, now paved as modern highways, for moving trade goods throughout the region. From three thousand years ago, this trade included exotic goods that suggest a ranked society, such as that of the modern Tsimshian. Indeed, amber, jet beads, and shells occurred in some graves and not others. Important people, both men and women, wore labrets—plugs of stone or inlaid wood buttoned into the lower lip. In recent times, however, only women wore labrets.

Armor and weapons also appeared in these graves, indicating an increase in warfare. Trophy heads and rod armor imply ripples of influence from the Old Bering Sea complex on both sides of the Pacific (1000 B.C.), which in turn had connections with Shang China (1600 B.C.). Indeed, Frederica de Laguna, during a lifetime of research in the Pacific Northwest, noted a shared ancestral foundation for the cultures of the Inuit, Aleut, and northern Northwest Coast.[3] Such associations suggest the origins of both crest hats and masks, as interpreted below. Over time, the Tsimshian, of course, developed their own styles and meanings, building upon this remote Asian stimulus.

Plank houses and towns grew larger after twenty-five hundred years ago, indicating population increase, and woodworking tools became more complex, suggesting the elaboration of the "formline" art style for which the Tsimshian are famous. Social ranks were indicated by differences in house size and imported goods. Just as in historic times, the largest houses were in the middle of the row of dwellings facing the beach. The chief of a town, now as in the distant past, lived in the center of his or her people. Raiding and warfare also increased, as indicated by broken, fractured, and battle-scarred bones. The surmise is that Tlingit neighbors to the north were in the path for the transmission of Asian military strategies and used them on the Tsimshian, who, in turn, used them on the Haidas of the Queen Charlotte archipelago to the west and on various Kwakiutlan tribes to the south. Slavery was almost surely one of the motivations for these attacks, providing extra labor for the elaboration of chiefly prestige.

Indeed, in conjunction with research along the coast, extensive archaeological work within the confines of Kitselas Canyon has been used to test hypotheses about the development of ranked society among the Tsimshian. Coupland (1988) looked at the factors of residential permanency, storage of surplus, population aggregation in towns, household or house size variability, and prestige indicators to suggest that, beginning three thousand years ago, intensive specialization led to social ranking within Tsimshian towns.

In the process, utilization of a broad range of foods began to narrow toward the use of shellfish, about four thousand years ago, and of salmon, fifteen hundred years later. Coinciding with this specialization, ranking provided the means for restricting access to the resource, now defined as corporate property, and for encouraging more intensive production, under the direction of leaders, to benefit not just individuals, but also house, town, and community.

At its maximum, resource diversity included land and sea-mammal hunting, river and ocean fishing, and shellfish collecting, until a shift toward intensification and corporate group formation channelled access to the most important resources, particularly salmon, after twenty-five hundred years ago. Though Coupland postulates an intermediate stage of corporate bands before the emergence of ranked leaders, social inequality was long characteristic of the Northwest Coast. Indeed, the antiquity of specialized leaders or chiefs associated with corporate houses connected by intermarriage within communities, later localized as towns, is supported by the ancient combination of planked houses bonded with named territories, the scarcity of habitable sites along the coast, and the expected inequality among all ranked positions.

As with the coast itself, where impossible terrain and tides restricted access to various resources, so the mesh between the Tsimshians and their habitat encouraged the same kinds of differentiation within their society, a feature of the region more significant for human history than the testing of more globally derived hypotheses.

In sum, by two thousand years ago, society along much of the Skeena River had stabilized. Economic territories were obviously claimed by houses, and the entire region had blended into a system of shared or compatible beliefs and practices that persisted until the Russians, Spaniards, and English began claiming rights about A.D. 1750.

Since then, an entirely different series of changes began as Tsimshian left the sites of their winter villages and moved to the trading post at Fort (later Port) Simpson, run by the Hudson's Bay Company (Fisher 1977; Grumet 1975, 1982; Meilleur 1980). Town chiefs appointed heirs to manage either the new neighborhood or the old town, thus elevating themselves into the role of tribal chiefs. These new ranks required confirmation in the old way, by lavish generosity at public displays called potlatches, which now took on aspects of rivalry and confrontation so as to sort out the relative rankings of tribes and chiefs. From this melee emerged a Tsimshian "high chief" named Ligeex, of the Gispaxlo'ots Eagle crest. The previous title for this tribal chief, Nisbalas, had been shamed when its holder had been beheaded for insulting members of the Raven crest. Through a series of potlatches, a foreign name from the Kitimat, inherited through a captured Gispaxlo'ots Eagle wife, was substituted as the tribal chiefly name. In the course of establishing the name of Ligeex into public approval, the Gispaxlo'ots tribe moved to the forefront of the Coast Tsimshian and its chief became the high chief.[4]

Other changes were introduced in religion. For several years after 1800, a series of prophets called Bini preached an accommodation of European and traditional beliefs (Miller 1984c),[5] but these attempts did not last long. The Hudson's Bay Company arrived in the 1830s, and, most importantly, in the 1850s, William Duncan, a remarkable Victorian lay missionary, settled among the Coast Tsimshian, learned the language, and created a cooperative Christian community that still exists in Alaska. In hindsight, it appears that Duncan was so successful because he replaced Ligeex, who became a convert, as high chief of the Tsimshian.

For millennia, therefore, the Tsimshian have displayed an elegance and elaboration of culture in the midst of changes (Hawthorn, Belshaw, and Jamieson 1958; Knight 1978). The inherent beauty and subsequent success, based on their abilities, remain apparent. What has complicated the analysis of Tsimshian genius, however, has been this facility to adapt to new conditions by modifying old ones in creative ways.

For two decades, I have been concerned with a model (Miller 1979) for the wholeness and integrity of a culture, yet it was only recently that I came to understand how the Tsimshian fit that construct. Each culture relies on an axiomatic tension between symbolic categories to confer order and meaning on its world. This tension is an echo for the culture, reverberating throughout its expressions of people, institutions, and environments.

The echo and its emanations consist of a set of three interrelated parts that form a matrix—a nested sequence of relationships such that one member is defined as closed, exclusive, marked, limited, and specific in opposition to another which is open, inclusive, unmarked, unlimited, and generic. Intermediate between these two is a third member that permeates, blends, and mediates.

For example, in most human cultures, the "left" is constrained as 'sinister', the "right" is preferred, and the backbone or heart is their link. Often, "woman" is a special case (exclusive) of "man" (inclusive), while their children serve to unite them, along with "gender benders" like berdaches or hermaphrodites.

Most generally, "woman," "left," "plants," and "summer" are equated as marked exclusive categories in contrast to "man," "right," "animals," and "winter," which are unmarked and inclusive. Mediating these were the heart, the hearth, the sun, and, for the Tsimshian, Heaven as the ultimate source of inclosive health, life, well-being, and light.

Based on previous research, five Tsimshianic (*sm'algyax* 'real language') terms express the building blocks of their cultural system. Two of them are contextual, namely the potlatch (*yaawk*) and the *halait* ('winter ceremonial'). In the aftermath of conversion to Christianity, moreover, halait became a very complex term, also serving as a label for the various privileged orders or priesthoods that were insignia of royal or chiefly status.

The other three words refer to the crucial concepts of the crests (*ptex*), the primordial wonders or spirits (*naxnox*), and light (*goypax*), this last the all-pervading source and summary of this culture.[6] While these three terms were long recognized by scholars as vital to understanding this culture, their inter-relations were not fully appreciated as long as each was treated as a separate entity. Often, naxnox and halait were confused or treated as aspects of each other. Yet naxnox were clearly more integral to the other systems since, as spirits, they provided, during encounters with human ancestors, the images that became the crests shown off at potlatches or the wonders masks and displays of halait winter dramatizations.[7] The assumption was that these three concepts formed a V diverging from the naxnox (wonders):

crests                halait

naxnox

Yet this mediation by naxnox was offset by another system based on the primary referents of these categories. For crests, a hat—carved, painted, or woven with the totem of the house—was its most important expression; for wonders, it was a mask; and for the halait it was a carved, inlaid, and painted frontlet worn over the forehead. The frontlet, therefore, mediated between the hat and the mask, as the forehead is situated between the head and the face.

In time, however, it became apparent that these V-shaped arrangements were integrated into a larger whole because they were branches of a common trunk, which was a beam of light.

As for other coastal First Nations, Tsimshian culture was created when Raven established the rules and routines of the modern world, empowering it when he released a blinding flash of brightness after stealing the sun, moon, and stars.

Raven himself was sent by Heaven, the ultimate source of this illumination, and the foremost of the naxnox spirits, who themselves provide the justifications for most of the crests, inherited through the mother, and for the various masked wonder displays, associated with fathers, which the Tsimshian renounced when they became Christians. Upriver, however, the Gitksan have continued their masked naxnox (wonders) in a Christian context.

Both crests and wonders were displayed during potlatches, while the naxnox themselves appeared in both fall and winter displays. At one time, naxnox masks, displayed only among the holders of these names, were also the focus of unique winter dramatizations. Since many of the Heavenly naxnox were described as "shining youths," the association of the naxnox with light was clearly evident.

Raven or Giant, who polished up the Tsimshian world, was a double foreigner, both a naxnox from Heaven and an adopted Haida. Overall, he is a curious figure for setting the world right. Since he was also a glutton with loose morals, at least when young, belief in him dealt with great complexities. Still, it was important that Raven began with another tribe because it was the slaves of that tribe who set him on his amoral course. Thus, all the bad things that initiated the Raven of myth were done by other peoples. What the Tsimshian got were the benefits, however inadvertent, that improved on this initial wrongdoing.

For the Tsimshian, there is no creation or origin as such. Rather, most of the patterns of the Tsimshian world were in place, literally, long before Raven came from Heaven. Roles, ranks, households, and resource harvesting were all taken for granted.

What Raven provided, instead, were refinements and improvements to the known world. Later, other sacred histories (*adawx*), some recounted below, take up the tale and add other niceties, like painted house fronts, chiefly robes, rules for respecting certain foods, marriage and dynastic alliances, and, most recently, Christian civilization.

Yet Raven retains priority of place among the Tsimshian because he brought the one thing that created Tsimshian culture: he brought light into the world, with branchings from its beam providing the major institutions of Tsimshian culture.

In 1993, I taught a class on the Tsimshian and Haida languages to native speakers in Prince Rupert. Since the class emphasized both language and culture, students asked why, if you could diagram a sentence, you could not also diagram a culture. Using my first draft of this book, I tried to do that for the Tsimshian, emphasizing the axis of light. Class discussion then led to branchings, based on images that had more to do with water flow than conifers, yet both were recognized as vital to their homelands. Whether correct or not, the image led to much talk about native culture and, in this way, serves the useful purpose of keeping the discussion of culture alive, even if some scholars now say that culture does not otherwise exist except through such discourse and debate.

Therefore, after being field and classroom tested, the best representation of Tsimshian culture, useful but not absolute, draws upon indigenous trees and rivers to provide a model for the culture that branches at different places and times to reflect the pressures and enhancements of changing climates and local conditions, yet always reaching for the light. Each of the branches represents a discrete category reflected in the language and the culture. In addition, the relationships within and among the branches express both internal structurings and historical changes. The trunk is the axial beam of light defining the overall

HEAVEN
LIGHT

WUTA-

SM-

PRIVILEGES

HALAIT

SKY

CAVE

WONDERS

FOREST

NAXNOX

SEA

ORCA

CRESTS

WOLF

PTEX

RAVEN

EAGLE

MOTHER

**HOUSE**

FATHER

SUBSTANCE

SPIRIT

*1. Tsimshian Culture*

system. Its analogy in the art is the center line which orients all carvings made by Tsimshians (cf. Jensen 1992:28). Major nodes along the beam include Heaven, the sun, the hearth of a house, and the heart of a person.

In all, the overall diagram includes four units (beam and three limbs), dividing the maternal substantial from the paternal spiritual. Such fourfold separations derived from a basic division into two were a pervasive characteristic of Tsimshian culture.

Moreover, the stemming beam of light and the three other branches intertwined within the house, the minimal unit of Tsimshian society. On the left are the fourfold crests (*ptex*), inherited through mothers, divided into semi-moieties. On the right side are the wonders (*naxnox*) and privileges (*halait*), for which fathers had responsibility. Each institutional segment has its correlated artifacts and clothing, discussed in later sections.

The crests still include a distinctive hat and robes decorated with the emblems of the patron animal or ancestor, the now-disavowed wonders were masks and props for astounding dramatic feats, and the halait consisted either of frontlet, chilkat robe,[8] and raven rattle defining chiefly status or of woven cedar bark rings, varying in color and style according to membership in a particular secret order.

The lowest branch is that of the crests, expressing the socialization of peoples, both human and spirit, within their overall environment. These crests are divided into the semi-moieties of Orca-Wolf and Raven-Eagle. Inherited matrilineally, proximity to these ranked crests is mirrored in the social classes of royals, nobles, commoners, and slaves, with the most prestigious crests associated with the royal status. For hundreds of years, Tsimshians have been involved in the system of hereditary crests that forged the regional international kinship of the north Pacific.

On the other side of the beam, associated with male activities, is the branch of wonders, based upon access to the naxnox, who are segmented by habitats into those of the sea, of the forest, of mountain caverns, and of the sky. Many of these naxnox partake of chaos, disorder, and antisocial demeanors, yet some, particularly their chiefs, anciently interacted with humans to establish crests or displays of wonders as specified in *adawx* ('sacred history').

The third, most dynamic, of the branches is that of the *halait,* a complex term referring to all manifestations of the supernatural, rather than the beings themselves *(naxnox)*. The primary branch consists of the shamans, called *swansk halait,* who partook in all sources of power.

Shamanism, in turn, gave rise to one kind of halait, known as the *smhalait* ('real halait'), whose insignia of frontlet, raven rattle, and chilkat robe indicated the chief in his or her priestly winter guise. Supposedly developed along the Nass River,[9] the *smhalait* diffused to other First Nations as an indication of chiefly status so that now Tlingit chiefs are laid out in frontlets instead of crest hats. William Beynon, a native Tsimshian linguist, consistently translated initiation into the *smhalait* as being "elevated" by virtue of ascension to Heaven.

The other halait, the '*wii-* or *wuta-* ('great', singular or plural) halaits, diffused from the Kwakiutlan dancing societies during the past few centuries, and, for the Tsimshian, are attributed to the Wütsdaa at Bella Bella. The four *wutahalait* of the Tsimshian match the four crests, indicating a consistent patterning based on fours.[10] The insignia of these international orders are cedar bark rings, headbands, and color associations to indicate membership in either the Cannibals (*xgyet, xgyedmhalait*), Dog Eaters (*nutim*), Destroyers (*ludzista*), or Dancers (*miła*).

Overall, halait (closest to the Light) is most *inclosive* (Miller 1979), wonders (naxnox) are *inclusive* because of their associations with power, and the crests are *exclusive,* being transmitted through women. Indeed, at the basic expressive level, the genius of Tsimshian culture, expressing different ways of dealing with light, is the matrix of lid, lens, and loop represented by crests, wonders, and privileges.

In the past, crests were kept in special boxes or rooms within the house, while wonders were kept away from the house, often in the woods, when not in actual use. Important insignia of the priesthoods were wide cedar bark rings (loops), variously colored and worn across the body, to indicate membership. Presumably, as a loop, such a ring represented access to the endless flow of light, personally available to the initiate.

After this insight into the modalities of handling light, other facets of Tsimshian culture fell into place, since the trunk was explicitly a beam of light. This kind of rich imagery, elaborating on basic themes, and ambiguity, confounding these basics, was and is inherent to north Pacific cultures, as shown repeatedly in their pictorial art and verbal literature.

After William Duncan precipitated the sweeping conversion of Tsimshians, the halait were banned.[11] Yet, by virtue of his stated purpose of leading the Tsimshian from "darkness" into the "light," the structural integrity of the overall relationships remained, with the light of God replacing the light of Heaven, and with white-robed angels substituting for shining youths.

As a consequence of the fur trade and conversion to Christianity, however, only the crests branch has survived to this day. Angels have replaced the naxnox, at least in public, while various Christian sects have been grafted in place of the halait.

In a fascinating statement about equivalences, Louis Clifton, deceased Eagle chief at Hartley Bay, once said that there are only four valid religions for Tsimshians: these were the Anglican, the Catholic, the Methodist, and the Salvation Army. While reflecting the churches that had missionized among the Tsimshian, his statement draws parallels which confirm the model of Tsimshian culture as a branching system expressed most fully in fourfold divisions. In other words, while Tsimshians are aware of the many religions available in today's world, Clifton insisted that only four of them were primary. Such ranked differentiations were and are typical of the Tsimshian outlook.

In all, after ten thousand years of adaptation, including three thousand years of domestic stability, and after several centuries of cataclysm arising from the decimation of European intrusion and disease, the structural integrity and creative vitality of the Tsimshian have remained largely intact.

Recently, Marjorie Halpin argued against the hegemony of Franz Boas's rule-based paradigm of Northwest Coast art as "natural species used as heraldic emblems of social groups" (1994:8), insisting instead that the native view be privileged in regarding this art as "ambiguous, imaginative, unstable, poetic, endlessly variable, changing, and productive of the new, the unexpected" (1994:6). In particular, she charged that Boas treated the art in isolation instead of linking it to the *adawx,* sacred histories about spirit encounters owned by a house, that motivate and authenticate art works, now as well as in the past. It is the *adawx* that specify places, resources, crests, and spirits who benefit ancestors and the house, explicitly linked together by a totem pole carved with crests, dedicated and set in the ground to face the river or beach.

In part, Boas, working at Columbia University in New York City, missed this complexity because he was involved in the larger project of receiving Tsimshian texts from Henry Tate, a Christian convert who shared his own biases. The precedence of the *adawx* was explicitly noted, however, by Marius Barbeau of the Canadian National Museum, who had the skilled advice of William Beynon, an educated chief who both sent texts through the mails and worked beside Barbeau along the Skeena and Nass Rivers. In turn, however, Beynon helped to train Boas's students, particularly Viola Garfield and Amelia Susman, after Boas sent them to British Columbia for fieldwork.

While the generic crests of the four semi-moieties—Orca Killerwhale and Grizzly, Raven and Frog, Eagle and Beaver, or Wolf and Black Bear—do conform to the Boas paradigm, various specific crests of the nobility do not, giving full play to ambiguity in the interests of house prestige.

Denying the validity of the culture concept, Halpin doubted Boasian efforts to record data and analyze a master plan from them. Yet she failed to note that Beynon himself had much the same goal in mind. Other natives had similar goals of making sense of Tsimshian traditions, particularly as these were being threatened or eroded by Euro-Canadian society.

Moreover, any concerned scholar seeks coherence from data, a comprehension just complicated enough to allow for the flux between whole and parts, joined together or acting separately. As both poet and scholar know, creativity comes not from random chaos but from novel variation within set confines. Virtuosity consists of knowing the rules so well that they can be challenged and maneuvered in creative ways. Admittedly, the vast majority of people acted on vague notions, but a few especially strove for an overall understanding. Quality of mind was more important than prestige, although a few wise leaders, particularly in old age, did achieve a synthesis of their knowledge of the culture. In other situations, one crippled or physically handicapped might compensate with their mind to achieve another kind of mobility.

In all cases, the intent was not a static summary, but rather a mature statement that others could discuss, debate, and refine. My model of Tsimshian culture as institutions branching from a beam of light is intended to do no more or less than to stimulate continued discussion of Tsimshian vitality and eloquence. Holism makes special demands on understanding, particularly since details function as contributions to the whole. The argument, therefore, is more complicated and sweeping, unlike the dismembered topics treated in most studies, which argue from deliberately partial information. My goal here is not the final word, but rather a masterful taking stock, as expressed throughout this book, so that others can go on.

From this introduction, we turn to the "Background" of Tsimshian society in place and time. Next we look at the "Beaming" of light, defining Tsimshian ancestral culture. Under "Branching Limbs," the articulation of Tsimshian culture is viewed in terms of the present and past system of hereditary houses, crests, and clans; the now-abandoned systems of the wonder (*naxnox*) masks and displays; and the privileged halait elevations. "Reflections" considers how the branchings have been embodied within a generalized person, in important historic figures, and in artistic expression. Lastly, in "Conclusions" I draw regional comparisons using this model of Tsimshian culture and recent work with the Haida and Tlingit.

# 1. Background

For thousands of years the homeland of the Tsimshian, with their towns, forts, and camps, has been the north Pacific coast between the Skeena and Nass Rivers, along with numerous offshore islands. People traveled widely along these waterways, to visit, trade, and feast, and to engage in subsistence activities whenever a particular resource was ready for harvest.

Of the four Tsimshian groups (Nishga, Gitksan, Coast, and Southern), the last three were along the Skeena, while the first was located along the Nass (see appendix).

The Skeena is about 150 miles long, and enters the Pacific through offshore islands (Large 1981). The Coast Tsimshian located their winter towns near each other along Metlakatla ('calm narrows') in the vicinity of modern Prince Rupert harbor. During the summer, each town scattered to camps at ancestral territories along tributaries of the Skeena.

The Southern Tsimshian had their towns and territories on islands and bays along the coast below the mouth of the Skeena.

Above the Canyon of the Skeena (near Terrace, British Columbia) were the Gitksan, linguistic and cultural relatives of the Tsimshian, who shared this eastern cultural interface with interior Athapaskans who had adapted to some coastal traditions.

The Nass runs roughly parallel to the Skeena, is about 180 miles long, and flows through 20 miles of the Portland Canal before reaching the open sea. The Nishga occupied the upper Nass Valley, moving downriver in historic times.

Throughout the region the bordering terrain consists of high and rugged mountains covered with thick evergreen forests and alpine snow fields. The undergrowth is dense with thickets and brambles that made travel impossible except by canoe or along ancient trails, most of which are now paved highways.

The environment is rich in a variety of plants and animals whose habitats were the coast, rivers, and mountain slopes. Both marine and land mammals were important in the diet, while fish, primarily five species of salmon, were the preferred and most abundant food.[1]

The climate is mild because of the Japanese current, but rainfall is heavy for most the year. Winters were particularly bleak, but were enlivened by religious and social ceremonials attended by both local relatives and foreign guests.

THE TSIMSHIAN

Nine "tribes" along the lower Skeena River composed the Coast Tsimshian.[2] Indeed, the term *Tsimshian* comes from *ts'm-* 'those inside' + *ksiaan* 'the Skeena', and refers particularly to the estuary below the canyon of the river (Dorsey 1897; Duff 1964b; Dunn 1979a; Boas 1911; Niblack 1890).

Until a few years ago, the existence of another language on the coast, now called Southern Tsimshian, went unrecognized (Dunn 1979b). It was spoken in three or so villages on islands and inlets south of the mouth of the Skeena. Once the missionary William Duncan (Usher 1971, 1974; Barnett 1940, 1942; Beynon 1941; Pierce 1933) began to use Coast Tsimshian for Christian liturgy, it acquired added prestige that enabled it to supplant Southern Tsimshian in these more remote towns (Miller 1978:25).

For the interior, the Gitksan (<*git-* 'people' + *ksan* 'of the Skeena') live along the upper Skeena (Hindle and Rigsby 1973; Barbeau 1928, 1929, 1958, 1961), an area which included an intercultural zone with Athapaskan speakers who "Tsimshianized" aspects of their lives in consequence of trade, marriage, and other contacts (Miller 1984b:xviii, 1981b). Along the Nass were the Nishga (also Niska, Nishka, and, officially, Nisga'a) who lived along its upper end until many relocated to the trading and mission posts established near its mouth, which had once been Tlingit. Indeed, the very name of the Nass is Tlingit (*naas* 'intestine'), in the sense of "food belly," because of the abundance of fish there (Emmons 1991:8). The Tsimshian name for this river is *klusms* (Dunn 1978), though it is seldom used except by native fishermen. The Nass run of candlefish (*oolichan,* also *eulachon, ulaken,* and, in quasi-English, *hooligans*), largest on the coast, drew many tribes together each spring (Sapir

2. *Ecstall River. This meandering tributary of the Skeena passes through the tree-filled and snow-covered mountains of the interior coast. (Photo by Jay Miller.)*

1915; Tarpent 1982; McNeary 1976a, 1976b; Nisga'a Tribal Council 1992, 1993; F. Stewart 1975; H. Stewart 1977).

While other tribes of the Pacific Northwest had three social classes (leaders, commoners, and slaves), the Tsimshian had four: royalty, nobility, commoners, and slaves. The distinction between royal and noble developed a century ago as a consequence of population amalgamations near traders, transport routes, and missions.

However, the Tsimshian of the lower Skeena and Nass Rivers are unique. They developed lineage political leadership into village chiefship, probably early in the eighteenth century. Before the beginning of the nineteenth century this had developed further into tribal chiefship. . . . Chiefs of the Skeena villages appointed representatives from among their heirs to take over chiefships in the new villages. A few senior chiefs emigrated and left leadership of the old village in the hands

of successors. In either case, senior chiefs continued to exercise authority over the younger men, at least in the early period of the splitting of
the villages. At this stage tribal chieftainship emerged and the tribal
chief was regarded as the active leader of his tribesmen regardless of
where they lived. (Garfield 1966:33–34)

In this context, chiefs who had never had to live together on a day-to-
day basis gave increasingly extravagant potlatches (public feasts to witness
changes in rank and personnel) in order to sort out their relative positions in
the overall hierarchy. It was this "rivalry potlatching," especially among the
Kwakwaka'wakw (Kwakiutls), that caught the attention of whites, leading to
the misunderstandings that led to the banning of the potlatch in Canada until it
was decriminalized in 1951.

During the process whereby royalty emerged from nobility, the secret societies or *wutahalait* orders were borrowed from neighboring tribes and influenced by the older *smhalait* or "real halait" emblems of chiefly rank. In this
way, the earlier triads of class and cult common to other north Pacific nations
became the fourfold pattern of the Tsimshian. New crests involving humans
and fabulous creatures, called combination monsters, were also being created
to distinguish emerging royalty (Halpin 1984:33).

Moreover, during these times of stress and instability, the Coast Tsimshian
gained confidence from their enhanced leadership. Such was the context for
the angry response a Gitksan directed at John Adams:

> When I discussed my model of the conflicts created in Gitksan soci-
> ety by imbalances of population and the problems of succession which
> result, one of my informants became furious with me: Who was I to ac-
> cuse the Natives of having such problems? Didn't Whites have these
> same problems, too? Weren't the deaths of Martin Luther King and both
> Kennedys due to jealousy? Why couldn't Whites learn what the Natives
> had learned: that to avoid such problems it is necessary to install a king
> who is so high above everybody else that nobody can touch him. (Adams
> 1973:112)

Garfield (1966:26) estimated thirty tribal chiefs for the Coast, Nishga, and
Gitksan. Each had an unblemished pedigree from a long line of chiefs. Each
was expected to be "skilled in all things, energetic and ambitious" (1966:17).
As a group they were "able leaders, good speakers, haughty and proud before
strangers, and humble and generous toward tribesmen. The ideal leader was an

able organizer and speaker, and a model of good taste and conduct" (1966: 27). Among the Gitksan, the Gitsegukla History (1979:37) states that a chief had to prove wisdom (*wii ho'osxw*), kindness (*amma'gawd*), and strength (*dahx'get, daxgyet*) to gain respect (*an thlx'ooms*).

Each leader had four named spiritual aspects, distinguished as *sm* 'real'. As *smgigyet* or house chiefs, they conducted feasts and namings; as *naxnox* dancers, they performed in masked winter ceremonials. As *smhalait,* they wore a carved frontlet and robes, and "with the raven rattle as symbol of power, they initiated young people into ritual roles. The final formal named role for a leader was the *wihalait* or 'great dancer', the leader of the four secret societies, into which many of the people were initiated" (Halpin and Seguin 1990:279).

There were several hundred lineage and house heads, who managed the societal routines and made up the nobility. Together with craft and resource specialists, they made up the advisory council that served each of the town and tribal chiefs. These specialists included shamans, carpenters, carvers, painters, musicians, composers, herbalists, midwives, and astronomers (McNeary 1976b:156; J. Miller 1992).[3] Each of these specialists had responsibility for some aspect of the world, but the overall system was coordinated by the chief of the town, assisted by those of the houses.

Since Coast Tsimshian tribes and towns functioned in terms of their constituent ranked houses, territories and trade routes were under the control of the house chiefs, along with all of their other responsibilities in maintaining the living traditions of the sacred histories. Both water and land routes were owned and defended by the house, while trade alliances were confirmed by royal marriages between households resident at the extremes of the rivers and tribal territories.

In addition to marital ties, alliances were also strengthened by the bestowal of names and privileges, by feasting, and by ceremonial displays. Thus, the name of Seeks, a relative of Ts'ibasaa when everyone lived at Temlaxham, was given to a Tlingit chief who became known as Shakes. Similarly at strategic locations along inland trails, chiefs built feast houses where friendship-making (*ne-amex*) halaits could be held. Though based on clan and kinship solidarity rites, these particular halaits were characterized by mistrust. At this ritual, a stranger was invited in, seated on a woven cedarbark mat, and entertained by a display of the host's halait, by feasting, and by the bestowing of gifts. Of course, in addition to forging a new alliance, the rite was also a warning about the consequences of the theft of local resources.

Border zones were bicultural and bilingual, at the least. The Southern Tsimshians at Gitisu neighbored the Kwakiutlan Xaixais, before they moved together at Klemtu (China Hat). Tlingits and Nishgas were north of the Coast Tsimshian, with Gitksans to the east. While widely separated by Hecate Strait, a few Tsimshian towns nevertheless had close ties with Haida communities. In turn, some of the interior nations forged alliances with Athapaskan hunters even further inland. Thus, the Gitksan traded with the Wet'suwet'en, who traded with the Kaska; the Nishga chief named Mountain monopolized trade with the Tsetsaut; and Tlingit chiefs contacted the Gunana (their term for Alaskan Athapaskans).

The Kitselas at the Canyon of the Skeena had a distinct identity which was fostered by their crucial position along the river. Their royal house was founded by a Fireweed lineage, which had fled Temlaxham and which had extensive kin ties with royalty along the lower Skeena and at Kitkatla. Later Githawn, a famous chief, founded an Eagle royal house there and established alliances with Ravens upriver among the Gitksan. Each spring, the Kitselas opened the annual trade with the Gitksan, and only afterward could the Tsimshian trade upriver.

Such trade became the monopoly of the Gispaxlo'ots[4] and of Ligeex, who several times tried to vanquish the Kitselas and the Kispiox. During one foray, Ligeex arrived in front of Kispiox with umbrellas, which he used as a naxnox display to lure the townspeople into an ambush, but, though the attack was brutal, the victory was not complete. Eventually, Ligeex resorted to feasts and marriages arranged through his daughter-in-law and other relatives to establish an alliance with the Kitselas.

In general, coastal towns specialized in various kinds of seafoods and marine goods (dried cockles, clams, grease, dried candlefish, seaweed, dried herring eggs, and shells) traded to interior chiefs in return for prestigious furs, hides, and copper.[5]

With the arrival of the fur trade, guns, clothes, and iron pots became coveted items. While Saaban, a Raven from Kitkatla, had the first reported encounter with a European ship near the southern end of Pitt Island, the most famous leader of the early era was Ts'ibasaa, a Kitkatla Blackfish chief. He spent a year on a trading ship and learned to speak some English. When he returned safely, he potlatched the new name of Hale, and created a halait in which he wore a top hat, cutaway coat, and pants. He correctly realized that such "fancy" attire had prestige among Europeans, and so adopted it as his own. He acquired a gun very early in the trade and used it to intimidate the Nishga at

Fishery Bay on the Nass in order to retain the Tsimshian camp at Red Bluff for candlefish (Marsden n.d.).

## THE SEASONAL ROUND

The Coast Tsimshian wintered together along the shores of Metlakatla Pass near Prince Rupert harbor. From there, after the ice broke up, they went to an-cestral neighborhoods along the mouth of the Nass River to catch and process candlefish.[6] During the fishery the Nishga camped on Fishery Bay, while the Coast Tsimshian occupied camps downriver at Red Bluff (McNeary 1976b: 151). The Tsimshian term for candlefish means 'savior' and was later applied to Jesus Christ. Coming as the initial bounty of a new year, this fish saved na-tive peoples from starvation and want. The Tsimshian control of the candlefish trade also made them wealthy. The first fish caught by a man was given to the oldest child of his eldest brother, who gave him gifts in return. Everyone was busy during the runs either drying the fish or rendering them for their oil, usu-ally called grease. Every household had a recipe for rendering these fish, pre-scribing a set number of days for them to decompose in pits before they were boiled and pressed to render the oil. Women did the rendering, pressing the hot mass to extract the oil.[7]

The grease was stored in boxes at the winter towns while en route to gather seaweed from owned locations along the coast. Most of May was spent drying and storing seaweed, particularly kelp. Men also fished for halibut at secret spots located by triangulating off landmarks. Women sliced the halibut into thin strips for drying. A few early salmon were caught by trolling.

The cambium or innermost layer of hemlock, spruce, and certain pines was also stripped off and eaten, while the inner bark of red cedar was stored for winter weaving into baskets, mats, and clothing. The Gitksan also gathered maple bark and roots for basketry.

During the herring runs, spawn was gathered from sea grass or kelp. Some-times branches were suspended in the water and taken up when covered with herring roe.

Early in June, the eggs of seagulls and other shore birds were gathered. These were eaten fresh. During low tides in summer, abalone was col-lected from offshore rocks. Fresh greens and shoots were eaten as they became available.

As the salmon runs approached, Tsimshians moved to their home territories along tributaries of the Skeena and the Nass. Each house owned fishing sites

*3. Candlefishery on the Nass River. Overview of the camp, probably at Red Bluff.
(Photographed by Richard Maynard in 1884; courtesy of the Museum of Northern
British Columbia.)*

occupied by standing habitations or by house frames walled over during the
fishing season. The town chief coordinated the activities of member houses.
He, or sometimes she, was advised by specialists who predicted the weather
and monitored local conditions to determine peak availability of various resources. Salmon from different streams had slightly varied flavors, and these
tasty nuances were appreciated by native peoples.

Women gathered a variety of berries all summer long from patches owned
by their houses. Berry picking began with salmonberries and ended with crab
apples and high-bush cranberries in the fall. A woman gave the first berry she
picked to a sister (herself a mainstay of that other crest) of her husband or father, who reciprocated with lavish gifts. Berries were dried and stored loose, or
were preserved in boxes filled with candlefish oil.

September and October were busy times as quantities of salmon were
processed for storing. Chum salmon was preserved in smoke houses, as were
shellfish.

In the fall, families moved to owned hunting territories. Permission was granted for the asking, and sons had rights to hunt on lands owned by their father's house. Throughout, hunters were under strict religious discipline. They fasted, prayed, consumed emetics made from hellebore, and slept apart from their wives, who were also subject to restrictions. The mortal danger to a husband caused by an unfaithful wife is detailed in the sacred histories of many houses, particularly that of the Heavenly Children. Animals were believed to favor only men who had followed all of the necessary rituals.[8]

Animals hunted included deer, elk, mountain goat, mountain sheep, bear, porcupine, raccoon, marmot (lacking among the Southern Tsimshian), hare, lynx, beaver, marten, and mink (Compton 1993; Compton and Tarpent 1994). Marine species taken were seal, sea lion, and sea otter. Waterfowl such as swan, geese, and ducks were also eaten. Because the hunting of sea lions and mountain goats required endurance and courage, these activities were appropriate to chiefs and their princely heirs.

The upriver Gitksan and Nishga did more hunting, providing beaver, marmot, and moose meat to be traded for the meat of marine mammals and for shellfish from the coast. Women collected soapberries for the trade.

By November, coastal towns had gathered at their fall villages for feasts, festivals, and games. The Coast Tsimshian congregated at the place that later became Port Essington (from *spaksut* 'place for autumn'; Clayton 1989; Harris 1990). There the strictures of communal life were instituted again as the chiefs took charge of social activities.

Then everyone moved to the winter towns, with the Coast Tsimshian occupying their locations at Metlakatla, their social and ceremonial center. Shellfish was collected all winter long during low tides, but mostly people lived on stored foods. At leisure, women wove baskets and mats, while men carved and made tools. Most evenings were devoted to story telling and family amusements, including gambling contests.

The move to the winter towns shifted attention from the economic to the spiritual realm. Chiefs, known as *smgigyet* 'real people' during the summer, became *smhalait* 'real halait' or priests for the winter. Feasts and potlatches were replaced by naxnox displays exhibiting masks and wonders devised by specialized artists.

The ownership of sacred histories (*adawx*)—detailing names, locations, and the rights to art forms—was the basis of each house among the Tsimshian and other tribes from northern California to Alaska. For the Tsimshian, renowned for their consummate artistry, these histories were manifested in crests that included architectural details, garments, designs, songs, dances, and dramatic displays. The basis for each was an encounter between a named ancestor and a naxnox who gifted the family with something that became a crest. The naxnox itself was often represented by a mask that was worn when the house hosted events. Generally, the crest was something inherited through a long line of women, and communally owned, while the naxnox was direct and personal, allowing for individual creativity within the more complex and rigid system of crests. Since the histories had to be recited whenever crests were displayed, information of general value was included for the public, but only direct heirs within the family knew the esoteric knowledge that went with each crest. In addition, practical knowledge about the locations mentioned in the histories and the peculiarities of their resources were only transmitted from leaders to their heirs.

Because salmon was and is the primary food resource, many houses have histories that involve encounters with Salmon spirits. Among the best known is that involving a boy who mistreated a piece of salmon, often moldy, even though that was the only food available. After he was taken to live with the Salmon people, he learned many of the rules mentioned in the composite Tsimshian version of the tale given below.[9] While these observances have been abandoned in the commercial fishery, many of them are still followed at home.

*Salmon*

Famine stalked the towns along the Skeena River. What little food people had stored was used up during the winter. Starvation loomed during the spring.

A chief and his wife had one child, a son. The chief loved him very much and purchased a slave to look after him. The slave also loved the boy.

The people of the town left to gather inner bark, which was a food used in times of famine. The prince stayed behind to make arrows, at which he was very proficient. His slave looked after him. When they were alone, the slave began to cry because he was very hungry. The prince never ate much so he suffered less. Soon, however, the slave's crying interrupted the boy's concentration. He decided to look for food. He opened every one of his mother's boxes, but they were all empty until, inside the last box, there was a smaller one which contained a folded up spring salmon. The boy unfolded it, took a piece, and gave it to the slave, who became quiet. He put the rest of the salmon back and resumed making arrows.

That night everyone returned. The mother went to the big box, saying, "I have saved a treat for a time like this. We will have salmon with our bark."

When she unfolded the salmon, however, she was horrified to find a piece missing. Irate, she scolded her son, who admitted taking the piece and giving it to his slave. Now angry, she scolded him even more because feeding a slave was a worse thing to do. The father told her to stop, but she continued.

Now the prince decided to run away. He told his slave he would leave after dark and go alone. Late at night the boy left. His slave began to cry and soon woke the house. The father asked why he was in sorrow and the slave told him that his son had run away. The chief ordered everyone up to search, but they never found the boy.

After he left, the prince hid in the woods and then followed a trail to the shore, waiting there until dawn. In the dark, a canoe approached and pulled in where the boy waited. Four men were in the canoe and the one in the bow said, "Your father calls for you, young prince. We will take you to him. Get in and go to sleep. We will arrive safely." The boy got in and went to sleep. He was very tired.

With the light, they arrived in front of a large village. All of the houses were painted with pictures of salmon. The chief lived in the middle of the row in the biggest house. The boy was invited in and went to the man, who was lying down along the rear wall. He was ill. The boy was given a seat nearby.

Soon he felt someone poking his side and looked down. Mouse Woman asked him, "Do you know where you are and how you came to be here?" The boy did not. "Give me your woolen earrings. Place them in the fire and I will tell you." The prince did so. Mouse Woman took the singed wool and explained, "Yesterday when you unfolded the salmon from the box, the chief of the Spring Salmon got better. He has been sick for two years, ever since your mother put his blanket of flesh in that box. For salmon to return, their flesh must be consumed and their bones must be placed in a fire so that salmon will be reborn as a healthy individual." Then she left.

The prince was fed and made welcome. He was to live with the Salmon for a year and learn their ways.

The next day, the boy was hungry. The chief said, "Go behind the house and find the children playing. Select a plump one and club him. He will be your meal. Cook and eat him. Then take a drink of fresh water to help him to be reborn. Gather up every bit of bone and put it in the fire. Then everything will be as it was."

The boy went behind the house and did as he was instructed. As the child was clubbed, it became a salmon. The prince ate, took a drink, and gathered the bones. When he went back to the house, he saw a child crying, "Oh, my eye, my eye, it hurts so much." Then the prince knew he had missed a piece. He went back to the fire and found the eye in the pit and burned it. When he returned to the house, the boy was entirely healed.

Meanwhile, the chief was sending scouts to the Skeena River to see if the salmon were running. The boy was confused until Mouse Woman came. She explained, "The Salmon here wait for ice to leave the river and then they send scouts. What humans see as the leaves of cottonwood trees are the salmon that these beings fish for." Then boy understood the multiple realities of the Salmon.

The scouts returned with the news that the time was not right. The boy was hungry and clubbed another child to eat. When he went back into the house, the child was limping. The prince went, found the missing bone, and burned it. The child was restored.

Finally, the scouts returned with good news. The chief called everyone in the town and announced the date they would leave for the Skeena. Then the first salmon of the season was ritually welcomed and eaten.

During the year, the Tsimshian chief and his wife had mourned greatly. They hired many shamans to locate their son or find out his condition. None could do so. Finally, a great shaman was summoned and he came. He put on his crown of grizzly bear claws, placed eagle down on his head, donned his dancing apron, and painted his face red. He took his rattle in his right hand and an eagle tail in his left one. While his companions drummed, he danced around the fire. He sang three songs and then stood still.[10]

After a time, he went to the parents and said, "Your son lives. He has been taken to the village of the Spring Salmon, where the chief is ill because you have kept his flesh in a box for two years. You must eat it now so that the Salmon chief will revive. Then your son will be brought back." The shaman left and the couple ate the dried salmon.

A few days later the shaman returned with more news. "The chief of the Salmon is much improved. Soon he will bring the boy home. Tell all of your brave men to fast and pray starting now. Tell them to take hellebore and make themselves pure. Husbands and wives must sleep apart. Everyone must be prepared for a wondrous challenge. Old women must make the salmon nets ready. Women who are menstruating must stay away from the gear. Old men must collect poles for the weirs. Everyone must do what they can to help."

Every night the shaman returned to say whether the salmon had left for the Skeena. Finally, he came and said, "The Salmon left today and will visit their villages for a few days before arriving at the mouth of the river."

Indeed, the canoes of Salmon people had left the town. Along the way, the chief visited the villages of the other Salmon. First he came to the home of the Silver Salmon, who said they would leave soon. As they left the Silver's town, the chief took a pebble from his own mouth and gave it to the prince, who placed it in his mouth. "This pebble will make you hard and strong. It will protect you from everything," the chief explained.

Other villages were visited. The Humpback Salmon said they would not start until after the Steelheads had passed. The houses of the Dog Salmon were painted with rainbows and they said they would follow the Humpbacks. The Coho houses were decorated with crooked snouts and they said they would wait until the fall to go to the Skeena. The village of the Trout had houses carved with stars and they said they would lead the Springs into the river. As the Springs and Trout left, they met the Steelhead returning from their time on the river.

Many canoes were gathered at the mouths of the Skeena and the chief went to each one. Each canoe announced its destination, naming a specific tributary of the Skeena. As they did so, the chief described the conditions distinctive of that waterway. For example, those who were going into the Ecstall River were told that their flesh would be harder than wood.

The shaman noted the movements of the Salmon while in his trance. When they neared the town, he called for everyone to be prepared. Men went to the fishing platforms and women got ready to cut up the fish and dry them for storage. Many fish were caught.

The shaman himself went down to the river with a net on the end of a long pole. He waited for the Salmon chief, who came upriver and saw the net of the shaman stretching from bank to bank. It magically blocked the river. The Salmon chief knew that his time had come. He turned to the prince and said, "My son, I will now take you home. Do not let your father dry my flesh. Have him invite all the people to a feast and make sure that everyone has a taste of my flesh. Then they must drink fresh water to help me revive. All of my bones must be burned in a fire."

The shaman felt the Salmon chief strike the net and pulled, but it was so heavy he called for help to haul it in. After placing the salmon on the platform, the shaman instructed everyone. "This is the chief and he carries the prince. Treat him gently. Do not hurt the prince. Call four shamans to help me with this work. Bring me the new cedar bark mat, my grizzly claw crown, my eagle down, my red ocher, my dancing apron, my rattle, and my eagle tail." This was done.

The shaman got dressed. The other four shamans took the salmon and placed it on the mat. Each carried a corner and they went to the house of the chief, led by the old shaman. Inside the house, all the young people were asked to leave. Only the old people stayed. All of the shamans, dressed in their special attire, walked around the fire four times.

Two old women who were shamans were selected to cut the fish with mussel-shell knives. Everyone was very quiet. One of the women called the honored names of the Salmon chief—Quartz Nose, Two Gills on Back, Lightening Following One Another, Three Jumps. They cut the salmon along the belly and removed the distended stomach. One woman cut up the fish and the other opened the stomach. Inside was a tiny child several inches long. All of the shamans shook their rattles and the old shaman sang as he walked around the child, who began to grow quickly. Soon the prince was his former size.

He told of his adventures with the Salmon people. He warned of the need to consume all the flesh within a year, to drink fresh water after eating salmon, and to burn every single one of the bones. He explained that the Salmon were people, that when they seemed to be jumping from the water, they were actually standing up in their canoes to look ahead. Every kind of Salmon had a town of its own with its own chief, but the chief of the Spring Salmon lived farthest out and was the leader of all the Salmon. Astonished, the people listened and learned.

The prince lived in the town for some time. As long as he kept the pebble in his mouth, he had no need of food. He resumed the making of fine arrows. He called together four companions and went to hunt eagles so he would have feathers for his fletching. They went into the mountains and dug a pit. One of them would hide in the pit and they would cover it over.[11] When an eagle came to take the bait, the man would grab it by the feet and pull it into the pit to be clubbed. They were very successful, but the others did not realize what they were using as bait. The prince turned himself into a salmon to lure eagles from the sky.

One day, as they prepared to go hunting, the prince took the pebble from his mouth and put it into the mouth of his most trusted friend. Then they went off to trap eagles. That day, an eagle killed the prince, who died as a salmon. Atop the pit, his companions found the body of the prince with his mouth full of blood.

With great sorrow, they carried the body home. After a time of mourning, the body was placed in a box and left upon four posts set into the beach. The companions stayed under the box for days, but eventually three of them went home. The fourth one, who had the pebble in his mouth, remained.

Early one morning, the friend heard canoes approaching. The Salmon people had come to take the prince back home. The friend crept into the canoe. No one could see or hear him. The friend went to the town of the Spring Salmon. He was ignored and began to become homesick. Then he took the pebble and put it into the mouth of the prince, who could see and talk with him. The friend was told to go behind the village when he was hungry and club a child to roast and eat as a salmon. After drinking fresh water, all of the bones were to be burned. The friend was very careful to follow all of the rules.

Yet the friend became more and more homesick. The prince promised to take him home in the spring. The Skeena was then frozen and ice prevented any travel by canoe. Meanwhile, the prince told the friend many of the rules that humans had to follow to show respect for the salmon and other fish.

For example, in the Canyon of the Skeena only mussel shell knives could be use to cut the heads and tails off each salmon. The tails must not be broken off. If a stone or bone knife was used, thunder, lightning, and heavy rains would flood the villages.

Once there was drumming from a house at the end of the town. The prince told his friend to peek inside by looking through a knothole. Inside the Salmon were dancing and making herring roe. The Salmon had filled the house with eagle down and were wearing shiny garments set with abalone. When the friend stuck a hemlock twig into the knothole, it came out filed with herring eggs.

When spring began, the prince volunteered to be one of the scouts. They left in a new canoe and the friend went along. There was floating ice in the Skeena, but the prince urged the scouts to go far enough upriver to deliver his friend home. This task was dangerous, but they succeeded.

The friend went home and told the people about life among the Spring Salmon. Now people know the rules that must be obeyed so that the salmon will stay healthy and return each year.

## 2. Beaming

As Marjorie Halpin, after a thorough study of Tsimshian materials, concluded, "Light is thus a principal attribute of divinity, and implies power and (male) potency. Light and seeing are direct oppositions to such naxnox qualities as death and darkness, although in a religious sense they may be the same" (1981:284).

Creation was not a particular concern of the Tsimshian. Rather, the qualities and interrelationships of the universe received special attention in a series of *adawx,* sacred histories, which explained how things came to be as they are now and which ancestor of what house was involved in the process. Thus, in addition to general accounts of the rearranging of the universe, specific accounts, owned by named houses, indicated that everyone inhabited a world of the ancestors' making. While every habitat of sky, earth, and sea had its owners, leaders, and occupants, the being called Heaven, the source and deification of light, had priority among these chiefs. For Tsimshian (as for neighboring Tlingit, Haida, and others), the Raven naxnox or spirit known initially as Txaamsm and then as Wiget, literally *'wiigyet* 'big person', did much to establish the present universe. Of all of his actions, the seminal one was the theft of bright light.

*Raven*

The world was unformed and in perpetual twilight.[1] Many things existed in the sky, earth, and sea, but they were unconnected and the most advantageous were selfishly guarded from general knowledge. Only the members of chiefly families were distinct individuals.

At one town, the chief and his wife were in mourning. Their only son had died. He was much loved and had shown great ability. Hearing the constant wailing of the chief and his wife made everyone sad.

Every day, the parents walked from their house to the tree that, in its upper branches, held the burial box of their son. As they went, they would sob and moan. Sometimes the wife would wail. They did this for a long time.

One day the wife awoke and began to wail, walking toward the burial tree. When she arrived, she saw a boy sitting on the box. His body shone as brightly as flames. Stunned, she stopped her crying and rushed back home. "Husband," she called, "Our son has returned." The man went back with her and everyone followed to find a boy sitting on the box. "Is it true that you have returned, my son?" the chief asked.

"Yes, I have come back," the boy replied. "Heaven felt your sorrow and sent me back. At first he was angry about the noise you caused, but, once he understood, he took pity."

"Come home with us," the man said. The boy climbed down and followed them. Everyone was amazed and pleased. The boy was given the place of honor in the house and esteemed as much if not more than the one who had died.

Because he was a shining youth from heaven, his own power provided for all of his needs. He did not eat. Sometimes he would chew some fat, but he never swallowed. He had no need for food. His mother was concerned that she could not feed and care for her child. She encouraged him to eat, but he always refused.

Finally, the couple decided to host a great feast to confirm their son in his position. Everyone was invited. The best of food was served and large quantities were available.

At the feast, the father urged the boy to eat something to honor the event, but he refused. The mother also coaxed him, but he refused. Then the mother's brother asked and he agreed. The mother ordered a slave to select the best morsels and place them in a carved wooden bowl for the boy.

This slave was mean and decided to take revenge for his lot in life. He selected the best of foods and then scratched a scab from his ankle. He hid the scab in the food. The boy, to be polite and show respect for his uncle, tasted the food. He barely put it on his tongue.

Yet, in a short time, he asked for more food. His father was pleased. His mother was delighted. More food was served to him. Then he asked for more. Soon he had eaten all of the feast food. He ate all of the food in the house. Foods were brought from other houses in the village and he ate those too. Soon, everyone realized, the village would have no food and starve.

The chief decided to send his son away. He announced to the people at the feast that henceforth his son would be known as Wiget (Giant, literally 'big person'), and he would be of high rank. The father gave him provisions. A sea lion bladder was filled with seeds and eggs. "Scatter these up and down the coast, my son, and you will never lack for food," the father explained. The son was given a stone to swallow so he would be impervious. Fine garments and clothes were also given to him. Then Wiget left.

Because he was a naxnox child of heaven, he could still fly, even though he was now more human and constantly ravenous. He scattered the seeds and eggs along the coast. Then he began his adventures. His desire for food took him all over. Sometimes he accomplished things for selfish reasons and sometimes for inadvertent ones. As he matured, he developed a moral sense that made him more kind.

At this time, useful aspects of many parts of the world were guarded by owners, wealthy chiefs who used them only for personal gain. Wiget went to these people and took away their properties for the common good. For example, he visited Tide Woman who kept the tides roped until she desired shellfish. Then she released the rope and gathered food at low tide. Wiget tricked her into releasing the rope so that the tide could find its own schedule. Further tidal fluctuations are the result of her wiggling around because she was made to sit on a spiny sea urchin. In consequence, humans can gather food at low tide.

Wiget came upon a rock and an elderberry bush who were both about to give birth.[2] He touched the bush and she delivered first. Therefore, humans do not live long and elderberries soon grow on their graves. If Stone had delivered first, than humans would have been hard and long-lived. Only their stone-like teeth and nails serve to remind humans of what might have been.

Wiget heard that a powerful chief near the headwaters of the Nass River owned the daylight (*goypax* 'brightness'). He went there but was refused entrance into this house. Wiget went into the woods and thought about what he might do. Soon the daughter of the chief came to fetch water in a wooden box. Wiget changed himself into an evergreen needle and floated into the box. Later when the daughter drank, she swallowed the needle. Soon she knew that she was pregnant.

Her father was outraged, but the daughter assured him that she had never known a man. The chief decided that divine intervention must have been involved, so he awaited the arrival of his first grandchild.

After the boy was born, he grew quickly and became precocious. His grandfather was delighted, even though a wise old woman warned him several times, "Look at that baby's eyes. They are bright and alert. They remind me of that Wiget who is going everywhere connecting up the world. I warn you that baby is not normal." But the chief ignored her warnings.

Every day at dinner time, the chief ordered a slave to take down the box of daylight from where it hung and place it on the floor. Then he would tilt the lid and light would flood the room so everyone could see and enjoy their meal.

As the boy got older, he became sickly and cried all the time. His grandfather was greatly concerned. During one meal, the crying child grabbed the box and became quiet. The chief and his household were relieved. Thereafter, whenever the child cried, he was given the guarded box. After some time, a slave no longer stood beside the box, nor were members of the household wary that the box was off its hook. This was what Wiget wanted.

Once, when everyone was occupied, the baby began to cry. He was given the box. Slowly and carefully, he moved the box from the rear wall, where the chief and his family lived, to the middle of the house under the smoke hole. When the box was directly under the hole, Wiget flew up and squawked. This sound alerted the chief and he used his power to make Wiget return. After a brief contest of willpower, Wiget broke free and flew away. Because he had been detained in the smoke hole, his cloak became black and shiny. Ravens, who take after Wiget, now have the same glossy feather covering.

Wiget flew downriver with the box. At the mouth of the Nass, many of the unformed beings were fishing. Wiget called to them, "Give me some fish and I will give you a wonderful gift that will change your lives forever and make things easier."

The beings complained, "We have been working very hard to get these fish. You only want to trick us. If we give you fish, you will get something for nothing. Now go away and leave us alone."

Wiget was upset by this reply and tried to explain, "I am trying to make the world a better place. I am working to make things connect and work together. If I am not fed, I can not work well. I am only asking for your help so that I, in turn, can help you."

The beings were rude and insulting. They sent Wiget away. Very angry, he shouted back, "Very well. I will show you how powerful I am. I will teach you an important lesson."

With that rebuke, Wiget smashed the box and daylight (here called *maax*)[3] emerged with a bright flash. Some creatures were blinded. Others were permanently changed into animals or trees or plants depending upon what they were doing at that moment. The beings who had been most offensive stayed much as they had been and became the frogs of today.[4]

Even though humans began to prosper because Wiget killed or changed the monsters of the ancient times, they did not always respect Wiget. Once he was so hungry he dove into the sea and ate the bait from halibut hooks. One fisherman hooked Wiget and broke off his bill. After a difficult time, Wiget retrieved his jaw and reattached it.

When the world had become a better and more interrelated place, Wiget called all of the spirits into his house and celebrated the first potlatch. He fed and entertained them. In return, the naxnox promised never to harm humans without provocation. Some monsters were turned to stone and others were sent to live far away from humans. At the very end, Wiget went to live far out to sea. Some say that he also turned to stone, but others report that a man in despair met Wiget in an isolated valley just after guns came to the Tsimshian. No one knows for sure and, as always when Wiget is involved, no one ever will be sure.

### Heaven

A game played with sticks and a ball preoccupied the children in ancient times.[5] They had fun, but sometimes they became obnoxiously loud. Soon, Heaven himself took offense. He was annoyed by all the noise the children made. They showed no respect.

Heaven sent down a feather. It floated over the children just out of reach. The children stopped their play and jumped for it. Finally, one boy got it and stuck it in his hair. The children resumed play, but when they became noisy, the boy with the feather in his hair started to rise. Higher and higher he went. Another child grabbed the feet of the boy, but he too rose. He was stuck and could not let go. Other children in turn grabbed the feet of those who rose before. Adults rushed out and grabbed the feet of the last child. All of them rose into the air. The town was empty except for dogs howling at the sky.

A few days before, a girl had been secluded in a menstrual hut, tended only by her grandmother. They were away from the town and so were spared. When her time was over, the women went back to the town and found it empty. They walked through the street crying. The grandmother suspected that the noisy children had been the cause of this destruction. She had warned them to be quiet. Now their people had been destroyed. Tools lay where they had been dropped, indicating how quickly everyone had disappeared.

The girl took up wedges made of crab apple wood, sloe wood, and spruce wood.[6] She gathered a small grinding stone and a tiny knife. As she cried, a bit of mucus fell on the ground and she picked it up. She took these things from around her house. She hugged these mementos of her people close to her, clutching them for four days and nights.

Then she knew that she was pregnant. Her grandmother nursed her until she gave birth to six children, five boys and a girl. The boys were called Crabapple, Sloebush, Spruce, Little Mountain, and Mucus. The girl was Little Knife. They grew up quickly. Soon they too played ball. As soon as they became noisy, their mother shouted, "Stop that noise at once. Such behavior killed your grandfathers. Heaven was offended." The children became quiet.

On another day, however, during a particularly exciting game, they would not listen and became very noisy. They were young adults and strong.

Heaven heard them, became annoyed, and sent down the feather. It floated and swooped over the children. Crabapple grabbed it and placed it on his head. They resumed playing and making noise. The eldest began to rise in the air. Sloebush rushed to grab his brother's legs, but he too rose even though he had set his roots into the ground. When he could stand no more, he asked his brothers to break his roots. Then he rose. Spruce grabbed hold and when he could endure no more asked for his roots to be broken. He rose. Little Mountain grabbed on and became a weight, but he too rose. Mucus grabbed on and tried to stick to the ground, but he rose up.

Finally, the girl rushed up and climbed over all her brothers to reach Crabapple. She used her hands to cut the feather. They all fell to the ground. They did not go to Heaven. The cut feather stayed on the head of Crabapple and he changed his name to Rotten Feather.

After the children landed, many bones fell out of the sky. These were the villagers from before. Rotten Feather waved his head over them four times and these people returned to life. They thanked the children, who went traveling over the earth and found places to stay.

Rotten Feather went to find a wife. His feather helped to get him into a well-protected village, where he married the daughter of a woman chief. At night, suspecting the worst, Rotten Feather let down his own top knot and arranged the hair of his bride like his had been. During the night, the mother came and cut off the head that she thought belonged to her son-in-law. Rotten Feather escaped, taking the labret of his wife as a token. Thereafter, he was called Labret.

In his travels, he heard of the beautiful woman who was the wife of Sleep. He decided to marry her. When he got to her house, she was pleased with him and agreed to marry him. They took Sleep's canoe, which went fast, all by itself.

Sleep was unaware of their escape. He slept all of the time. His chamber pot and maul had the responsibility for waking him up if there was danger or need. The chamber pot knocked Sleep on the head and spilled urine over his face, but Sleep did not respond. Then the maul struck Sleep on the head repeatedly until he woke up. Maul said, "Labret took your wife."

Sleep rushed to his own canoe to pursue the couple, but it was gone. He took another canoe. He went very fast and saw them at a distance. He called, "Stop, Labret, or I will put rocks in your way." Labret ignored him. Then Sleep placed a mountain in front of them. Labret used his feather and the mountain cracked open.

Next Sleep threw his comb to make a dense forest in the way. With his feather, Labret made an easy passage through the trees. They escaped and lived a long time. Even now the Gispwudwada Blackfish display the mask of Sleep, whose eyes open and close, at their feasts to show that they are related to this couple.

ILLUMINATION

Such sacred histories, each claimed by a house, consider many themes important to the Tsimshian, but all trace the beginnings of their culture to the empowering burst of brightness that Raven brought to the world.

Initially, I suspected that the Tsimshian tension or echo was based on dimensions of form, wherein the crests were the vertical, represented by carved poles and the lineality of a person under a hat; the wonders were the horizontal, treating the face and mask as expressions of a perpendicular axis; and the halait was their crossed intersection. This hypothesis, however, proved false because it did not account for the symbolic importance of doorways and openings, nor for the lack of crosses and intersections in the iconography.

During the feasting season of 1982, I attended an important installation in one of the Southern Tsimshian villages. Traditional costumes were much in evidence, making this event all the more impressive. The new crest leader and his close kinsmen were dressed in apparel decorated with appliqués of shiny buttons outlining their Eagle crest.

Over their ordinary clothes, each wore pieces of decorated cloth as a wide band around the head, a large blanket over the torso, an apron, and anklets. In all, the person looked like a cylinder wrapped in the heraldic emblems of his matrilineage. The parallel to a totem pole was obvious, but the symbolism was much more potent. After all, beneath or inside the crests was a human being, a comparison all the more noteworthy because the finer totem poles are hollowed out along the back and their carved crests seem to surround "nothing."

These insights led me to the overall system after I had read a paper prepared by Carol McClaren (n.d.) to accompany an illustrated lecture about the raven rattle. Together with the chilkat cape and the frontlet, the rattle is supposed to have originated among the Nishga, and diffused widely along the coast as the insignia of high rank throughout the regional hierarchy.

For all of its elaborate surface iconography, McClaren, following Marjorie Halpin, showed that the rattle was basically a hollow tube surrounded by intertwined figures on one side and by the carved body of the raven on the other. She saw this tube as a channel for light and the carvings around it as masks.

She notes that light is a pervasive symbol among the Tsimshian, and I concur. A favorite expression of the naxnox was to have a mask, apparently blind, suddenly see. In the instance told above, the mask of Sleep wakes up when his eyes open. Moreover, the most famous example is the pair of nested stone masks reunited by Wilson Duff (Abbott 1981), discussed in chapter 3.

In myths, wondrous sky beings first appear accompanied by four bolts of thunder and lighting. Light is also emphasized in references to shining surfaces, like those of beads, shells, mirrors, crystals, and water creatures, particularly the glistening bodies of salmon.

With this realization, I understood that the opposition between crests and wonders, mediated by halait, expressed different ways of handling reflected light. A crest represented something encountered by an ancestor and taken into the matriline. It became guarded property, exclusive to a household. The wonder, in contrast, acted as a lens for intensifying this essence from the past. Crests were static because they were fixed commodities, but wonders were dynamic, expressing an ongoing relation with the supernatural. Crests could also be wonders that had been harnessed. Overall, the process was bidirectional. Before Raven stole the sun, moon, and stars, they had been kept in boxes, much as crests are now.

BRIGHTNESS

In all, therefore, for Tsimshian culture, light (*goypah, goypax*) was and is the mediator with universal potency, a manifestation of the divinity, called Heaven, that pervades everything. In the earlier literature, this potency has been called power, but that seems to be too specific a reference. Light has neutral associations and an ambiguity of source that make privilege or potency a more appropriate term for it. Boas noted:

> In the religious beliefs of the Tsimshian, Heaven plays an important role. He watches the acts of mankind, and sends down helpers known as nExnox. Practically any natural object may be a nExnox, but in the tales the most important ones are shining youths, strokes of lightning, and animals. The term nExnox designates anything mysterious. . . . Heaven rules the destinies of mankind, has taught man to distinguish between good and bad, and given religious laws and institutions. Heaven is gratified by the mere existence of man. He is worshiped by offerings and prayer, the smoke rising from fires being especially agreeable to him. Murderers, adulterers, and those who behave foolishly, talking to no purpose, and making noise at night, are especially hateful to him. . . . His messengers, particularly Sun and Moon, must be treated with respect. Man makes himself agreeable to the deity by cleanliness. (Boas 1916:543)

Aspects of Heaven are expressed in the translation of *laxa* as "heaven, sky, storm." The most important of the human chiefs were closely identified with Heaven through halait names incorporating the term *laxha* (Dunn 1978: 57, 58).

> *laxha* (la[x]: "on, on top of"—and ha: "sky," "atmosphere," "air," "wind") is often loosely translated "heavens," but it could also mean more precisely "sky on top" or "atmosphere" or "beyond the air." In any case, among the Tsimshian the identification of the great *halait* (*wihalait* or *semhalait*) with the "Sky" rather than with definite spirits or *naxnoq* which could be linked with houses or lineages would help solve a question asked by Boas about the control over the naxnoq by the house or the clan. The houses would own the naxnoq names and powers manifestations as they do crests; but the "Sky" naxnoq would be called only by the high-ranking chiefs. It would stand beside and beyond the crest system as a rank prerogative rather than a house privilege. (Guédon 1984a:156)

The use of abalone, copper, and polished surfaces on chiefly artifacts provides further support for the mediation of light. Salmon, which spawn and die yet return each year, are also important mediators, highlighted by the iridescent quality of their wet skin. Among the Nishga, a polished slate mirror was called *nahawn,* "indicating the shining skin of a fresh salmon, from *na-* a prefix indicating properties of; *hawn* 'salmon' [also, generic fish] referring to its reflective quality" (Emmons 1921:20-21; Marie-Lucie Tarpent, personal communication 12 June 1987).

Crystals are a particularly important emblem of the priestly power of chiefs on the Northwest Coast, and of shamans everywhere. The Nu-chah-nulth (Westcoasters, Nootkas) keep crystals *(hin'a)* as family treasures and display them in Wolf Rituals (Arima 1983:187), and the Nuxalk (Bella Coolas) used a pair of crystals for initiations (McIlwraith 1948: plate 4).

During the early days of contact, glass windows installed in traditional plank houses greatly enhanced the prestige of the householders. It is easy to see why. Painted house fronts were among the greatest crests since they were constantly on display. A glass window letting in light was itself doubly wondrous, as an object and as a symbol. Previously, the equivalent in prestige was the multifaceted quartz crystal. The Tsimshian still apply the same word to both (Garfield 1939:336, 1966:11). Thus, at a halait initiation conducted under the naxnox name of All Bright Heavens: "The power which came to the chief was represented by a large piece of white quartz crystal *(tkwa)* given him by his supernatural spirit and brought from the mountains at Ginadoiks River. He had two, the larger one being used here as it called for more compensation and, of course, was more powerful than the smaller one. For the use of the stronger power he received four moose and caribou skins, whereas he would have received two for the weaker" (Garfield 1939:306).

*Crystals*

Because we know so little about these important items (cf. Levi 1978), an account by Rev. William Collison (1981:197–200) will be quoted at length to describe the events after a Nishga hunter found a cave full of crystals. It nicely illustrates the association of crystals as lenses with wholeness, mind, light, and potency.

After the discovery was announced, an expedition was mounted by the most important leaders, with the promise "that the leading chief of every crest and clan who joined in the expedition should receive a share in this wonderful discovery" (1981:196). "The canoes which had been sent to summon the chiefs were manned by young braves, who cried aloud in front of the various camps, that the leading chief had discovered the Gan-sha-goibakim-Lakah, or that which enlightened the heavens" (1981:195). A slave called Zidahak was put in a basket and lowered to the front of the cave, but he piled so many crystals around himself that the rope broke and he was killed. "There they found him, a mangled mass, but on unfolding his inner garment, or what remained of it, they found six of the smaller but more perfectly formed crystals lodged, three under each arm, where he had clasped them even in his death fall" (1981:199). After cremating the slave's remains (usually a privilege of royalty), everyone went home. The six crystals were displayed in the house of the leading chief until a council was held to name and distribute them.

The first crystal was named Aizuli, or the Eldest, and was presented to Chief Neishlishyan, or the Grandfather of the Mind. Of this crystal a chant or song was composed by the music master of his tribe, which was sung on special occasions, as when a potlatch was made.

The second stalactite was named Tka-ga-Koidix or the Coming of the Whole. This was presented to Chief Gadonai, and a song was also made for it.

The third crystal stalactite was named How-how-imsh-im laub, or the Lion Stone,[7] and was presented to Chief Klaitak, the predecessor of the chief who narrated the incident. A chant was also composed by the music master of the tribe for this crystal.

The fourth crystal was named Daow-im Lakah, the Ice of Heaven, and was presented to Chief Gwaksho, who was the chief bear hunter on the river, and killed a bear on one occasion without any weapon but his teeth.

The fifth crystal was named Kalga Lagim Lakah, the Great Fire Glass of Heaven, and was presented to Chief Neish-lak-an-noish, who was a [Coast] Tsimshian chief, but had married a Nishga chieftainess. This chief was famed for his skill as a carver and designer in gold, silver, and wood.

The sixth and last of the crystal stalactites was named Gwe-yel, and was presented to Chief Ginzadak, who after a hard life of raiding and fighting with other tribes at length became a Christian.

A song was composed by the music masters of the camps in commemoration of the finding of the crystals, and the circumstances connected with it. This song was named Maouk, and was sung annually by the tribes when they assembled for the potlatch, or Yiaak [*yaawk*], on the lower river. They were generally known as Giatkadeen, or The People Of The Valley. (1981:199–200)

Collison was privileged to see the Lion Stone (the third crystal mentioned) and described it as thus: "The stalactite was eight to ten inches in diameter. It was hexagonal in shape, and looked like cut glass" (1981:200).

As prisms refracting the enlightenment of the Tsimshian, crystals are eyes on the culture. They transmit light and so mediate the contrastive systems of crests and wonders, of vertex and vortex, of lid and lens.

*Source*

The source of light was variously called Heaven, Sky Chief, or the Sun, but this was not the only one. The Tsimshian also speak of *gal* (Miller 1981b: 154), whose name is invoked when a bear is killed. As a gesture of respect, the bear's tongue is cut into four sections, each of which is offered to a corner of the universe while thanks are given to *gal,* whose name has two possible, inter-related etymologies, one linking it to *gool* 'loon', and the other to *gal* 'space, empty'. Since loons moved between land, water, and air, they expressed the all pervading aspects of light. Moreover, the meaning of "space, empty" accords well with other features of the culture.[8]

As important as the house is for the social organization, it is equally so for the cosmology since the Tsimshian world consisted of inter-nested houses, each with a doorway, fireplace, and smokehole for the transmission of light. In addition, corners played an important role in ritual because they marked the areas where light was most contained. Royal children usually had four companions so each could stand in a different corner when access to power required total protection of the heir. Similarly, there is also an implied equation of the human body with a hollow tube, as George MacDonald (1981, 1984b) explored for the linkages of body, house, and cosmos.

In this manner, the house also provided an image of mediation. In the same way that an empty house "contained nothing," so, too, the universe itself can be described as hollow. What makes them both habitable is light, illuminating the void. As the hearth was the source for light and sociability in the house, so the Sun or a more abstract source produced the light that filled the universe.

As a hole had an edge and a hollow tube had sides, so the Tsimshian universe had a confining border, linking contents and container. The Tsimshian universe was comforting because, while it might seem empty, it was nonetheless bounded. It was hollow, but rimmed. As Seguin has noted, citing Boas (1916), the container and the contents were treated as a unit among the Tsimshian. "Indeed, Tsimshian oral traditions are explicit about the fact that a food without a proper container is ideologically no better than an empty container" (1984a:316).

Farber has also observed that Tsimshian culture "revolves around an organizing principle, the action of embodiment and containment. A subtle and mutually defining relationship exists between contained and container, 'reality' in some senses is that which can be contained, so, by extension, containers are reality purveyors. Containers can be physical, conceptual, or linguistic—an acting human, a box, a house, a lineage, a moral imperative or prerogative, or a word" (1984:316).

Further, Jensen (1980:182) noted the importance of distinctions between "empty" and "filled" in Tsimshian Raven sagas. Above all, of course, these statements indicate that contents and container were equally important to the Tsimshian and that one could not occur without the other.

On this basis, the symbolic importance of vessels, hollows, tubes, and passages among the Tsimshian becomes clear. They are the means for collecting or transmitting light and privilege. Ultimately, of course, the universe was itself container and light its contents.

In both their art (Holm 1965; McClaren 1978) and their mythology (Boas 1895, 1902, 1912, 1916, 1974; Spier 1931; Cove 1985; Barbeau 1929, 1950, 1958; Barbeau and Beynon 1987a, 1987b; J. Miller 1989), Tsimshians traced the beginnings of their culture to the efforts, often unrestrained, of Raven, who came to earth as a "shining youth."

Ultimately, the Tsimshian echo or axiomatic tension was a semantic equation based on light such that crest = lid (*ptex* = *haap*), wonder = lens (*naxnox* = *ts'al*), and privilege = loop (*halait* = *lui*).[9] John Cove, in his phenomenological study of "what does it mean to be human" for the Tsimshian, discussed these modalities as "totemic," "shamanic," and "privileged" (1987:10).

The human body consisted of fragile flesh, blood, and bone because elderberry gave birth first. As a reminder of what might have been, however, humans still have stone-like teeth and nails on fingers and toes. Moreover, noble women wore labrets, often of stone or inlaid wood, in the lower lip, with the lip-plugs of royal women being the biggest and most elaborate of all. Weighing on the lip, the labret represented the heaviness of royal status and served as a reminder to speak and eat carefully.

For all noble children, added status was conferred by having their ears pierced and their skin tattooed under the auspices of their father's kin, using designs from their mother's households.

In this manner, children were elevated to join the "real beings," the immortal spirits with a humanoid form concealed under the guise of another species. Thereby, some humans shared in the same primordial culture as the naxnox. While their species "blanket" might be consumed by others, their souls lived on.

The hallmark species, throughout the region, was the salmon, who spawn and die, yet return every year, have iridescent or shiny skin, and share language, society, and habitat with humans. When salmon left their villages beyond the sea, each species came in sequence to the rivers where they saw floating cottonwood leaves as their own kind of salmon. They left their villages as humans paddling canoes, but capsized to assume salmon form. After they died or were caught, their souls returned to the villages as humans, provided that Tsimshian burned the bones.[10]

Such immortality of souls rested on a belief in cycles of reincarnation, provided that remains were treated with proper respect and everything edible was consumed. Salmon stored for the winter must be eaten, as was explained in the story about a boy who refused to eat a piece of moldy salmon and was taken to live with the salmon for the year.

Mortals, therefore, nourished spirits as well as themselves by eating food from nature. By devouring outer coverings between species, the immortal essence of "real beings" was renewed and revived. At potlatches and winter ceremonials, when people were given real names, quantities of food were distributed among assembled friends and relatives. In doing so, they were literally nourishing body and soul—the bodies of other mortals and the souls of immortals.

Because there were only a fixed number of real names and associated places (seats) in each Tsimshian house, Adams (1973:4) has argued that during potlatches, when reality was conferred on a successor, people were also being redistributed. As fortunes and conflicts shifted, ordinary people bettered their positions by changing allegiances and moving to other houses where they had matrilineal claims. At such public feasts, by acting with the hosts rather than with the guests, a person indicated a new membership.

Periodic scrambling among lesser mortals, therefore, allowed the perpetuation of elite status among the holders of real names. In the process, *baa'lx* ('a soul') became reincarnated at birth in people related through women. While there was a tendency for succession to follow birth order, with younger brothers inheriting before elder sister's sons, transmission was not automatic. A man of ability might advance beyond his birth order, providing, first of all, that he was among the eligible successors.

Birthmarks suggesting pierced ears, scars, or tattoos were an advantage in claiming inheritance, as were proper training in family traditions and demonstrated managerial abilities.

In some cases, the evidence of birthmarks could be very compelling. A great-grandmother at the village of Hartley Bay had a pair of scars on either side of her hip in the place where her great aunt was pierced by an enemy arrow (cf. Seguin 1984b: 121). Unlike the Gitksan along the upper Skeena River, who trace such reincarnations among a close group of relations, the Coast Tsimshian are more diffuse about the lines of transmission.

Family support was also important and is now often expressed by a dream in which a deceased relative appears to a pregnant girl or to a senior woman and announces an intention to reincarnate. This dream mobilizes the family of the newborn to insure that the child assumes his or her rightful place in society.

Similar social concern also applied to the deceased.[11] In the past, Tsimshian nobles were cremated and each town had a special location shielded from the wind where a fire, tended by paternal relatives, consumed the body. Here again it was the kin of the father who eased the spiritual transition between worlds of reality.

In some cases, before cremation, the chest of a chief was cut open, internal organs removed, the heart buried, and the cavity filled with cedar bark to aid combustion (Garfield 1939:241). During cremation, all halait insignia were burned with the body because these were personally acquired, unlike a person's crests or wonders which were passed on by inheritance. Ashes and other remains were placed at the top of a mortuary pole.

Thus freed of one mortal container, the soul was ready to occupy another form and be reincarnated at the birth of the next holder of that particular real name. Significantly, this process occurred through the medium of fire, which consumed one life and kindled another. As a source of light, flames created the most real way to enable reincarnation.

With fire came reality. The hearth fire fed a family, day after day, at the same time that it transmitted food and forms between worlds. Flames, always new, symbolized the endless repetitions of reality that were enabled and perpetuated.

# 3. Branching Limbs

The "house," the basic social unit among the Tsimshian (and other Northwest Coast societies), was and is where the various branches of the culture intertwine. In full, a "house" was a building (or buildings if there were cadet branches), a membership, a territory, and a repository for hereditary treasures.

## Building

Every house had a series of locations at various resource areas, but the most important one was located in a winter town. Arranged in a row or rows facing the water with the forest behind, each house had much the same structure.

Tsimshian houses were huge rectangular constructions covered with overlapping cedar planks set in a framework of grooved beams. Four posts served to hold up the gabled roof and provided decorated surfaces for displaying carved and painted emblems passed down through women ancestors. The outside front of an elite house was also painted with the design that symbolized the most important crest of the house, which usually provided its name.

Inside, the house was divided on the basis of rank into family spaces, either as places on the wide bunks along the walls or in separate planked cubicals for more privacy. Family areas might also be divided by hanging woven cedar mats abutting the walls. In the most imposing of houses (*da'ax, da'ak*), these bunks formed tiers like bleachers along the sides of a deeply excavated

*4. Cedarplank House. One of the last traditional-style houses at Port Simpson had an eagle painted on the front and a pole with a carved beaver at its base. Canoes rest on the beach. Known as the Sgagweet Eagle House, it displayed the giibilk crest of the name title Nis'wiibaas. (Courtesy of the Museum of Northern British Columbia.)*

interior. The Gitisu had a famous house with ten levels (accordingly named "ten steps down") along the sides. These deep houses both were warmer during the winter and added to the prestige of the owner since he could shelter a larger constituency. The upriver Nishga made good use of these buried houses during the winter (McNeary 1976b:78).

Ranks were graded from front to back and from center to sides. Traditionally, these ranks distinguished nobles, commoners, and slaves, but during the past century a royalty emerged from the nobility as a consequence of a protective stance assumed after English settlement. Not true social classes, these ranks were more like categories of persons, with almost everyone belonging to the nobility. Commoners were more like marginals in that they had no family pedigrees to claim. Slaves constituted probably five percent of the population (McNeary 1976b: 136).

Slaves and low-class people slept near the door, which was drafty and vulnerable during attack. Commoners had spaces or cubicles along the sides. Important families were located along the back, protected and prominently in view. The family of the man (sometimes the woman) holding the foremost name, and thereby the "owner" of the house, lived in the back center. A special room occupied that end of the house, divided off from the public area by a carved and painted wooden screen, in which the treasured heirlooms and art were kept. The elite family had direct access to this cache and drew upon it for wearing apparel and display items at the feasts which they sponsored.[1]

Houses were built by cooperative labor. The home of a lineage was constructed by all the members of that kin group, thereby giving all members the right to live therein if they so chose. The home of a town chief was built by all the members of a town to show their allegiance with that leader. Men contributed materials and labor, along with goods to be given away at the dedication potlatch. According to McNeary (1976b: 128), Nishga houses belonged to the men, and, in fact, the core residents were males related as brothers and nephews.[2] At marriage, noble women moved to the home of their husband. Yet the house represented the matriclan. Therefore, after repair or completion, women and their older children, who constituted the lineage, came forward with mats, baskets, and food to supply the house. Furthermore, these furnishings were in keeping with the nearly universal equation of men with the outside and women with the inside. In the past decade, the chief of a Southern Tsimshian town built a new Euro-Canadian style home for his family. While he paid for the building, his wife paid for the furnishings.

The clans of fathers with children living within the house had special responsibilities. They provided some of the materials, helped out as needed, and carved all of the designs in the new house. If they did not do the actual artwork, they arranged to have it done. Members of other clans raised the corner posts and set the roof and wall boards, for which they were compensated at the dedication. Lineage members constructed the interior bunks or tiers and did the final finishing work. Thus, the main framework was built by members of other clans, while the inside was done by the house owners.

Andrew Nash   John Nash   James Percival   Philip Nash   Charlie Brown   Mrs. Eliza Woods   Matilda Peal
                                                                                        nee Brown
                                                                                        Aunt of the Chief

5. *Nishga Chiefs with Treasures. During a potlatch at Gitlaxdamiks, about 1903, a full range of house treasures and elite artifacts are on display. The copper (extreme left), box or chief's drum (extreme right), decorated tunics, and wooden chests were associated with crests, the masks represented the naxnox, and the frontlets, chilkat robes, raven rattle, and cedar neck or head rings indicated aspects of the halait. (Courtesy of the Museum of Northern British Columbia.)*

When all the materials were assembled, these other clansmen, especially those of the fathers, were invited to a feast that signaled the start of the house-raising. Everyone who came, whether they worked or not, received a gift. When the house was finished, a dedication potlatch was held to thank the workers and to formally name the house. The crests, privileges, and fame of the house and its illustrious ancestors were extolled.

Winter houses were occupied from about November to February, when the candlefish runs began in the Nass River. The house master supervised this movement, although each adult male had his own canoe for transporting his family and provisions. Gitksan villagers walked overland along the Grease Trail. At the Nass, each tribe had its own neighborhoods occupied by fishing cabins. Sometimes, families took the wall planks from their section of the winter house and used them to enclose an existing framework at the fishing camp.

By the 1870s, elite families at Port Simpson were building and occupying single-family dwellings built in European style. Wooden floors, doors, windows, and furniture became features of prestige. Moreover, Anglo-Canadian laws created many conflicts about the ownership and succession to these houses. Wives and children were expected to inherit, according to this law, while matrilineal succession meant that the homes of chiefs should pass to the nephew who inherited the name and position.

Chiefs used their own money to pay to have houses built and insisted that they had the right to sell and transfer these buildings as they wished. In consequence, people were less likely to engage in cooperative labor since they had no advantages or claims on the household as a result. During the past two centuries, wealth that had been spent on house building to add to the fame of a lineage was directed toward the ceremonies for installing or burying the chief.

Conflicts arose over the transmission of not only the building, but also the site where it stood. These places had been owned collectively by the lineage and clan.

A telling example involved Mark Luther (Garfield 1939:288–89), whose father was from Kitkatla. His mother belonged to the house of Grizzly Bear of the Raven clan of the Ginaxangiik. Just before 1900, Mark purchased the home of a Gitwilgyots woman chief at Port Simpson. When he went to take up residence with his new wife, he found the door padlocked. Undeterred, he broke into the house. Soon a group of elderly women of the Gitwilgyots came into the house and wandered from room to room weeping and lamenting their chiefs who had lived in the house. Mark Luther and the women ignored each other. Finally, he asked them to leave and they did. A new lock was installed, and he went back to the place where he was staying.

Several chiefs came to Mark Luther to ask that he give up the house in favor of the Gitwilgyots. He refused, citing Canadian law. Rumors spread that he had also purchased a pole associated with the house belonging to the Gitwilgyots, a great breach of etiquette. He denied the rumor, but conditions did not improve.

A meeting was held under the auspices of the missionary, a neutral party, to resolve the dispute. The lineage leaders explained that the house and property had long been used by their chiefs. The woman chief had no right to sell either, but these men knew that Mark Luther had bought from her in good faith. They offered him a partially built house and money, but he refused.

After a few days to calm down and talk with his wife, he decided to settle. The Gilwilgyots gave him a few hundred dollars and the village council gave him title to a vacant lot, where he built a new home for his family.

The chief kept the down payment, refusing to transfer it to the Gitwilgyots, who were upset with this haughty woman, but had no recourse to force compensation.

### Membership

Occupants of a house included the ranking name holder with his wife and children, his mother if widowed, his sisters (if divorced or widowed) together with their children, unmarried brothers, mother's sister's sons, and nephews with their families. These nephews were heirs to the house and one of them would, often after marriage, assume greater prominence in the affairs of the house and eventually succeed to the ranking name-title.

Every family had its own place along the sides of the house, while the leaders had ranked seats there during public events. Similarly, "The close relationship between a household group and a canoe party is noteworthy. A house chief became a canoe chief and every member of the party had an assigned seat in the canoe that corresponded to his seating rank within the house. Canoes, like houses, were named beings thought to have an existence and history of their own" (MacDonald 1979:13).[3]

Among the Coast Tsimshian, houses were ranked within each town, regardless of clans, while Gitksan house hierarchy was based on clan and the Nishga used a combination of both crest and clan depending on the town (Halpin 1973:285–87).

Among the Coast Tsimshian, the memberships of a person were fourfold: own side (crest) of own house, other side (affines) of own house, own crest in other houses, and unrelated houses (Dunn 1984c:38, with diagrams). Each crest was chartered by an *adawx* (a saga, epic, or sacred history) narrating an account of the immortal names who stayed in a specific territory and interacted with a naxnox to gain the privileges of the house.

The crests and epics "commemorate the group's origins, odysseys from ancient villages, moments when the people drew upon the assistance of spirit power, the defeat of neighboring peoples who threatened their security, or the discovery of new ways to survive the natural disasters they periodically experienced" (Gisday Wa and Delgam Uukw 1989:25). Crucial to each epic were the songs (*iimk'oyt*), sometimes called "dirges," which came from the breath of the ancestors and fused the past and the present into an emotional bond. Each crest represented the history, title, and authority of the house, along with its spirit power (*daxgyet*) passed through generations inheriting the same name-title.

Therefore, the house was "known by the hereditary name of the house head, and each succeeding candidate for the position assumed the [same] name, and the properties, duties and privileges that went with the name" (Halpin 1973: 23). Other members, if freeborn and not slaves, strove to have at least two names, a *waa* (from *waa* 'hip') from their *ptex* crest, and another from the naxnox, used respectively in summer and winter. If privileged to belong to a leading family, he or she also held a halait name.

Moving between the houses were members of the other freeborn class, the commoners, who shifted abodes with the seasons or in the hope of doing better in the household of another leader. They made up the labor force, serving those with claims to valued names and associated resources, but they were largely handicapped because they lacked important privileges or pedigrees of their own.

Marriages were carefully arranged between houses, particularly for leaders who used them to form social and political alliances. Royalty were expected to marry cross-cousins (Cove 1976; Rosman and Rubel 1971). The stated preference was for a man to marry into the category of mother's brother's daughter, but father's sister's daughter was also a possibility. Dunn has explained the advantages of each in terms of the fourfold house divisions listed above. The matrilateral preference

> will result in maximum retention of personal possessions within the house, and it will result in an absolutely equitable distribution of possessions to the four village divisions. Since it must now be clear that the purpose of the inheritance mechanism is to build the prestige of the deceased, to make him connotative grandfather and thus ancestor of all four parts of the village, a double motive for patrilateral marriage also becomes apparent: it will result in a greater distribution to the village quarter totally unrelated by tribe or house to the deceased and will thus in the logic of the potlatch accord him even greater prestige. Finally, this last quarter (unrelated, outside) contains the children of his own house. (1984c:54)

Among royalty, a man might marry a woman and have four children, then separate from her and marry again without stigma on either party (McNeary 1976b:163). Kwakiutls (Kwakwaka'wakw) did much the same thing to build up alliances with several families.

At the lowest extreme were the slaves, purchased from native traders or captured in raids. Most were women and children. Rarely, a Tsimshian man might commit a breach or insult that would force him to forfeit his freedom. If a highborn foreign woman were captured, she might quickly be married to a Tsimshian noble before the stigma of slavery became attached to her. In this way, slave raids sometimes also resulted in marriages between elite families from different tribes.[4] In other cases, the family was allowed to ransom a captive before he or she entered slavery. Similarly, a captive belonging to the same crest as one of the raiders might be released with gifts so as not to blemish their common kinship.

*Territory*

Usually, the saga specifies that the named ancestor visited or camped in the territory claimed by the house. The territory of a house could include halibut and cod banks, seaweed-gathering spots, sections of beachfront for salvage, salmon streams, berry-picking and hunting grounds, bathing places, cremation sites, cemeteries, and the actual place in the village where the house physically stood. The most important house was at the middle of the town, with houses of lessening rank at further removal from it.

*Repository*

By explicit analogy, a house was like a person (*gyet*). As a house had a central hearth, a person had a mind (*sigootk*), located in the heart (*goot*), like a flame of intelligence.

As a personalized building, the house represented the ancestry of the matriline, clan, and moiety. The four support posts were limbs, the ridge pole was the backbone, the rafters were ribs, and the walls were skin. The decorated front was the face, with the door serving as the mouth. Known only to the elite, secret tunnels, used for staging winter spectacles and for escape, represented digestive functions.

The ancestor was visualized as standing between the door and the central fire looking east to the rising sun.[5] West was in back, north on the left, and south on the right. The central vertical axis of the body linked the upper and lower worlds with the human world. The spine of the ancestor, like that of the current name holder, provided this direct link between worlds.

In the sky, the leader was Heaven; on earth, there were land and undersea owners or "Chiefs of Wealth." Every animal species had its own leaders who also occupied plankhouses like those of humans, also arranged by rank. Orcas and Eagles, at least, had the same four clans and moieties as the Tsimshian themselves.

As households formed towns and tribes, they were also organized in terms of kinship, economy, and religion. Significantly, these features also depended on names, relating to crests, wonders, and privileges. At present, however, only the crest names have survived the wholehearted conversion to Christianity.

As Lévi-Strauss aptly noted, this notion of the house was very close to that of feudal Europe, where the estate consisted of immaterial as well as material wealth, and its membership could be based on highly convoluted (if not outright fictive) kinship ties:

> The chief of the house is rich, sometimes immensely so, as Montesquieu observed when he analyzed Charlemagne's will; and in any case, rich enough for his fortune to constitute a political tool and a means of government. To paraphrase Girart de Roussillon: Gifts are his towers and his battlements. The wealth of the house also includes names, titles, and hereditary prerogatives—what used to be called "honours"—to which must be added, as with the Indians, goods of supernatural origin: Saint Martin's cloak, the Holy Ampulla, Saint Denis' banner, the crown of thorns, etc. (1982:176)

Crests and wonders pervaded all of Tsimshian culture and society. They influenced the individual during his or her seasonal activities in the summer or the winter, and correlated with events in the camp or the town. In terms of the arts, they were expressed in the difference between inherited art forms, made privately within the community, or wondrous displays prepared away from the town in such secrecy that any intruders were said to have been killed immediately. These secret artists were called *gitsontk,* and they "were exclusively noble and included all younger members of a particular house, with hereditary rights. Subsequently this was diluted by the addition of talented commoners, whose parents were able to pay the substantial sums involved in advanced initiation fees. These commoners then became 'noble' by courtesy" (Shane 1984:167).

According to Heber Clifton, Blackfish chief at Hartley Bay, the *gitsontk* "carved nothing but [naxnox] spirits, and worked in utter secrecy" (Barbeau 1950:789–90). They were specially trained, and anyone who encountered their workshops in the forest was killed. Conversely, if one of their wonders failed to perform or was found out in public, the *gitsontk* committed suicide. For example, a huge wooden whale was made to swim, dive, and spout. It appeared only at night, either illuminated by fires on shore or by moonlight, but, on one occasion, its fastenings came undone and the people inside it nearly died. Its makers jumped into the sea and drowned because of their shame.

The other artists were called *ukgyiɫae* and "their calling was to produce crests and totems. As there was no secrecy to their work, they could not carve naxnox" (Barbeau 1950:790).[6]

Among all of these artifacts, the most important of the crests were hats, worn on the head of the prime sponsor at a potlatch. Wonders, on the other hand, were primarily masks, worn over the face by the owner or a surrogate during a winter ceremonial. Halpin (1973:119) noted this contrast, as did Barbeau, who wrote that the heir of a mother's brother "had to accompany his uncle to all feasts and gatherings, at which he sat either in front of him or behind, depending on the nature of the feast. If it was a narhnorh [naxnox] (spirit) feast, where a narhnorh would be dramatized, then he would sit behind the uncle. If it was a yaeuk [potlatch], then he sat in front" (1950:134). Since the sister's son was more protected behind his uncle, this seating agrees with Halpin's interpretation that, "Whereas in the naxnox they had played the sacred game of boundary transgression and power release, in the potlatch they celebrated the boundaries" (1981:287). Furthermore, the seating arrangement also specified succession, since the next in line to the office sat either behind the holder at a potlatch or behind the heir at a naxnox display.

## CRESTS BRANCH

The crests were and are defined by matrilineal kinship and constitute the best known Tsimshian institution because they are the most public. The four clan crests were generally known by the animal that provided the predominant design, along with subsidiary designs, indicated here in parentheses. These crests are: Orca Blackfish (Grizzly, Grouse, Mosquito), Raven (Frog, Sculpin, Starfish), Eagle (Beaver, Halibut, Octopus), and Wolf (Bear, Crane, Owl) (Halpin 1984:26).

In the specific instance of Hartley Bay, the Blackfish crests were Sun, Stars, Rainbow, Grizzly, Fireweed, and the Fireweed Cane; those of Eagle were Whale, Dogfish, Beaver, Halibut, Frog, and the Cormorant Hat; those of Raven were Bullhead, Starfish, Frog, and Red Leggings dyed with sea lion blood; and the single Wolf family was submerged within the Blackfish (Hartley Bay School 1985a, 1985c).

Among the neighboring Haida, Tlingit, and Wakashans, crests were comparable units on the order of pseudo-species. To these horizontal categories, the Tsimshian added a ranked vertical one, so that crest names also implied social position and class membership (Halpin 1973, 1984:28).[7] In other words, particularized crests were unique to Tsimshian royalty, in contrast to the generic ones of the Haida and Tlingit. For example, a Tsimshian royal house crest was not simply "Blackfish," but rather "Two Blackfish Facing Each Other." Often, a royal crest was called "Prince of X," as with Prince of Blackfish, and decorated with abalone, copper, or white paint (Halpin 1984:31, 32) to provide light-reflecting surfaces. Usually, crest designs appeared on clothing, hats, house posts, house fronts, interior screens, canoes, drums, feast dishes, and freestanding poles.

Since chiefs were literally called "real people," it is significant that only they could wear the actual head or pelt of the crest animal, enhanced by decoration. While crest designs were applied to the clothing and house of their owner, they were most in evidence during a potlatch when changes in the names and statuses of householders were being witnessed by an audience of prestigious outsiders, who, in return, were compensated with food and gifts.

While all tools and utensils were decorated in some fashion, only those closest to the public image of the name-holder, aside from his economic role, could bear appropriate crests. Usually, the most important crest was a hat displaying the emblem or actual animal head. At a potlatch, the crest hat was worn by the senior name-holder, along with other "proofs" of his pedigree.

When Tsimshians from the different towns gathered at the new settlements, all four crests came together and were recorded for surviving communities. Increasingly, however, "Fieldwork done since the 1960s . . . suggests that, *at the village level,* Tsimshian society traditionally had a dual or moiety structure" (Halpin and Seguin 1990:274). Thus, traditional towns were divided into "sides" such that only two of the crests functioned as moieties (halves), distinguishing Owners from Others (Miller 1981b:158).

For the Coast, the Owners are Blackfish-Grizzly (*Gispwudwada*) and the significant Others are Raven (*Ganhada*), sometimes replaced by Eagle (*Laxsgiik* 'On The Eagle') or Wolf (*Laxgibuu* 'On The Wolf'). Tsimshian themselves have a sense that Blackfish and Raven are the original moieties, while Eagle derives from the Haida, and Wolf from interior Athapaskans. Several of the crest origins within the clans have been summarized by Garfield (1966: 18–22). For the coastal towns about 1850, comprising about fifteen tribes, 334 houses were divided among the four crests (Duff 1964a:67).

| Gispwudwada | Blackfish, Grizzly | 122 houses |
| Ganhada | Raven | 96 houses |
| Laxsgiik | Eagle | 74 houses |
| Laxgibuu | Wolf | 42 houses |

Among many Gitksan, Frog-Raven is the Owner, and Fireweed-Grizzly is the Other, probably in consequence of aboriginal conventions to allow for intermarriages among trader-nobles from coastal and interior communities (Miller 1981b) and facilitated by the "Macro-Crow kinship system" found among these matrilineal tribes (Dunn 1984a).[8]

As reassessed, therefore, the four crest groups, usually called phratries or matriclans, are better described as semi-moieties. Further, when elite marriages were arranged with Haida and Tlingit, Blackfish-Wolf were regarded as one moiety and Raven-Eagle as the other. Among both the Haida and the Tlingit, the Raven moiety is the Owners.

For example, at Hartley Bay in 1985, the immediate environs of the town were "owned" by the Orcas, as was the location of certain primary resources. Immediately adjacent to these were Eagle lands forming a wedge around the town. The Ravens had two pockets of land, one in Blackfish territory and the other in that of the Eagles. Blackfish and Eagle, therefore, predominated, functioning like moieties of the town (cf. Hartley Bay School 1985c:89).

On a larger scale, the Tsimshian oriented themselves by a conceptual framework based on the cardinal directions (MacDonald 1981:227), with the horizontal defined by a shaman facing east and the sunrise, so that west was to his or her back, north to the left and south to the right.[9] Aides stood in the four corners of the house to mobilize its powers. The sky itself was another house-like world, with the smoke holes of sky, earth, and underworld houses aligned to define the vertical, which was also marked by the polar star. In some places and times, this vertical was also represented by the fire of a house, the totem poles set up near the house, and the chiefly and shamanic leaders of the house in their ritual guises.

Since each of the four crests was internally ranked on the basis of prestige and royal status, with the most important crests held by the houses at the middle of the town, each crest must have represented aspects of the horizontal. Generally, as the primary coastal moieties, Blackfish belonged to the sea and the west, while Raven connoted the beach on the east where he was sent by his human father. In terms of sacred history, however, Raven was ubiquitous as a culture hero, while the founders of the Blackfish were located both far out to sea, as aquatic mammals, and deep in the interior along the Skeena, as Grizzlies, so they too were mediators. Among the Gitksan, Grizzly was of the east and Frog-Raven of the west. Wolf was associated with the forests and people of the north, and Eagle with the rivers and people of the south.

Of course, each crest drew its inspiration from spirits all over the landscape—from sky, land, sea, and caverns inhabited by various naxnox. Each account of an encounter specified the route taken to get there, and something of the terrain so that its cosmological significance could be ascertained. The use of canoes, snowshoes, trails, and particular hunting or fishing gear also helped to identify these habitats. For example, snowshoes and mountain goat gear implied mountains, as halibut lines indicated the sea.

Yet each crest had, and still has, a primary referent and set of associations in terms of the axial model, with vertical ranks occupied by its members as royals, nobles, and commoners, and with the horizontal ones arranged according to the placement of people within each house.

The crest system of hierarchically arranged art forms inherited through the mother was balanced by the wonder (naxnox) system displaying a mastery of spiritual power with a male or paternal emphasis.

While there were hundreds of named Tsimshian houses, each belonged to one of the four primary crests. Because research among the Tsimshian began in relocated communities like Port Simpson, decades passed before scholars realized that these four units, often called phratries, actually functioned like semi-moieties. This meant that the moieties of the Haidas and Tlingits had, and still have, direct analogues among the Tsimshian. As modern Tsimshian say, Blackfish and Wolf "go together," as do Raven and Eagle.[10]

According to *adawx* tradition, almost all crests originated at Prairie Town (Temlaxham), located along the upper Skeena River near modern Hazelton. Indeed, most houses trace their ancestry back to Prairie Town, but there are also other sagas about origins, as in the Nagunaks (Ngwinaks, Nugunaks) history of the Southern Tsimshian Gitisu given below. The Heavenly Children pacified the world and founded Prairie Town, which eventually outgrew its bounds while its members became guilty of overkill. The revenge of the Mountain Goats exemplifies the most typical of the outcomes, as does the flood caused by the Trout.

### Heavenly Children

After the time of Txaamsm, two villages lived across from each other along the Nass.[11] Both were very wealthy, each with many warriors who fought each other.

In one village was the woman chief named Gawo (Gawaw), who had four sons and a daughter. The boys were great hunters and kept their families well fed.

Once they went to hunt beavers. When they went to dismantle the beaver dam to expose their prey, however, the oldest brother was killed when a gnawed stake pierced his heart. As his brothers dug the body from the jumble of branches, they decided that their sister-in-law had been unfaithful. That was why their brother died. A hunter's luck depended on the sincerity of his wife.

The youngest brother decided to go back to the house they shared and watch their sister-in-law. He waited outside until night and then went in. First he went to his mother and told her that her oldest son was dead. She began to wail, but he asked her to be quiet. He inquired about the sister-in-law but the mother was sure that nothing was amiss. Going near the bed of his dead brother, however, the man heard laughter. Then he knew.

He waited until the couple was asleep. Then he cut off the head of the handsome man who was sleeping with his sister-in-law. Her lover was the son of the chief of the other town. Expensive earrings of abalone and blackfish teeth glinted in the fire light as the brother took the head out of the house.

Soon the unfaithful wife woke because her bed was wet. She was startled to find that blood soaked her covers. Quickly, she realized her lover was dead and his head was gone. Very much afraid, she arose and lifted the planks of her bed. She buried the body of the young man underneath and changed her bed clothes. Then she pretended to be asleep.

The next day, the brothers returned early, carrying the body of the eldest. The people mourned profoundly because he had been much loved and very generous.

While everyone was out of the house grieving, the youngest brother hung the severed head inside, high over the door in the shadows of the peak.

When the young prince did not return to his home, his father became concerned. Members of the prince's own crest showed little concern because they suspected that he might be hiding because of some shameful deed. His father, however, could express the depth of his emotional anguish. He ordered all fires to be extinguished, insisting that everyone mourn in darkness until they knew what had become of his son.

Everyone put out their fires, except those in the house of the brothers. They were discreet, but, every morning, they built up their fire. A little smoke drifted through the roof.

The chief saw this and sent a slave to investigate. He told her to ask for a flame so that they could light a fire when they needed to start one again.

The slave went to the house and asked for fire, as she had been instructed. The brothers nodded and pointed to the flames. While she bent down to light her torch, the slave looked around but she saw nothing. She went home and reported that nothing was suspicious except for the burning fire.

A few days later, the chief sent the slave again to get fire, giving the same reason. The slave did as instructed, but as she left the house something sticky struck her foot. She deliberately tripped when going through the door and her torch went out in the snow.

She turned around and went back to ask for fire again, explaining that she was only a clumsy slave and had fallen. Looking carefully over the door, she saw the oozing head of her prince. She ran through the door and across the ice to the home of her master. There she wailed that his son was dead and his head hung over the inside door of the house of Gawo.

The chief roared in his grief and summoned all of his warriors. Within moments, they fell upon the other town and killed everyone. Then they burned the town so that nothing was left.

Yet Gawo and her daughter survived. They hid in a tunnel under the house and when the ashes were cool they climbed out and ran into the woods. The old woman wailed constantly for all who died in her town, and, particularly, for her sons.

After a day of mourning, she began to think of their present condition and cried out, "Who will marry the daughter of Gawo?" She called this constantly.

Soon a wren came up to her and said, "I will marry your daughter." The woman asked, "What can you do? I need a son-in-law who will revenge my people and leave me heirs." Wren said, "When a hunter gets near an animal, I fly around and signal a warning." "Show me," the woman said. Wren did, but the woman was not impressed. "Leave us now. You will not do." Then she began her cry again.

Over the next few days, the birds who approached with offers of marriage got bigger and bigger. Each had a specialty. Hummingbird grabbed hairs from people, Sparrow wakened sleepers, Robin announced Summer, Mockingbird announced bad weather, Bluejay told when it was time to pick berries, and Eagle pecked out the eyes of enemies.

Then, the animals came, each one larger. Squirrel scattered nuts, Rabbit stared at people, Porcupine threw quills, Marmot watched the sun to foretell the weather, Otter drowned enemies, Beaver made trees fall, Wolf bit enemies, and Grizzly Bear ripped bodies apart. Gawo rejected all of these. Still she wailed and called.

The fourth time she shouted lightning flashed and thunder rolled. Four times it did this. Then a handsome man stood before her, wearing garments that shone like flames, and said, "I will marry your daughter."

The mother was frightened, but she asked, "What can you do?" "I can make the world turn over and kill all enemy warriors," he replied. "Show me," she asked and he did. Now she was satisfied. "You will be the one to marry my daughter."

"I will now take you to my father in Heaven," the man said. He placed the daughter under one arm and the mother under the other. "Do not look down when I fly up," he commanded, but the mother could not obey. Four times she looked, and four times they fell back to earth. The husband was angry. He pulled a branch from a tree and put the old woman inside. Ever since branches have creaked and moaned.

Then he took his wife to the sky. They lived in the house of his father, but they slept apart. One morning a ray of sun struck the girl's belly and she became pregnant. Soon she had four boys and two girls. They grew very quickly and their grandfather made houses for them, each decorated with the first crests that were ever seen. The house of the eldest had a carving of the sun and moon, the next younger had a carving of stars, the next a rainbow, and the youngest a carving of a mirage in the shape of a man. Each was also given a special weapon. From the oldest brother to the youngest these were a stone club, a sling shot, a spear, and the power to kill with his fist. Now they were ready to take revenge.

That night a heavy fog obscured the Nass River. Four loud noises were heard across the river where the destroyed town had been. Each was the sound of a house coming to earth. Youngsters joked that the enemy dead were restless that night, but the elders forbade such talk because something strange was happening.

The next morning, the fog lifted and revealed four new houses, painted and standing where the old village had been. The other village was afraid, but they decided to visit.

Leaders went across and were well received. The young men spoke nicely to them and the two women fed them great quantities of food. Everyone acted friendly.

The next day the towns decided to gamble. This was part of the plan. The

heavenly sons won every game and the proud people from across the river became more and more angry. One of the sky sisters had a slight limp and some
visitors began to make fun of her. Others scoffed at the success of the brothers.
Soon they came to blows. Each of the brothers used his wondrous weapon to
kill many people that day.

Their grandfather had given the heavenly children a box, called *tsüwan,* to
open when they were attacked. When the lid was removed, the earth turned
over and left the enemies underneath. When the brothers could fight no more,
they opened the box and the other town was destroyed.

Now the brothers traveled the earth. They founded the Gispwudwada crest.
Their sisters married and carried it into future generations. If people did not do
as they said, they fought them into submission. Soon the whole world was at
peace. The other crests were founded—the Ravens, Eagles, and Wolves—to
permit lawful intermarriage.

Joining together as the Gispwudwada were the Moon, Stars, Rainbow,
Grizzly Bear, and Blackfish. The Ganhada combined the Raven, Frog, Sea
Lion, and Starfish. With the Eagles went the Beaver, Halibut, and others. Wolf
and Crane went together.

Each member of a crest must marry a member of another crest. People were
proud of their crests and had them tattooed on their chests and hands. Some
designs decorated houses and other property.

When all had crests, the heavenly children held the first human potlatch.
Everyone displayed what they had and settled all differences. Yet still the
brothers fought other towns. Now their grandfather was uneasy that they
would not know when to stop. He decided to take them back to Heaven and he
did. Thus, if Tsimshian break any of the laws that he provided, he will be
angry and people will suffer.

The crests have very strict rules. Each has its own songs for victory in
battle, for paddling canoes, for the potlatch, for thanking an animal killed by a
hunter, for gambling, for dancing, for taking a name, for baby lullabies, for
ridiculing others, for having fun, for fishing, for mourning, and when longing
for friends.

Each crest has a drum to accompany singing, while women carry the tune
of the song. Men sing the songs of victory and paddling. In the same way,
names are passed on through women. A father will help his children all that he
can, but they belong to the crest of their mother and they take names from her
house.

That is the way the "heavenly children" made it to be.

*Goats*

While people lived at Temlaxham, some hunters found a hillside filled with mountain goats and killed them all except for a young kid which they brought back home and abused by shoving it repeatedly into a fire.[12] A kindhearted boy took the goat home and rubbed vermillion paint over its burns. Then he let it go. Other people were not as respectful. It was the custom, after goats were killed, for children to dance with goat skulls on their heads, mocking these animals. No one thought anything of these incidents because the people of Temlaxham had grown wasteful and had lost pride in themselves.

Several days later, two unknown men wearing white blankets came to the town to invite everyone to a feast. It was assumed that these were new neighbors introducing themselves, so the chiefs accepted. The messengers stayed four days and then led everyone over back trails until they came to a broad prairie with an elaborate house in the middle. Everyone went inside and saw that all was ready. A skin curtain hung along the back, hiding the stage. Singing was coming from behind it. Local people seated the visitors and made them comfortable.

A boy came to the boy who had been kind to the young kid, led him to a corner of the house, and sat beside him. This boy, who wore a white blanket with red marks on it, said, "Stay very close to me. Something is about to happen."

A huge mountain goat came from behind the curtain and walked slowly to the center of the house.[13] Everyone was amazed. The boy said to his visitor, "Pay very close attention. Something dreadful will happen. Hold tight to me. Hold on regardless. When you hear the song, be ready."

The host began to sing, "I shake my hooves on this side and on that side. Now the mountain will split." He lifted the curtain sharply and, at once, a mountain slide began.

Instead of being on a prairie, they were on the steep side of a mountain. The house collapsed and everyone was buried in the slide. The boy was saved, however, because he held tight to the kid whom he had saved from the fire. His kindness was returned.

The boys were safe in a rocky gorge. There they spent the night. In the morning, the boy was greeted by the goat kid that he had saved, still wearing red marks. The goat said, "It is all over. The rocks have settled. You can go home safely now." The boy walked to the edge of the ledge where he had spent the night and looked over the edge. It was a long way down and he was very frightened. His heart sank.

The boy looked back at the goat and cried, "If I go this way, I will surely fall and die. Is that what you want?" "No," the goat replied, "that is not my intention. I forget that humans are afraid of heights and lack our abilities." Then he sat down and took off his shoes and blanket. "Here, put these on," he told the boy. "These will do the trick." The boy put them on, but he was still afraid.

So the goat took his garments back and put them on. "I will show you how safe it is." Then he jumped all over the cliffs and from one peak to another. He walked down the rock slide as though it were level. He came back to the ledge. "See how easy it is," he exclaimed.

The boy put the blanket and shoes back on. The goat explained, "Now do as I did. Only you must say 'thumb sticking out' every time you jump. Every time you must say that. When you get to the bottom, place the blanket and shoes in a tree and I will find them again."

The boy jumped and said "thumb sticking out," but he was unsteady at first. Soon he gained confidence. Every time he said, "Thumb sticking out. Edge of the rock ledge," he did quite well. Soon he reached the bottom and left the blanket and shoes in a tree.

The bodies of his friends filled the base of the mountain. He could do nothing for them. He walked back to Temlaxham, where a few of the old and young had stayed. He told them the story of the revenge of the Mountain Goats and, for a time, people were again respectful, but it did not last.

### The Flood

Prairie Town again grew and prospered.[14] There were no enemies and there was no end of food. The population of the town grew larger and larger. Soon there were so many people that they could not keep track of each other. The elders ignored the children, who did many things which were forbidden. Everyone did as he or she pleased. Great chiefs would give feasts and kill many slaves. They wasted food. The people had become wicked.

One day some children went across the Skeena to play by themselves. One of them went for a drink at a small stream. There he saw many trout. He called to the others, and they began to fish for trout even though they already had plenty of food.

They abused the trout. When they caught a fish, they would put urine in its mouth and return it to the water to watch it writhe and die. They laughed and mocked the fish in its agony.

The trout had come to spawn that fine spring day, but they died instead.

Soon a black fog began and a strong wind blew. Then it began to rain torrents. The trout stream began to rise. The children drowned.

In the town, everyone began to prepare for a flood. They put provisions in their canoes, all of their crests, coppers, and other property. They made tents of elkskins within the canoes to keep off the rain. They floated and watched.

The water covered their houses. The poor people drowned because they had no canoes. The very old and the youngest died because they could not withstand the hardships.

For twenty days it rained. All the valleys flooded. All of the hills went under water. Foam was everywhere because the wind was violent and roiled up the water. Over the sound of the tempest, the people heard a sound like a bell ringing. This was Heaven warning everything to fear his wrath.

Canoes began to drift away because their anchor ropes were too short. Some left their canoes and went to the mountain tops, but they died of exposure. Eventually, all of the canoes were swept away from the town.

Then the storm grew quiet. The people of Prairie Town had been scattered from Alaska to the southern coast. They took with them their crests and their memories of the greatness of their town.

Everywhere there was only a vast expanse of clay. The animals had survived on the highest peaks, and they too came down. Only the fiercest monsters had drowned. The earth was so clean because an enormous whirlpool had formed at the end of the flood and sucked down all of the dead bodies of trees, birds, animals, and people.

The important people in the biggest canoes survived, although they wailed constantly for their dead. When the flood was gone, they landed in many places and started over again, living in their elkskin tents until they could find materials for houses.

While everyone had spoken the same language (Coast Tsimshian) in Prairie Town, every community now developed its own speech. Even though they have different languages, everyone knew who their relatives were because they shared the same crests.

Atop the highest mountain a boy and a girl had survived. When the water receded, they walked down to the river and became the parents of the tribes along the upper Nass and Skeena. Even they have the same crests as the people along the coast because they too began at Temlaxham.

After the deluge, Prairie Town Gispwudwada survivors had Grizzly as their primary crest, while coastal Gispwudwada had Blackfish Orca. To unify their traditions, new crests were created. These were Grizzly Bear of the Sea and Blackfish of the Lake.

The separate status of the Southern Tsimshian (Simonson 1973; Miller 1978, 1981a, 1981b, 1984c) is borne out by their distinctive account about an ancestor named Dragging Along Shore and his adventures with Gitnagunaks in the Moore Islands. While many of the Southern Tsimshian royal houses traced their name-titles back to Temlaxham, the local royalty acknowledged the Nagunaks source within Gitisu territory.[15] To illustrate this distinction, versions of the founding of Gitḵa'ata and the Gitisu epic will be presented. In particular, the epic of the localized winter, another of the tragedies at Temlaxham, provided the motivation for the southward migration.

### Gitḵa'ata

When everyone lived at Temlaxham, Nta'wiiwaap, a Gispwudwada, and his large family lived at Ksnga'at, a tributary river of the Skeena, and were prosperous because the weather was mild, food was abundant, and people lived in peace. A large salmon trap made of logs was full during the runs, and game was everywhere.

One spring, however, when the salmon were spawning, it began to snow. At the First Salmon ceremony, a young man held a spring salmon up to Heaven and rebuked him for sending the storm. The elders were angry with the man for his indiscretion, particularly when their rite had the attention of Heaven, but the other young men backed him up, saying that food would always be abundant.

But Heaven was offended. The weather grew colder and colder, and the snow became so deep that the salmon trap was crushed. Even the squirrels abandoned the region. Famine ruled. The houses were buried under the snow and everyone starved to death, except Nta'wiiwaap and his wife.[16] One day a robin appeared at the smokehole with a sprig of elderberries in its beak.[17] Then Nta'wiiwaap and his wife knew that it was summer all around them, so they dug their way out through the snow. Soon, they found the sun shining on a bright summer day, with everything blooming. The wife gave birth to a child, but it died. Nourishing herself on tiny fish, she fed Nta'wiiwaap with her milk.

Regaining their strength, they began to preserve food for their journey. Nta'wiiwaap made a canoe to carry these provisions. After going down the Skeena and across the Lakelse River, they came to the Ecstall River, making a winter hut beside a large lake. A daughter was born to them, and she grew up quickly. In the spring, the chief hunted mountain goats and saw smoke rising from a house. Curious, he made a sled to carry their food and led his family down the mountain. They found a river and saw a house on the other side. They called across, and some stocky young men came for them in a canoe. Inside the house, from the honored place at the back wall, a very old and short man greeted them. He told his slaves to feed the visitors.

When Nta'wiiwaap and family were finished, the old chief spoke to them. He explained that he was the son of the North Wind and asked to marry the daughter. Nta'wiiwaap agreed that his daughter could marry this naxnox. In time, Nta'wiiwaap and his wife died. The daughter had children, in sets of four, by her husband, and kept house for his brothers, the Northwest, Southwest, East, and West Winds. When these men traveled, they took the form of ducks.[18]

When the numerous children grew to be adults, they founded the town of Gitḵa'ata on the coast. These people explored their territory and K'ayamtkwa, brother of Nta'wiiwaap, found good hunting, particularly for sea otter, on Banks Island. He tried to claim it for his own use, but Nta'wiiwaap insisted that the best places had to be shared by all. K'ayamtkwa moved to Kitkatla, where he had a high rank.

The nearest neighbors of the Gitḵa'ata were fearsome members of the Wolf crest who had come from the Tlingits and were married to Eagles. After several skirmishes, Nt'a'wiwaap called together warriors from the Gitḵa'ata, Gitlope, and Kitamat, who drove these Wolves from Douglas Channel. The survivors joined another fortified Wolf town on Lowe Inlet (Kmodo). A rope, hung with rattling deer hooves and puffin beaks, stretched across Greenville Channel to warn the Wolves of approaching travelers. After careful planning, another raid led by Nta'wiiwaap destroyed that village and cut the rope, allowing free passage through the territory. In time, the Gitḵa'ata intermarried with the Wolves, who became absorbed into the tribe.

During the migration from Temlaxham, another group was led by 'Wamoodmɫk, a Blackfish, married to a Raven woman. Their first town in Gitḵa'ata territory was Tsetsat, now called Turtle Point, on Gil Island. Gunaxnuutk, brother of the chief, settled at Kitkatla. After the brothers separated, 'Wamoodmɫk acquired a crest called White Bear (*moksgmol*), inspired by a Kermode bear he had seen on Princess Royal Island. Gunaxnuutk coveted this crest and planned to shame his brother and take it.

One day while passing Tsetsat, he loudly commented on the temporary lean-to huts that these Gitka'ata were living in, calling them "raven snares" (*ganugaax*).

'Wamoodmłk heard the insult and responded by building an impressive house. When the building was finished, he had it covered over with branches and vegetation. Then he invited his brother and the Kitkatlas to a potlatch, announcing that he would take the name of Raven Snare.

When the Kitkatlas arrived, everything seemed the same and they became smug. 'Wamoodmłk invited his brother to come from the camp where the Kitkatlas were staying, and as Gunaxnuutk approached the beach, 'Wamoodmłk called to his men to uncover his "little raven snare." Immediately, all of the brush was removed to reveal a beautiful house with stars painted on the front. 'Wamoodmłk called out, "This is my 'raven snare' and it will be called Star House (*biyaalsmwaap*). I will take the name of Ganugaax and be its chief." Then he gave away wealth and property to all the guests. Gunaxnuutk presumed that he would receive the White Bear crest, but he left without it.

Eventually 'Wamoodmłk sought a new town, with salmon, berries, and seafoods nearby. He decided to move his people to the place where two rivers meet, went there, and placed a cane into the ground, proclaiming that his tribe would now become known as the Gitka'ata, the People of the Cane. The cane had come with the refugees from Temlaxham and represented their ancestry in the Fireweed clan.

'Wamoodmłk had another Star House built at the town, but it always faced the sun. The chief was concerned that the painting would dry and crack so he assigned a slave woman to throw water on the house front constantly. The woman became exhausted, but the chief would shout at her, saying, "Woman of the Tides, keep throwing water on the painting." The woman began to mourn her fate and her song became a dirge of the Gitka'ata royal house.

The brothers continued to bicker over the White Bear crest. Once, Gunaxnuutk went with a nephew to hunt. When a storm arose and capsized the canoe, Gunaxnuutk drowned but the nephew survived.

The Kitkatla blamed the Gitka'ata for the death because the nephew should have taken better care of his uncle. They planned to attack, but 'Wamoodmxl, seeing that his people were outnumbered, gave the new Gunaxnuutk the coveted crest as compensation. Since then Gunaxnuutk has used the White Bear crest at Kitkatla (Hartley Bay School 1987a).[19]

Even now the Gitka'ata, Kitkatla, Klemtu, and Metlakatla have close ties because many of their chiefs shared common origins from Prairie Town and their houses continue to intermarry.

*Nagunaks*

About the time of the Flood, a family lived among the Gitisu.[20] Their chief was named Dragging Along Shore (Dzagamsagisk), but the world was yet sparsely populated. The men went out to hunt sea lions, sea otters, and seals, but they could find none. The canoe of the chief stayed out with a crew of four, which included the chief, two other men of the Blackfish, and the steersman, who belonged to the Eagle crest. Even they eventually gave up and decided to turn back to their new town.

When evening came, they camped in their canoe at the foot of a steep mountain. The steersman said, "Let us cast anchor here." They all agreed. The four members of the crew went to sleep. The chief was in the bow.

Late at night, he awoke because a fish was splashing around the canoe. He looked and saw a blue cod. He was angry at the fish for waking him up. He reached out and grasped the cod. He scolded it for making noise and then damaged its fins. "Go away now," he said. "You will not bother me any more." Then the chief went back to sleep.

The crew did not know that their anchor had landed on the home of a powerful spirit called Gitnagunaks ('person under water'). He sent his slave to discover what made the noise because, after the anchor smashed onto the roof, it scraped along the surface all night.

The slave returned weeping. She was hurt and ashamed. She told the naxnox, "Men have anchored above us and their anchor is making all the noise. When I went to see them, the chief hurt me."

Gitnagunaks ordered his slaves to bring the canoe down into his house. They put it on the highest row of bunks along the inside of the house.

The steersman slept until water dripped into his eye. Awake, he looked around and saw a sea anemone above them. He was startled and looked carefully. The crew and canoe were inside a great house. Very quietly, he said to his companions, "Listen to me, but make no sound or movement. We are in great danger. Something has happened to us." Then the others secretly took in their surroundings. They began to cry.

After some time, the spirit chief called to his slaves, "Let my guests join me at the fire." He sat at the back of the house in the center. The slaves escorted them down. The men moved slowly, holding back panic. They sat by the fire.

The human chief felt something poking him. He looked down and saw Mouse Woman, who said, "Noble sir, throw your ear ornaments into the fire. I must receive a gift for the advice I will give." The chief took his earrings deco-

*6. Painted House Front. This facade probably depicts the encounter with Gitnagunaks in his house under the sea. As an origin tradition distinct from that of Temlaxham (Prairie Town), this epic legitimated most of the crests used on the coast and some of the secret priestly orders. (Photo courtesy of Bill Holm; from the collections of the Smithsonian Institution.)*

rated with wool and singed them in the fire. Then Mouse Woman took them for her nest.

She asked, "Do you know where you are? This is the home of Gitnagunaks, a mighty spirit. You anchored over this house last night and disturbed its quiet. When a slave girl was sent to investigate, you mutilated her. His slaves brought your canoe down here to teach you a lesson. You better offer him what you have in the canoe." Then Mouse Woman left.

The spirit ordered his slaves to boil four seals to feed the guests. They took four boxes and boiled the water with hot stones, adding a seal to each. While the seals were cooking, Mouse Woman returned and said to the chief, "Do not be afraid when they bring each of you a whole seal. Open your mouth as wide as you can and you will swallow the whole thing. It will not hurt you. Tell the others what I have said." The chief passed on this advice after Mouse Woman left.

The spirit ordered his slaves, "Take a seal to each man, who must eat it whole." When the slave bought a seal to Dragging Along Shore, he opened his mouth and swallowed it head first. The other two men did the same, but the steersman could not swallow his seal. He was an Eagle and lacked the abilities of the Blackfish.

The spirit chief observed this and said, "Cut up the seal so that this Eagle may eat it easily." Thus, the spirit began to love his guests.

Other spirits heard of these visitors and often asked the spirit to allow his guests to come out, but Gitnagunaks feared what these other spirits would do. They were dangerous.

Finally, he decided to hold a feast and told his household, "I will give a feast for my fellow chiefs in the rocks. I will invite them and show off my human guests. Then I will send all of my friends home, and the humans also." The members of the house consented and messengers were sent to the other spirit chiefs.

It seemed only a day that the men had been in the undersea house, but it was a year of human time. They were never hungry nor in want of anything.

The time for the feast came. The spirit told the men, "Get back into your canoe and watch what will now happen." When settled into the canoe, the human chief asked, "Shall I give you a gift, Great One?" "Do so," the spirit replied. Dragging Along Shore presented four coppers, mountain goat fat, red ocher, eagle down, and tobacco, along with a box each of candlefish grease, of crab apples, and of cranberries. Gitnagunaks was very happy. His house was full of rare items.

Then he announced, "My guests are coming. Open the door." When it was opened, water rushed in and filled the house. The humans were safe floating in their canoe. Then the waters left and the spirit chiefs of many places sat in their appropriate seats. Gitnagunaks greeted them wearing his blackfish robe covered all over with horns. "Thank you all for coming," he said. "I give this feast in honor of my brother, Dragging Along Shore and his nephew, and also for his Eagle brother-in-law, Holdamia. They brought me many coppers and costly provisions. I now wish to share with you these gifts."

After he gave away what the humans had provided, the spirit chief announced, "I will now give to my brother my blackfish garment covered with horns, my principal crest of the mermaid children swimming upriver, and my copper canoe, copper stern board, copper paddles, and the design of my house." Everyone was much pleased.

As a final token of esteem, the spirit chief asked all of the other spirits not to harm the members of the human crew. Instead they should give these hunters good luck whenever they saw them nearby.

"Open the doors," the spirit commanded and again the waters rushed inside. The men floated safely in their canoe. When the water receded, the other spirit monsters had gone away. Two new rooms now stood inside the house. One room was carved with two blackfish joined at the noses. This crest was called "Dash Against Each Other." The other room was carved with green seaweed and contained a copper canoe with a copper sternboard and a copper bailer.

The spirit turned to the chief and blessed him. "From now on you will receive everything that you need from your land. But you must never hurt any fish or anything else that you see in the water. If you do, you will be in grave danger. When you hunt, first offer burnt offerings. Then you will have good luck. If things become scarce, float over my house and make offerings to me. I will set things right. Tomorrow, I will send you home."

The spirit went to the Eagle steersman and said, "I give you my hat," and presented him with a large sea-apple shell with a living person in the center with a face like a man's. He also gave him a large box inlaid with abalone shell.

"Sleep in the canoe again tonight," the spirit said. As a precaution, the crew had slept in the canoe every night they had been in the house, and they continued to do so on the last one.

The next morning, the steersman awoke first and discovered that the canoe was in a mountain of foam. He called to his companions, "Alas, we are in danger." As the others awoke, the foam seemed to lessen. Unbeknownst to them, the foam was changing into a dense fog. Everyone was silent with fear.

Rolling thunder was heard and the fog vanished. Bright sunshine filled the day. The steersman saw that the hat of the chief was covered with all kinds of seaweed, anemones, and tide-pool life. The hats of the others were the same. The canoe was also filled with shore life.

The chief said, "Take up our paddles and let us go home." The paddles were also covered with sea life and were very heavy because they were solid copper. "Leave all of these creatures alone," the chief urged. He remembered the warning. As soon as the paddles touched the canoe, it rang like a bell and sped away as fast as a bird in flight. At midnight, they were back in the village.

They had been gone a year. The elder sisters of the chief had gone down to the beach every morning and wailed for their lost brother. That morning when they gathered, a monster floated in front of the town. It made a sound like a bell. The sisters ran back to their husbands, crying, "We are in danger. A monster waits near the beach."

The husbands went down and saw that this was true. To be sure, one of them called, "Who are you? Are you here to do us harm?" The crew called back. "We are the men who went with Chief Dragging Along Shore to hunt. Now we return and are safe."

The village heard and was excited. Everyone went down to the beach to welcome the crew. Some people drew back, however, because they were frightened by the sight of these men and their canoe covered with seaweed. Even their woven hats had seaweeds, shells, and creatures all over them.

The crew beached and young men tried to carry the canoe ashore, but it was much too heavy. Then the crew themselves lifted it ashore. Everyone was impressed by this feat.

At his house, the chief said, "All of those belonging to the Blackfish crest must be invited to a feast. Send messengers to all of them." These members came quickly. The chief fed them and then told of their adventures at Nagunaks. He told of the gifts from the spirit chief, both to the three men of the Blackfish and to the Eagle crest man. Then he asked, "My people, should I have a potlatch for the other crests and tell them of these things?" Everyone agreed that this should be done. Messengers were sent to other villages to invite the other crests.

All of the other chiefs came on the day appointed. Each wore the crests of his or her house. When all were seated in their official places, the Eagle man opened the box he had been given. A thick fog filled the house. All the chiefs were dumbstruck. The Eagle man closed the box, and the fog went away.

The house was now filled with seaweeds and shore creatures. The copper canoe rested on the first level of benches nearest the fire. A carved room stood at one side decorated with the facing killer whales. On the other side was a room with carved seaweeds. The chief appeared in his blackfish robe covered with horns. All the guests were also covered with seaweeds.

The chief intoned, "Henceforth, because of my adventure, I will be called Gitnagunaks, and the name will pass to my successor in our house of the Blackfish crest." Then all of the guests were given gifts and food to take home.

Later, Holdamia, the man of the Eagle crest, also held a potlatch. He showed everyone his copper paddle, his sea-apple hat, and his inlaid box that released the fog. He made Nagunaks one of the names of the Eagle crest.

The chief prospered. He had success whenever he hunted. His fame covered the world. He feasted many chiefs. Things went well for many years.

Then the chief began to hunt with a new crew. He had explained to them all of the prohibitions that needed to be observed to make sure that their success continued, but these men were foolish. By following the rules, the canoe had only to land and animals would meet them and fall dead. When they went for fish, these floated to the surface to be collected.

Once they were out hunting and had to make camp. As the men carried gear from the canoe, they found a bullhead aground in the shallows. One man clubbed it, but the others said, "We have plenty of fine fish, leave that worthless thing alone." "No," the man replied, "the chief said that we needed to take everything that we met while we hunted." The other men took the fish away and laughed at its agony. They cut its mouth on both sides to make it even wider.

The third man went to the chief to complain about what his companions were doing. The chief became very angry. "Now look what you have done," he screamed. "We are finished because you did not obey the simplest of instructions." He sent one of the men to the top of a hill to watch as everyone else left in the canoe. As they paddled around a point of land, this man saw a whirlpool open and swallow the entire canoe.

The man walked home and told what he had seen. The foolish men died in the whirlpool, but the chief went to live with Gitnagunaks forever.

OTHER CRESTS

Some crests originated among other tribes. The Wolf and its crests were frequently attributed to Athapaskans in the north, like the Tahltan, while many of the Eagle crests have Haida and southern affiliations. In every town of the Tsimshian, Tlingit, and Haida, moreover, one moiety was the Owner of the area in contrast to the Other. These moieties intermarried and performed services for each other.

For example, the Haida source of important Eagle crests among the Tsimshian, such as the Cormorant Hat, is treated in a famous epic about a haughty prince who abused a frog.

*Frog*

In a Haida village lived a chiefly couple and their children, a boy and a girl.[21] These children were much loved and pampered. They always wore the best of clothing.[22]

One fine spring day, the prince called together his companions and set out in a canoe to fish for trout. The prince sat in the bow, so he could direct their movements. He wore the Cormorant Hat, a great treasure decorated with abalone and copper. Using fish spears, they soon had many trout.

A particularly large trout went by and the prince tried to spear it. As his head tilted, his hat fell off and he missed. He put the hat back on and waited. Another large trout came by and the prince tried again. Again, his hat fell off and he missed. Two more large trout came by and twice more his hat fell off. Very angry, the prince ripped apart his hat and threw it away, saying, "Water, you do me no good. You just get in the way and the sun glancing off you hurts my eyes."

The companions were shocked at the outburst. The steersman retrieved the pieces of the hat and placed them in the back of the canoe. By now it was dusk, and the men took the canoe to a nearby campsite at the foot of a spruce tree. They gathered skunk cabbage leaves to use as platters and began to cook some trout. As the trout were cooked, each was placed on a leaf. A frog hopped out from the bushes, sat on the largest trout, and stayed there.[23]

The prince shouted at the frog to go away, but it just sat. The prince took the frog and threw it into the fire. The frog jumped out. The prince threw the frog back into the fire and held it there with a stick until it died. The steersman secretly threw the body of the frog into the bushes. Then all the men went to sleep.

The next morning, the prince told everyone to break camp and load the canoe. They were going home. They launched the canoe and had just started off when a voice called to them. A very pretty woman stood on the beach where they had camped and called to them, "Please take me with you, noble sirs." The prince was much taken with her beauty and ordered the canoe back to shore. As he leapt to grab the woman and take her on board, she disappeared. Where she had been, a frog hopped away.

The canoe left again and the same thing happened. Four times the woman appeared, called to them, and left a frog in her place. Then the canoe departed for good.

On a nearby point of land, the woman appeared again and shouted to the men. "Noble sirs, listen to me. Your prince insulted the water, a bad thing to do. Then he killed my child, who meant him no harm. Now all of you will pay. As you round the next point, your prince will fall back dead. At the next point, the next man will die. At the third point, the other middle man will die. Only the steersman will live to reach the village. He will tell about these events and then he too will die."

And so it came to pass. At each point, a man died. The steersman reached the village and everyone rushed to find out what had happened. He said nothing. He went to his father's house and motioned for all the people to be called together.

When all were assembled, he told the story and died. The bodies of these fine men were buried in the Haida way and the village moved away. The next morning, an old woman from the village came to the chief and told him to call together the people.

When everyone was together in the house of the chief, the old woman spoke. "My dear ones, I had a terrible dream last night. We will be destroyed. Only the princess, the sister of the slain son, will be saved, but we must dig a pit in the middle of this house and leave her there."

Immediately, the hole was dug and filled with food, coppers, furs, woven blankets, and family treasures. The princess was placed inside and the hole was covered.

Then the woman continued. "I saw fire fall on the mountain behind our village and spread from there. Everything was consumed." Even as she said these words, fire reached the peak and flowed down the mountain. It surrounded the village, burning the forest and the sea. No one escaped. It burned the entire village. As she died, the old woman sang a mourning song that the princess heard.

After some time, the land began to cool and the princess heard footsteps. She pushed away the covering and came out. She met a beautiful woman with a cane in her hand. The cane had a live eagle on the top, a live person in the middle, and a live frog on the bottom. She wore a huge hat, woven of spruce roots and painted green. She sang a song about the prince who burned up her child, a daughter. The princess also learned this song before the woman vanished.

The princess put on all of her costly garments and picked up some of her treasures. She left the destroyed village, singing the dirge she composed from the songs of the two women.

The princess came to a lake that glistened in the sun. A great roar came from the water and a Halibut spirit emerged looking like a painted house front. She took the design as a crest of her family. She added the incident to her dirge as she went on.

Beyond the lake, she walked until her garments were tattered. She was cold and hungry when she came to a glowing fire along a shore. She warmed herself at the fire. The body of a princess had recently been cremated there.

A canoe came by and saw her. They reported to the village that their dead princess had returned. The grieving parents arrived and were amazed at how similar the two girls looked. They were sure their daughter had returned. They gave the name of Omen to the princess.

In the spring, all the women went to pick strawberries. The princess stayed in the canoe. A storm came up suddenly and drove the canoe out to sea. The girl sang her dirge. From the sea came a loud noise. A huge eagle emerged with ten smaller eagles on its head. She took it for a crest and added the incident to her song.

Her canoe drifted until it came to Metlakatla, the winter abode of the Tsimshian towns near the mouth of the Skeena River. She was taken to the home of the chief of the Gitwilgyots, who was so taken with her that they married. They had three sons and two daughters.

The chief had five other wives and these women became very jealous of the princess. They were unkind to her. Once she was called a slave from the Haida, which was a grave insult. The princess brooded on these slights.

The children grew up and prospered. The eldest son became a great hunter and was very generous. To honor him, a feast was held to bestow the Cormorant Hat upon him and affirm his right to wear it. He was also given a cane like that used by the Frog Woman when she viewed the devastation at the burned-over village. His house front was painted like the Halibut of the Lake, while another crest was the Eagle of the Sea with ten eagles on its head.

The princess herself took two new names, Great Haida Woman and Picking Strawberries, to remind everyone of her adventures. The other wives were humbled. She sang the dirge that described all that she had experienced and her family remembered it for important events.

Years later, the princess called her children together and reminded them that the Tsimshian were not their people. The youngest son and daughter decided to return to the Haida. Their mother told them where her village had been and how to find the pit filled with the treasures of their house.

These youngsters made themselves ready and went by canoe to the Haida. They went across the ocean and found a town filled with people. They shouted from the bay that they were the children of the princess whose town had been burned by Frog Woman. They were made welcome by their uncles. The next day, the son went to the destroyed village and returned with the treasures of his family. He and his sister became great among the Haida Eagles, while the elder children established important Eagle crests among the Tsimshian.


## MARRIAGE ARRANGEMENTS

Marriage arrangements were a direct responsibility of the crests, but matters of rank and class also were involved. Royal marriages were political and social alliances with lasting consequences for all the houses and families involved. The greater needs of the community over those of the individual became the subject of an important history told for its general moral lesson.

### The Rejected Cousin

In major houses, the nephew of the chief was expected to marry the chief's daughter, his cousin, so that he would be sure to inherit the position of his uncle.[24]

In a large village, the only royalty were a brother, who had an only daughter, and a sister, who had an only son. These cousins were expected to marry. They grew up together, but when the time for the marriage proposal came, the daughter rejected her cousin, though he loved her very much. Her rejection was utter and complete because she was vain and selfish.

Still her cousin persisted and she decided to make a fool of him. She walked to the edge of the town and sat down. Soon her cousin joined her. He asked again for marriage. She smiled and said that if he truly wanted marriage he should slash one of his cheeks. He did so. Then she asked him to slash the other cheek. He did so. Then she asked him to cut off all his hair. He did so.

The princess laughed out loud and said that she could never marry anyone so ugly. The prince was humiliated and left. He wandered alone in the forest for many days. Then he came to a hut. A woman called to him from inside. She fed him and said that she felt sorrow for him because he was mocked by his own intended wife and cousin. She urged him to go to Chief Pestilence at the edge of the earth and ask to be cured. She told him not to be afraid.

"When you get to the house, boldly open the door and announce, 'Chief Pestilence, I have come to be made beautiful again.' Then walk to the rear of the house where the chief stays. Ignore all the maimed and crippled people living along the sides. They were not strong enough to get to the chief. Avoid them at all cost."

The prince went to the house and announced his request. People called to him from the sides, but he ignored them. Finally, from behind the screen at the rear of the house, Chief Pestilence emerged with his beautiful daughter. "Come here, my dear prince," the chief called. The man went to him and was given a seat to the right of the chief.

"Bring my bath," the chief said. Slaves brought a large wooden tub filled with water. The prince was placed in it and the water began to boil of its own accord. The prince was boiled to bare bones. These bones were removed by slaves and the chief arranged them on a wide board. Then his daughter jumped over them four times.[25] The prince was restored, white and shiny. He was more handsome than before.

"Bring me my crystal comb," the chief ordered, and, holding it firmly, he combed the prince's hair until it was long and flowing. "Now stay with us for a day or two, my prince." What were two days in that house were two years in the human world.

The prince left the house with his good looks and many gifts. He went back to his village. Everyone was taken with his beauty. He was welcomed and feasted in every house. Even his cousin now wanted to marry him, but he ignored her. The princess still slept in the cubicle set against the wall above the bed of her parents. A woman slave slept at the foot of the ladder each night to guard her virtue. The princess sent this slave to tell the prince of her desire for marriage. The prince paid no attention. Then the princess sent word that she would do whatever the prince desired.

The prince sent back word that she should do to herself what she had had him do to himself. She slashed her cheeks and cut her hair. The princess sent the hair to the prince, who laughed out loud and mocked his cousin. He would never marry anyone so ugly.

Now the princess was ashamed. She and her slave left the village. She wanted to hang herself, but the slave convinced her to seek the house of Chief Pestilence. For many days they walked. If they saw anyone or any house, they avoided it. The princess was too ashamed to be seen and too haughty to ask for help. That was her undoing.

Eventually, they reached the house of Chief Pestilence but she had no understanding of what she must do. She entered and responded to all the maimed people. They grabbed her, broke her back, and made her crippled. They broke her arms and legs and twisted her mouth. They did much the same to the slave woman. Then they threw them out of the house. After many days, they limped back to their town, where the princess died.

Therefore, a law was made that marriages would be arranged for the benefit of the crest and family, not according to the whims of individuals. If a couple were to marry, their parents discussed the arrangements. Their uncles also conferred. Then all of the relatives on both sides met and agreed.

At the time of the marriage, the families staged a mock fight to get rid of any resentment. Rocks were thrown and any scars that resulted became emblems of the marriage pledge.

The bride was carried in state to the place of the wedding. Sometimes she sat on a board laid across two canoes that were paddled to the beach in front of the town of the groom. Sometimes she was carried on a fine robe by eight princes. The bride sat on the left and the groom on the right. They sat together for four days, without eating or drinking. They were not to laugh, although children teased them to do so. Meanwhile, their families visited, sang, and celebrated. On the fourth day, they feasted and exchanged treasures and gifts. Then the couple was truly married and the families were united.

WHY HATS?

In the rainy climate of the Pacific Northwest, hats have long been required coverings. Their necessity, however, became elaborated as these human societies became more complexly organized, with the rain hat becoming the basis of the major crests.

The development of the primary crest, such as the Cormorant Hat of the Eagles, mentioned in the Frog *adawx* among the Tsimshian and their neighbors, harkened back to a much older tradition. While it was true that "hats make the man" in many cultures, along the north Pacific coast the power of such hats derived from beliefs inherent in the religion of hunting.

As Fitzhugh and Crowell have noted, "The animal-spirit basis of these hats is more than 2,500 years old in the Bering Sea" (1988:164). Worn by sea hunters, visors and caps served both to keep glare out of the eyes and to camouflage the hunter. Sometimes the hat acted as a decoy. Furthermore, each hat was carefully decorated to evoke both the animal hunted and, sometimes, the spirit who acted as benefactor to the hunter by giving him success. In all, the cap functioned both as a disguise and a charm.

From these beginnings, as a manifestation of the transfer of personal power among hunter, hunted, and spirit ally, this hat became institutionalized among the Northwest Coast tribes as an emblem of the crest, house, and moiety. The success of an ancestor became inherited matrilineally by descendants who were members of a corporate body. By changing an individualized spirit into a badge of corporate membership, and by adding it to the naxnox, kinship units

*7. Basketry Hat with Painted Crest. Often woven from cedar or spruce roots, hats were standard rain gear along the coast. When painted and embellished with formline designs, however, they served as crest hats, which tended to be larger than those worn every day. (Photo courtesy of Bill Holm.)*

were distinguished by household and town. What had been a token of individual success became an emblem of family pride.

To the south, among the Nuchahnulth of the west coast of Vancouver Island, chiefs signaled their fame as whale harpooners by wearing elaborate conical hats decorated with bulbous tops. Woven into the hats were the designs of a canoe full of men pursuing a whale. Since sons inherited from fathers along the central coast, the paternal whaling tradition among the elite was perpetuated by these hats.

With the development of the formline style, the representation of these figures became less naturalistic and idiosyncratic. Animals became identifiable on the basis of standard characteristics. A specific encounter now became a generic one. Thereafter, in wavy outline, ovoids, and paints, the being became less unique except in terms of stylistics that distinguished the art of one town or tribe from that of another.

Yet the importance of hats remained, initially, to easily represent a manifestation of power, and, later, its transfer from one head to another. Over time,

*8. Carved Squirrel Hat. More elaborate crest hats were carved from wood and decorated with additional materials, as with this Squirrel, carved from cedar, holding a pine cone. (Photo courtesy of Bill Holm and the Royal British Columbia Museum, #12146.)*

however, utilitarian functions, requiring light weight and durability, were replaced by artistic considerations that resulted in heavy hats of carved and decorated wood. Some were so huge and heavy that they were held against the body of the host at a potlatch, rather than being worn on the head. Still, the actual physical contact was important so that the success and power represented by the headgear could pass from one generation to the next in a public forum where witnesses could attest to the transferral.[26]

## POTLATCH

No single word evokes the complexity of and confusion about the cultures of the Pacific Northwest more than "potlatch," derived from the term meaning 'to give' in Chinook Jargon, the trade vocabulary of the region. Outlawed by missionaries and the government, likened to a banking system by past scholars, and equated with wasteful extravagance by settlers, the potlatch was merely a public forum for bringing people together to eat, celebrate, and observe how important names, positions, and times of life or death were dealt with in an orderly fashion. Members of the elite served as witnesses to these events and were charged, by virtue of accepting food and gifts, to state publicly that these transfers and observances were legal, binding, and legitimate.

More than this, the potlatch brought together the living and the dead and all other important relationships in the world to renew and respect all aspects of, quite literally, the universe. As all realms of nature occupied a house and all beings had a human form under their varied appearances, so the house where a potlatch was being held became a microcosm of all these other houses and beings and, for the moment, represented all of them.

Early missionaries opposed the potlatch as much for what they saw as its "worship of the dead," a misunderstanding of the role of the ancestors, as for the seemingly senseless abandon with which hosts gave gifts to guests. Families would spend years amassing furs, baskets, robes, ornaments, and treasures such as coppers, and then give these all away in a few hours. While Europeans admired the thrift and industry that made the collection possible, they were dumbstruck that all of this effort benefited others.

Modern Tsimshians gave up the potlatch as such, once they became Christians, and instead celebrate changes in the social fabric with feasts, which emphasize the food rather than the crest aspects of these events. Now, services, prayers, and parables take the place once occupied by naxnox displays within halait contexts. Formerly, the fall potlatches were balanced off against the winter halait, but now feasts take the place of both.

According to Garfield (1939: 192–219), the major potlatch in the career of a chief was held to celebrate the building of the house of his crest. Later, when the Euro-Canadian style of parent-to-child (including father-to-son) inheritance was adopted, and families built their own homes, this lavishness was transferred to the ceremonies of installation and memorial for a chief, including the raising of totem poles. With the law against potlatching, granite gravestones carved as crests were, and still are, installed much as poles had been in the past.

In addition, potlatches could be held for many other events, ranging from the piercing of a child's ears and nose to acquiring a copper or assembling a war expedition. The first appearance of a baby, however illegitimate, lying upon a copper at a potlatch purged the family record of blemish. Such was the power of the potlatch among the wealthy. It removed the taint of capture and slavery and confirmed heirs to titles that were in dispute. Indeed, an important aspect of high status among the Tsimshian was this ability to manipulate the rules to personal advantage and to use wealth and resources to achieve the appearance of order in their family and household relationships.

Most potlatches were small affairs held among the members of a house, related crest houses, and their in-laws (affines). Important families, however, invited widely, preferring to have guests from different houses, towns, and tribes, along with foreign nations. The food served was often collected from the territories of the house. By consuming it, guests acknowledged the rights of the house to these lands and resources.

Among all the relatives who contributed to a potlatch, fathers played a significant role in organizing and contributing to the potlatches and halaits of their children because this was the one place were a man could stand out and do something apart from his own crest.

People were involved in potlatches before birth, since the announcement of a pregnancy could be an occasion for one. Later, the birth and namings were similarly commemorated. Noble children had the helix and lobe of each ear perforated at a potlatch. The higher the rank, the more holes were made. Commoners and others who lacked such piercings could be insulted by calling them "no ears" (*wah 'tsmuu*), a term now applied to oblivious whites and other "crazies" insensitive to Tsimshian ways. Such additional holes were believed to aid hearing and understanding, providing a mark of wisdom. At potlatches and other public events, nobles wore elaborate goat wool earrings decorated with abalone shell. In sacred histories, Mouse Woman demanded these in payment for giving advice and used them to improve her home nest. So important were these marks of rank that, after they converted to Christianity, several important families held this potlatch but did not allow their daughters ears to be pierced. Thus, traditional social etiquette and the local missionary were both satisfied.

In addition to ears, children had other piercings. Girls had the lower lip pierced to wear a labret (a stone or wooden plug), which increased in size with age and rank. Aged royal women wore huge labrets as an obvious mark of prestige. A woman without a labret was said to be "without a mouth." Boys had a hole made in the nasal septum to wear a straight feather, bone, or shell. The boy's ceremony was more prestigious than that of the girl but required fewer people. For the girl, a different paternal aunt was asked to pierce each hole, and all of the father's sisters contributed the earrings and other gifts.

Tattooing involved a similarly elaborate ceremony, with the father's family playing a prominent role. Today, however, a feast is held after someone has gone to a tattoo parlor and had a crest design applied by machine needles.

The first kill by a boy or the first berry picked by a girl might also be the occasion of a small potlatch among chiefly families. Today, this first success is marked in public by gifts to elders, who pray for continued luck for the child. Today, a succession of feasts and dinners are held to celebrate namings, puberty for a girl, and marriage for a couple.

In the past, people could only benefit from potlatches at which their chiefs were guests if they had been previously recognized as tribal and town members by hosting a potlatch of their own, wearing their hair like that of a warrior. On the other hand, once this was done, that person was ever after expected to contribute to any potlatches hosted by his or her chief and tribe.

When a chief hosted a potlatch, he began preparations several years before. He told his tribe his plans, and each person made a contribution according to their rank in the town of their name and house. Every donation was announced in public so everyone could keep track of the fund. Everyone who was not feeble or infirm also was given an assigned role to perform during the event, such as herald, usher, or provider of certain foods. The chief, of course, gave the most, followed by his nephews who were in line to inherit the title. These contributions moved only up the ranks, since members of a tribe always supplied their chief, but he or she did not reciprocate downward. Everyone was expected to contribute to events hosted by the chief, but otherwise every host acted alone when sponsoring a feast.

Preparations might involve elaborate trading. In one instance, candlefish were caught on the Nass and rendered into oil, while some fish were dried and traded to Haidas for clothes, which were traded to the Nishga for marmot (groundhog) skins, the minimal unit of value in this system.[27] These furs were then traded for large woolen blankets, moose hides, and caribou skins. Crab and wild plants were traded to the Hudson's Bay Company for tobacco. Soapberries were collected to make a delicacy called "Indian ice cream," which was mixed in a new canoe to serve the multitudes at the feast. Seaweed was dried and stored, as were berries. Famed composers were hired and came to live in the house so that everyone could learn new songs and dances to provide entertainment before the crest songs were performed. Carvers were also hired to make feast and potlatch bowls and utensils. They too were fed by the house but paid by the father of the host.

The actual potlatch might last for days, with special songs sung on the beach to greet the arriving guests or in the house to welcome them. Skits and newly composed songs were performed at the beginning to make everyone relaxed. Quantities of food were served before the "business" began. The children to be named, the adults taking higher-ranked names, and the positions to be filled were all introduced and proclaimed before elite witnesses. During interludes, the lack of success by members of other crests and clans, or promises not fulfilled, were alluded to in special songs that exalted the hosts and embarrassed these guests. At the very end, all of the gifts that had been collected were given out, the elite witnesses receiving more than others. Everyone received something, but commoners got only tokens. Later, at home, the chiefs would further distribute what they received to members of their house, town, or tribe.

Southern Tsimshian describe feasts as being either happy, like that just described, or sad, for a funeral or memorial. Similarly, William Beynon listed three types of feasts for the Coast Tsimshian: black or mourning, memorial, and red or completion (Cove 1987:144), depending on the color of the face paint worn by the hosts. Completion refers to the end of a potlatch series resulting in the final assumption of a hereditary name-title. As the black feast was sad, so the red feast was happy. The memorial feast was a transitional category, used as the need arose to extol the family or crest during a time of conflict. For example, the former wife of the Nishga chief Sagewan ('mountain') held a memorial for her dead brother to assert her own high rank after she divorced the chief.

During the time that the Tsimshian were consolidating at the trading post at Fort Simpson, the potlatch took on many aspects of rivalry as chiefs attempted to sort out relative rankings among themselves. Ligeex emerged as the high chief of the Coast Tsimshian, while Ts'ibasaa of the Kitkatla, Nek̲t of the Gitksan, and Sagewan of the Nishga rose to prominence in their own groups. Chiefs set out to permanently shame or vanquish their rivals, at least in the eyes of the public. Indications are, however, that the chiefs kept a check on each other so as to maintain their own exalted status.

At these rivalry potlatches, slaves were killed, valuable goods destroyed, and guests humiliated, often by serving them vast quantities of rum. Since refusing food at a feast was an insult, guests had no choice but to drink all that was given them and to suffer the consequences as best they could.[28] These rum feasts received much negative commentary from missionaries, agents, and traders, who nevertheless sold alcohol to the hosts.

Because of his status, Ligeex hosted some of the most elaborate potlatches of the Tsimshian (Barbeau and Beynon 1987b:92–94). At such events, his important crests included both the Frog Hat and a cane topped by a Frog, together with the Beaver Hat, which was held on Ligeex's head by a member from each of the four crests to show that Ligeex "was the highest in rank among all the clans" and "that he alone is the head chief of all the Tsimshian" (Boas 1916:272, 512).

*Ligeex's Potlatch, 1860s*

One of the line of Eagle chiefs called Ligeex hosted a potlatch, possibly in 1866 after he was paid by the Hudson's Bay Company for his trade monopoly on the Skeena River. This potlatch was notable for the formality and dignity which was required because it included so many chiefs.

A year before, Ligeex called a meeting of his Gispaxlo'ots tribe, and after he had fed everyone, he announced his plans. Families offered to help, and suggested which members should be named, elevated, or confirmed in higher ranks at the event.

Next, he held a feast for members of his father's Raven crest to ask their help and assign each one certain tasks, such as announcing, organizing, contributing particular foods, or commissioning carvings.

Meanwhile Ligeex continued to collect foods and gifts. When the date was set, tribesmen were sent as messengers, each accompanied by a lesser chief so that the other chiefs would not feel slighted, to invite towns and tribes. Arriving in front of the town, the lower ranking chief stood in the bow of the canoe, wearing a chilkat robe, using his raven rattle, and singing a naxnox song to the accompaniment of hidden whistles. He called out the name of the town chief three times, inviting him and his people to the potlatch. The fourth time, the chief responded by sending a messenger to the beach to invite the visitors into his house. He fed them and gave them gifts to take back to Ligeex.

The chiefs of each town gathered their families and advisors and paddled to Ligeex's town. Each canoe waited in front of the beach until Ligeex's sister and other ranking women came down to greet them by dancing and singing. The sister, wearing a mask, acted as though she were grabbing one of Ligeex's naxnox, called All Calm Heavens, from the air and throwing it toward the guests. The arriving chief acted as though he caught it, wrestled with it, and threw it back to the sister.[29] Then the canoes beached and the guests were welcomed.

Inside the house, they were treated to displays of other names and spirits owned by Ligeex. After this dancing and singing, the guests were well fed. That night, chiefs stayed in homes of crest relatives while other visitors camped on the beach, supplied with wood and food by the hosts.

The next day, a feast was held on the beach. That night, a challenge feast was held with Ligeex boasting of his fame and belittling everyone else. Guests were seated by rank, and some were singled out to receive huge ladles full of candlefish grease mixed with snow brought from the mountain tops.

Ligeex's people came in dressed for war, with their hair bound up, but scattered eagle down everywhere to indicate their peaceful intent. After taunting songs and overeating, gifts were distributed, accompanied by jokes about the shortcomings of the guests. Every item was counted out while a song was sung, the better to overwhelm the guests with the wealth of Ligeex, since most of these offerings came from his own supply. Many goods had been hidden behind a rear partition, and these were now thrown into the room. Soon the pile was so high that the roof boards had to be removed. Ligeex taunted that he had thousands of items while other chiefs had only hundreds.

A Raven man assigned this task then announced all of the names and histories that Ligeex claimed. Then all of his coppers were shown and named. Children of Ligeex's crest were brought forward and named. Any pregnant Eagle woman was given the names of a boy and a girl to give to the newborn according to its gender. While the guests relaxed, members of the tribe made a final tally of the remaining gifts. Bundles of sticks had previously been assembled to represent each group of guests, divided by house and lineage. Quantities also varied by tribe, from most to less, according to a ranking ranging from the Kitkatla, the tribe of Ligeex's wife, to the Gitlaan, a small group because most had converted to Christianity and forsaken potlatching.[30]

The final day was spent giving out these gifts to the chiefs, for the benefit of themselves and their tribes. Speeches of thanks by tribal spokesmen followed, and a feast ended the event. Then the hosts helped to pack all the canoes, and the guests left.

A short time later, Ligeex held a feast for the Eagles to thank them for their help. Every man was given some food as a gift.

*Hartley Bay (Txałgiu), 1978*

During 27–30 December 1978, the town chief of this community was involved in a series of feasts, each hosted by one of the crests, that culminated in his assuming the highest ranking name among the Blackfish. Born an Eagle, this chief was adopted by his own father to lead the Blackfish and become chief of the town.[31]

The occasion provided a means to compare the publications about Tsimshian potlatches with actual contemporary events. Among those described for the past and the present were commemorations such as the potlatch proper or *yaawk,* the religious power displays called *halait,* and the humiliation-challenge-rum feasts called *la'ax.* However, Southern Tsimshian in this town agreed that these events were no longer held. Instead, their modern events were called *luulgit* 'a feast'. Elders said that a *yaawk* was a feast held for guests from outside the village—an external potlatch, while the *luulgit* was a feast held by one of the crests for other residents of their town—an internal potlatch. Potlatches had been prohibited by the Indian agents and by missionaries, and modern elders felt that feasts were more in keeping with their Christian faith.

The sequence of events was the same on each day of the feasting, while the host group differed from one day to the next. The interactions of these crest groups indicate that the community functions as though divided into moieties of Killerwhale and Eagle. The Killerwhales or Blackfish claim a local origin, establishing them as Owners, while the Eagles mention connections to ancient Haida towns. The single resident Wolf family, whose members came from Port Essington, are treated as members of the Killerwhales when they are not being reminded that, according to ancestry, they are foreigners. The Ravens, who maintain an active presence, are chided that some of them speak like Kitkatlas, where many of them were born, and so are reminded, humorously, that they are also Others.

Sometime during lunch, from eleven to two o'clock, two messengers visited each home, stood before the head of every family present, and addressed him or her in Tsimshian by the correct hereditary name-title, inviting them and theirs to the community hall for a feast at four o'clock that afternoon.

Between 4:00 and 4:30 P.M., people arrived at the hall to be welcomed in Tsimshian by official ushers who seated them at one of twenty-four tables. Younger, less prestigious people sat at the side tables, more important older ones at tables in the middle, and those of the host group sat at tables near the door.

Between 4:30 and 6:00 P.M., various forms of entertainment were held, including speeches, dances, songs, skits, and good-natured insults. At 6:00, the native minister said grace, and dinner was served by the woman in charge of each table. Additional helpings were strongly encouraged. About 7:00, the take-home food (*xsoo*) was passed out, consisting of mandarin oranges and apples. Everyone received about a dozen, which they nibbled on during speeches or took home. Until 8:30–9:00 P.M., hereditary names were publicly assumed, and various important men and women stood individually to deliver

*9. Tables Set for a Feast. The "old hall" at Hartley Bay awaits the arrival of guests in 1976. (Photo by Jay Miller.)*

speeches of thanks to the hosts, to scold the young for ignoring their past, or to call attention to someone for compliments or criticism.

About 9:30 P.M., a half hour after everyone had left the hall, the members of the crest hosting the feast on the following night were expected to gather together to plan their entertainment and prepare their feast: cutting up meat, vegetables, and baked goods. The food would be cooked on the stoves of crest members throughout the village for most of the next day.

Each day the feast was hosted by a different kin group. On 27 December, the hosts were the Ravens (Ganhada), and they served clam chowder. The Ravens had decided to have a happy feast, so all the crest groups prepared skits. When everyone was seated, each crest group sent in a tableful of representatives. The Ganhada came as "Chief Dan George and His Tribe of Savages." The Eagles came as the "Clam Diggers Union" in fisherman hats and slickers, carrying "on strike" signs. The Gispwudwada came as the "Blackfish Tribe Disco Dancers," lead by the oldest women in the town. The humor was slapstick and self-deprecatory. A good time was had by all.

On 28 December, the Blackfish sponsored the feast, serving beef stew. The feast was more serious, although banter focused on the author, who inadvertently insulted the town chief by acting like a host instead of a guest.[32]

On 29 December, the town chief sponsored his own feast to assume his great name. His family served roast beef, turnips, potatoes, carrots, biscuits, candy, and fruitcake. During the meal, the chief went to selected tables with bowls of spare ribs. After dinner, the chief was named by four rather than the usual two sponsors, and other members of his family were also given hereditary names.

On 30 December, the Eagles sponsored the feast, serving beef soup. Names were given to several members of the crew of the missionary launch named after the Reverend Thomas Crosby.

The highlight of this feast was the revival of a dance that had not been held for about twenty-five years, the "Eagle Drinking Song," which was composed by an Eagle chief after he became a reformed alcoholic. Originally, only the song was to be performed because the mime of drunken comportment would have been too expensive as the audience would have to be paid off so the shame of being drunk in public, even as a sham, could not be used against the Eagles. By that evening, however, the Eagles had decided on the full performance. The song was both haunting and melodic, accompanied by a saxophone rather than a drum. As each dancer appeared more unsteady, members of the audience rushed to support them. Everyone went to an Eagle whose father belonged to his or her own crest group and supported him or her so that they would not bring shame to their fathers. Afterwards, each supporter was paid from five to ten dollars, "out of respect for their fathers," by the dancer for their kindness.

In this way, the ancient obligations of own crest to father's crest continue to be observed among contemporary Tsimshians.

## WONDERS BRANCH

Often, in the sacred history of a house, a human ancestress and male naxnox beget an heir, as illustrated by the famous account of the name of Asdiwal. In Tsimshian speech, *naxnox* is used as a generic term for anything dealing with the supernatural, including, but not limited to, the immortal beings who transfer it, the encounters when and where it is acquired, and the artifacts made to display this linkage. Accordingly, *naxnox* is "supernatural; having supernatural power; a supernatural being" (Dunn 1978:79).

During the movement from summer camps to winter towns, Coast Tsimshian would spend time together at fall gatherings where they feasted, played games, and enjoyed various dramatic naxnox displays involving puppets, effigies, and other wonders. The fall place (*spaksuut*) for the Coast Tsimshian was located at what became Port Essington. The Gitḵa'ata now live at the place, modern Hartley Bay, where their fall site had been. If more information were available, it is likely that these fall gatherings were contests where the wonders (specifically, the cultural display of naxnox) had full outlet, in contradistinction to the crests used at potlatches and the halait of winter ceremonials. Further, while the halait were the privilege of the high chiefs, participation in the wonder displays was more open, allowing a greater range of house members to take part in the displays.[33]

William Beynon (mss.: text 185:57–58) provides the most explicit discussion of the naxnox among the Coast Tsimshian. He noted that a "nack-nock" was not a crest because it was individually owned, and inheritable by only one person provided it was validated with a potlatch. Each name had one or more masks and costumes that were dramatized in public with songs (*ks-naɫk*), which "were" the breath of the associated spirit. Only other holders of naxnox names could attend these events, dressed according to the dictates of their own spirits. At each enactment, the full history of the name was recounted. Most often such names originated from a hunting territory and were used to denote sole ownership of it.

Among the modern Gitksan, each naxnox name also possesses a reserved seat at feasts, along with a ritualized mask display.[34] "Most names of adult men and women have naxnox which go with them. Each such name entitles the holder of it to a 'reserved seat' at feasts. A naxnox is both a particular spirit whose power the owner of the name is supposed to inherit when he takes the name, and is also a 'show' or dramatization of the power of that spirit. Naxnox are shown in connection with the raising of totem poles or gravestones and the performances are considered to be very amusing" (Adams 1973:41–42).

Henry Tate provided an example of how this was done among the Coast Tsimshian for the naxnox name of Changing Mind:

Lu-na-gisEm gad (Changing Mind).—When Lu-na-gisEm gad appears, one mask representing a man stands on the right-hand side of the house, that of the women on the left-hand side. The two masks have one song, because they belong together. As soon as the name of the mask is mentioned in the song, the faces of both of them change. The man's mask becomes a woman's mask, and the woman's mask a man's mask. This is repeated four times; and while this change in the mask goes on, the people of the chief's tribe change their faces also. Men have women's faces, and women have men's faces, during the singing. This is the work and the power of Lu-na-gisEm gad. (Boas 1916:556–57) [35]

The elaboration of such displays was the responsibility of a group of nobles trained as artists (*gitsontk* 'person hidden') who worked in secret (Shane 1984:167). Because of this guild, Tsimshian masks are remarkably consistent among all four of the divisions. Each has "a broad face with stretched, narrow-lipped mouth, an aquiline nose, and cheeks formed of three intersecting planes" (Holm 1987:132; cf. Wingert 1966).

A favorite manifestation of the naxnox was to have a mask, apparently blind, suddenly see. The most famous example of this is the pair of nested stone masks reunited by Wilson Duff (Halpin 1981; Abbott 1981). Laboriously carved, the outer mask is solid, while the inner one has holes bored for the eyes. Worn together, at a critical moment the outer mask was removed and hidden so that the inner one reflected the light of the fire through these eyeholes.

Unifying the different types of naxnox was a concern with rebirth (Adams (1973:47) or, more correctly, the elaboration of death, both physical and cultural. In the native idiom, for example, people are given to the names, not names to people, because a name was and is eternal, briefly recalled and renewed at each bestowal on a human.

In her careful analysis of the naxnox system, Halpin concludes that:

> The entire naxnox naming system was a metaphorical elaboration on the theme of death. The various physical infirmities represented by naxnox names—old age, lameness, deafness, smallpox, etc.—were metaphors of physical death. The various cultural infirmities represented by naxnox names—selfishness, drunkenness, insanity, etc.—were metaphors of non-sense or meaninglessness; that is, cultural death. The relationship between the two can be expressed as follows: insanity:cultural death::infirmity:physical death. What the Tsimshian collectively overcame was death, which they negated through culture, the only context within which human life is possible. . . . The naxnox naming system and its ritual dramatization were continual reminders of the necessity of living within the rules of Tsimshian culture, and the resultant specter of death if these rules were ignored or violated. (n.d.:15–16)

When translating the term *naxnox* into English, modern Gitksan have decided to use "power" or "powers." After considerable discussion with Coast Tsimshian, however, "wonder," "wonders," or "wondrous" seem to be better translations, depending on context. Naxnox are generic and inclusive, within *inclosive* (Miller 1979) expressions of halait potency. For clarity, naxnox themselves are the spirits, sometimes called "powers," while their human representation is here called "wonders."

### Gunaxnesemgyet

While living at the village called Sgasa'mnt on Aristazabal Island, where the Gitisu hunted hair seal, fur seal, sea otter, and other marine mammals, a crew of seal hunters set out.[36] Halfway there, over a shallow spot, the steersman saw a sea anemone with a hair seal in its mouth. He urged the crew to take the seal, but they scoffed at him. "Can't we get our own seals? Why bother with some stupid seal that got stuck in an anemone?" The man fell silent and the canoe continued on.

The sea anemone had actually been a naxnox, who was offended by their remarks and took revenge.

The crew only intended to camp for one night. That was all the food that they had. During the night, a huge storm struck and lasted several days. Their food was quickly gone and the storm prevented them from getting more. They began to comb the beaches, but only the steersman found food. He brought back four sea urchins, which he shared. They went to look for fern roots, but only the steersman found any. He shared the four he gathered. No more food was found, so the men starved. Three of them died. The steersman waited with their bodies, assuming that he would soon join them in death.

Weak and frail, he waited. Eventually he heard someone approaching. It was a hair seal. Summoning all of his strength, the man killed it with his war club. He skinned and cleaned it before cooking pieces of meat. When the meal was ready, he placed bowls in front of each of the dead men, saying "Brothers, eat. Now we have plenty of food. Enjoy."

Suddenly the storm stopped and everything became calm. The man went down to the beach to launch the canoe. He carried all of the dead men to the place they had occupied in the canoe and placed paddles in their hands. Then he pushed off and paddled back to their village.

As he approached home, a man in a shiny canoe overtook them. He asked, "Why do these other men not move?" The steersman, who was wise, answered,

"Great naxnox, my companions insulted what a spirit offered to them. They died in a great storm. Only I survive."

"Let me look at them," said the naxnox. As he touched each of the bodies with his spear, the man awoke. Then he spat into his own hands and wiped their eyes. Their sight was restored. They were revived.[37]

Next the naxnox said, "Give me your canoe and take mine." Then he gave his club to the steersman, saying, "When you get to the village, you must not go near your wives. Observe this rule according to your position. The bowman must abstain for a day, the next man for two days, the third for three days, and the steersman for four. Each day you must wash yourselves with the juice of devil's club (hellebore). If you fail to do this, you will die again." The spirit disappeared and the men continued on in the new canoe.

At the village, everyone was in mourning because the crew was presumed dead. The men thought they had been gone for four days, but in human time it had been four years. Their wives were eager to see them, but the men followed the rules given by the naxnox.

On the second day, however, the bowman fell dead after he went back to his wife. Each day after, another man died after returning to his wife. The steersman now realized that the rule applied for four years, not four days. The man told his wife, but before the four years ended, he went to her and said, "We will now make a son and I will die. Name him Gunaxnesemgyet. Take the boy to his grandfather and give him the canoe and club I received."

The wife became pregnant and the man died. The woman moved in with her uncle, a great chief, but he was mean. He kept the mother and son in a corner of the house, a humiliating location for a woman of her rank, but the uncle was embarrassed by his nephew. The woman followed her husband's instructions. Every day she made the boy take hellebore, a powerful voiding plant, so he had constant diarrhea. He stank and so did the place where he lived.

When the boy was grown, he gathered three companions and went to his mother. "I am ready to travel. Give me the canoe and club that my father left for me." She conferred these on him and the crew left during a time of famine.

After going some distance, they saw seals on a rock. The boy hurled the club, it killed all the seals, and he brought them back to the canoe. The crew headed back home, arriving at dusk. The boy told his mother of his success and she went to the uncle. "My son went out to wander and found some seals. They are on the beach. Your slaves can bring them up."

The uncle was suspicious. "How can such a sickly crybaby find seals? My best hunters have found nothing. You probably exaggerate. It is probably some trifle." But the chief sent his slaves to the beach. To the wonder of all, they returned with many seals.

The next day, the boy went out again and returned with more seals. Every day, he provided meat. Soon sea lions and large animals were added. He always left very early and came back after dark so no one would see his club and canoe.

Once, however, he had not gone far before he filled the canoe with meat. Then he came back during the day and all marveled at the shiny canoe. His mother announced his name of Gunaxnesemgyet in public and told of the special gifts left by his father.

The uncle was impressed and married the boy to his daughter. They were happy.

Then, one day, a white otter swam in front of the village. Every day it did this, passing very swiftly so that none could kill it. Gunaxnesemgyet went after it and found it sleeping on the water. His club killed it.

When he brought it on shore, his wife offered to clean it. At the edge of the water, while she paused to urinate, the otter drifted away. As the woman rushed after it, the otter, which had two fins, stole her away. The people ran to tell her husband, who set out to save his wife.

He followed the otter until it submerged over the spouting hole of a spirit called Kwok. There he anchored the canoe and climbed down the anchor rope. At the bottom he encountered a giant mussel guarding the entrance. He distracted it by singing his song, "I will grant favors to mussels around here." Then he took some snuff and rubbed it on the mussel, which died. Next he came to a giant clam and killed it the same way.

He came to a trail and followed it. He heard women calling out, "We can smell Gunaxnesemgyet." These women were blind, but when he rubbed some of his spit on their eyes, they could see. "We will help you recover your wife. They are going to make a Blackfish of her. The chief captured her by sending his giant slave in the form of an otter. If you hurry, you can save her."

He went on and came to a giant crane, which was blind. Using his spit, he restored its sight. It said, "If you hurry, you can save your wife. They are going to make a Blackfish of her. A giant slave guards her, but if you trip him, he will be unable to rise again."

He got to the home of the chief and peeked through a crack in the wall. Inside, everyone was making a Blackfish cloak to cover his wife and change her. He could not see her until he looked up. She was hanging on the smoking racks to dry thoroughly before they changed her shape.

When he saw a chance, he rushed inside and put out the fire. He grabbed his wife and ran outside. They went along until they came to the giant slave, who was splitting wood, and tripped him up. He fell, never to rise. The man took the copper wedge the slave was using.

The people rushing after the couple found their way blocked by the prone slave. After running around him, they came to the crane who also lay across the trail. Further on, the newly sighted women, who were geese, also blocked the trail. The couple reached the anchor and yanked the rope. The crew pulled them up and into the canoe.

The couple lived happily in the town. Soon a son was born to them. The man continued to hunt. He killed many seals, but his wife would only eat the sexual organs of male seals. She relished these greatly. In time, a handsome young man would visit the wife while the husband was hunting. His wife was unfaithful. This adultery went on for a long time.

Eventually, the son went to his father and said, "Your wife, my mother, has been sleeping with another man. They play all night and, in the morning, he goes into the hills."

The next day, the man said, "I will hunt sea otter. I will be gone many days." Then his crew left the village. Instead of going far, however, they pulled into a nearby beach and waited until night. They went back to the village and the man went to his house. His wife and her young lover were asleep. Gunaxnesemgyet cut off the lover's head and his organs. The wife awoke to find the bed slippery. She took her dead lover and hid him in the smoking racks.

When her husband returned, she gobbled the organs that she thought came from seals, but they were from her paramour. Soon she died.

The lover had belonged to the Wolf clan, which suspected the worst. They sent a slave to the town of Gunaxnesemgyet and she entered each home asking for fire. In the house of Gunaxnesemgyet, she saw the body of the prince and returned with the news.[38]

That night, a woman's voice called from afar, "Return only the garment of my brother to me." Everyone wondered what this meant, but none acted on the plea.

The Wolves called in all the creatures of the forest and the sea. They agreed to attack Gunaxnesemgyet, who took refuge in his great house. The animals came and began to undermine it. Just before it collapsed, the man and his son fled to the beach and left in the canoe, taking along the club. The water animals rushed after him, but just when they were about to overtake him, he beached the canoe on a rocky spur that was a *spanaxnox,* the abode of a naxnox, and found refuge there. The muddy bar turned to sand, which further delayed the pursuing animals.

The home of this naxnox was full of people, but it was a hard life because the spirit had forbidden people to use water. If anyone did, they drowned. Oblivious to the warnings, Gunaxnesemgyet got water for his son, who was very thirsty. The chief was outraged and challenged Gunaxnesemgyet to a contest the next day. Each sat on one side of the house and threw their clubs, each of which had a name, at each other. Gunaxnesemgyet caught that of the chief and was safe. The chief was killed. Gunaxnesemgyet married the widow of the chief and took over the house.

With his new wealth and followers, he planned a raid on the Stikine River. Among the residents of the house were many hermaphrodites (*kanawdzet*), kept as slaves. To thwart their new chief, they made him forget his club when he left for the raid. The women found it and decided to follow the warriors to return the club to Gunaxnesemgyet.

The women had gone a long way when they found many tall cedar trees with good bark for making mats and baskets. The women gathered a great deal of bark, and took it home, forgetting about the club. This lapse was also due to the hermaphrodites.

On the Stikine, the expedition was easily defeated. The head of Gunaxnesemgyet was cut off and placed at the top of a cedar tree where it cries out whenever invaders approach, "This is the end of Gunaxnesemgyet."

### Asdiwal

During a winter famine, two noble women were suffering.[39] They lived apart in distant villages, but each suspecting that the other had food, each one decided to visit the other. Starting from their respective homes, each walked along the same frozen river until they met halfway. (We know they are high class because they do not "just give up.") They were prudent, building a flimsy shelter, and generous, sharing the one rotten berry they were able to find. They were also pious, placing offerings in the fire. They began to pray and sacrificed red paint, eagle feathers, and inner cedar bark as it was used for dancing ornaments. The next morning, the younger woman showed her prestige and industry by searching for food because persistence, prudence, and piety were hallmarks of elite status.

She was rewarded by finding a small animal under the bark of a tree. Every day, she returned to this tree to find more and bigger animals. They had been put there by the man who came each night to sleep with her. The man was a naxnox, often taking the form of a bird associated with good luck, and he represented the typical equation of wonders, men, and fatherhood. When the woman became pregnant and gave birth to a son, he was named Asdiwal at his father's request. Thus, the name came from the naxnox into the house of the mother. His father also provided magical hunting gear, a basis for later crests. In some versions, he gave two tiny hunting dogs (Red and Spot) who changed into huge mastiffs on command.

The women grew wealthy from the food they were able to store. When the husband left, they went to their clan house and put on a feast, announcing in public the boy's name of Asdiwal.

The boy grew quickly into a skillful hunter. He married and lived in the mountains hunting bears and goats. He was lavish with his bounty. One day a white bear appeared and he stalked it, aware that white was emblematic of the most noble of spirits and crests. Following it into the sky (Heaven) to the home of the Sun, he married Evening Star, Sun's daughter, who warned him to beware of the tests about to be imposed by her father. Such tests had been fatal to previous grooms, but Asdiwal triumphed to win the approval of the Sun.

Later, he successfully hunted goats on a mountain of shiny mica. The goats were in the midst of a shamanic curing ceremony, so he presumably learned their songs and dances before killing all of the participants except two. On other occasions, he safely returned from dangerous trips to collect fat, water, and firewood. His own father saved him from being baked alive by giving him a piece of magic ice. Throughout, he encountered shiny surfaces, reflective of light.

After a time, Asdiwal grew homesick and came back to earth with his wife. They arrived with food during a winter famine and saved the community. At a feast, he took the name of "Potlatch Giver." Daily, his wife tested her husband's faithfulness by dipping a feather into clear water. One day, it came out slimy, proving that Asdiwal had been unfaithful, and she left. Asdiwal followed after her, but fell out of the sky and died. The Sun fished up the bones through a hearth, revived him, and reunited the couple, who lived in the sky until Asdiwal became homesick again.

His wife took him back to earth and left. Since his mother was dead, Asdiwal went traveling. He married the daughter of a chief and went mountain-goat hunting with his four brothers-in-law. He provided so well by his hunting that his brothers-in-law grew jealous and finally abandoned him just after he killed four bears.

Rescued by four brothers from Kitkatla, island people still renowned as sea-mammal hunters, Asdiwal gave each of them a slain bear and married their sister. The couple had a son named Wox. Asdiwal's hunting prowess led to his winning of a contest with his new brothers-in-law, who became jealous and abandoned him on a rocky reef inhabited by sea lions. As waves threatened to drown him, his father turned Asdiwal into a bird and helped to save him.

A mouse summoned the hunter into the home of the chief. At first Asdiwal could only hear her, but then he saw the mouse by looking through a hole in his covering. Presumably, the importance of the hole was that it let in special light.

The chief of the sea lions had a house inside the rock at a *spanaxnox* where most of the inhabitants were ill. Unseen by them, this epidemic was caused by the wounds and barbs inflicted by Asdiwal, who acted like a shaman and cured the human-looking sea lions (using the mountain goat rite), while deftly removing his barbs from their bodies. The chief sent Asdiwal back to shore in a vessel that was his own sea-lion stomach, a pun on whose stomach usually contained whom.

Upon reaching land, Asdiwal met his grieving wife and son and plotted revenge. While his wife made offerings, he lured her brothers (except the kind, youngest one, in some versions) to their deaths by having them pursue magical killer whales he carved from wood and animated.

Asdiwal went off again and settled in another town, gave a potlatch, and assumed the chiefly name of "Stone Slinger." His son joined him there and inherited his extraordinary hunting gear. One day while out hunting, Asdiwal forgot his snowshoes and became stranded on a mountain top. There, his body, staff, and dogs turned to stone and his soul (or one of them) flew off to be with his father.[40]

WHY MASKS?

The wearing of masks, the primary expression of the naxnox, has long intrigued scholars, as it has the Tsimshian themselves. Today, some people will say that they have noticed that the most shy and awkward person will perform well in public if he or she is wearing a mask. As Christians, modern Tsimshian regard such masks only as disguises, not as the symbols of great power that these carved faces had been for their ancestors. Indeed, most coast people plead ignorance and disinterest when asked about the ancient system of naxnox displays. A few will also say that they are afraid of such things because

*10. Twin Stone Masks. This famous pair, carved of solid granite, represent the best
known of the* naxnox *or spirit personifications. The outer mask is blind, while the
inner one has eyeholes that allowed the impersonator suddenly to see when the
outer mask was hidden under his cloak, exemplifying the Tsimshian theme of
illumination. (Photo courtesy of Bill Holm, with permission of Musée d'Homme,
#81.22.1, and Canadian Museum of Civilizations.)*

people have forgotten how to treat them with respect. There is always the danger that these powers, once summoned, however innocently, are likely to hurt,
maim, or kill all those involved. Yet there are hints about the system and how
it worked in the notes of William Beynon (mss.). Among the Gitksan, today, a
version of the belief and display continues.

Moreover, the Tsimshian use of masks is an aspect of a larger and more
intriguing pattern. In human societies, as a rule, masks are characteristic of
matrilineal societies. Why this is so was first pondered by Elizabeth Tooker,
although she came to no ready conclusion. Relying on the Tsimshian and comparative evidence, however, the system can be seen as an expression of beliefs
about relationships with the father and, through him, with the spirits.

In her famous article, Tooker explored "an association between the use of
masks in religious ritual and the presence of matrilineal institutions" (1968:
1170) in Native North America.

She recalled that Fritz Graebner, an early German anthropologist, noted an
association between secret societies with masks and matrilineal moieties as a

feature of his East Papuan or Matrilineal Two-Class kulturkreis (culture circle), but when Alfred Kroeber and Catherine Holt tested for such an association, they found no correlation between masks and moieties in general.

Looking again at Kroeber and Holt's data, Tooker factored specifically for matrilineal moieties and found that "although masks are frequently found in societies that lack matrilineal moieties, it is of some interest that no society that has matrilineal moieties lacks masks" (1968:1170). According to her "Table 2, Masks and Matrilineal Moieties in a Sample of North American Cultures," the five representatives were Haida, Hidatsa, Iroquois, Mandan, and Tlingit (1968:1171).

Moreover, looking at the relationship between masks and general matrilineality, particularly among the Pueblos, she found evidence "that the more important matrilineal institutions are in the organization of a society, the more important masking will also be in the religious ritual of that society" (1968: 1170). Her "Table 3, Masks and Matrilineality in a Sample of North American Cultures," includes twelve representatives, the same five (Haida, Hidatsa, Iroquois, Mandan, Tlingit) along with seven others (Crow, Delaware, Hopi, Kutchin, Navaho, Tsimshian, Zuni) (1968:1172).

While "no present anthropological theory adequately accounts for" this linkage, she suggested that "it seems most likely that there is at least one intermediary variable that can be ascertained only through further study" since neither masking nor matrilineality is causal for the other (1968:1173).

As a source for this variable, she pointed to the role of male authority in matrilineal societies, where "Men do not propitiate the gods; they become the gods by the mere act of putting on the mask" and "men and spirits together work to keep the world in order" (1968:1174).

To pursue, again, this line of reasoning, we first need to correct for previous data. For example, while the Tsimshian were once described as having four clans, this is more a consequence of anthropologists working in resettled communities than of ethnographic reality (Miller and Eastman 1984). In Tsimshian terms, their society consists of moieties whose emblems were names and crests, traced through the mother, while the emblems of the wonder-based names were masks, traced to a male, often a supernatural father, in the sacred histories of the household.

Even within the matrilines, regard was also accorded to the father's side, a source of help, both financial and spiritual. According to Adams, "there are essential spiritual and physical components of every Gitksan which come from the father as well as from the mother. A child who is living in his father's village will not be harmed because he has some of the look and character of his father's people, some of his spiritual qualities, in the literal sense, which will return to his father's people eventually" (1973:39). Among the Tsimshian, therefore, there is an equation of moieties and masks, but with the twist that the masks are specifically equated with men.

Aside from Tooker's surmise about the linkage of masks with men in a context of matrilineality, there have been few theories of masking. Among those most distinctive is that of Laura Makarius, who argues that "masks represent instruments of protection" from the violation of taboos, the most basic of which for her is the shedding of blood (1983:195). In contexts fraught with ambivalence, masks themselves become sources of danger and, hence, are treated with reverence and fear (1983:200).

While Makarius may help to explain masking connotations, she does not address the intent of mask use in specific societies, particularly matrilineal ones. Fathers, standing outside the vital social fabric, become sources of power, aliens charged with energies at the limits of the known and related universe. Their connections with the body of the community are both spiritual and superficial (or external) since substance comes internally from women, passed on matrilineally. It is just this superficiality that encourages the use of masks, the face of Otherness representing a link based on appearance, on analogy but not on identity.

The clearest statement in the literature is not from the Americas, but from Papua New Guinea, Graebner's first area of interest. According to Nancy Munn, "Whereas the child's bond to the mother is an intrinsic one of material substance and continuity, the ideal relationship to the father is one of likeness to someone extrinsic to one's own bodily self. . . . Ideally, a child's face (*magi-*, a term that also denotes appearance) should resemble its father's" (1986: 142–43). That such a statement does apply in the Americas is supported by comments from the Tlingit with "reference to a resemblance between his or her face and those of his or her classificatory fathers" (Kan 1989:67). Ronald Olson noted that "A special relationship holds between a person and his [or her] father's clansmen. . . . This relationship may also be on a joking plane. Thus a person might say to his father's brother (or anyone he called by that term) . . . child of Kagwantan, his face. This is making fun of the face of the person addressed, teasing him. If he resented it he might reply . . . from among you, I look the same" (1967:16).

Since Tooker published her article, more has been written about American masking (cf. Crumrine and Halpin 1983) and its various tribal contexts (Fenton 1987). These studies demonstrate that well-developed masking traditions were rarely simple. Raymond Fogelson (Fogelson and Bell 1983:54) observed a distinction, common among Eastern tribes, between carved wooden masks and woven cornhusk or cut-gourd masks. The former were associated with the forests and male activities such as hunting, while the latter were associated with clearings and female efforts such as farming. Even so, the husk or gourd masks were worn by men representing both men and women beings.

Among the Iroquois, genders are reversed from those expected by Anglo-Americans. For Iroquois, female is the unmarked, inclusive, or general category, while male is marked, exclusive, and specific. It is therefore entirely appropriate for Bushyhead husk masks, woven of corn husks and associated with females and plants, to represent both men and women beings. Moreover, in keeping with their Otherness, the Bushyheads were believed to be "a people from the other side of the world where the seasons are reversed" who taught humans "the arts of hunting and agriculture" (Fenton 1987:54). Thus, even when the symbolic equation of the Bushyheads was with women, who did the farming among the Iroquois, it was men who expressed the relationship.

In matrilineal societies, women were substance and men were surface. For a child to admit kinship with a father, he had to rely on external characteristics. In the interest of saving face and claiming affection, masks were used to convey the complexities of such superficial imaging. In this instance, at least, masks had a profundity which was fully intended to be only skin deep.

Among the Tsimshian, therefore, masks represented the naxnox and as such they were associated with the fathers in various sacred house histories. Masks imaged and conveyed male power, both from ancestors in the past and to heirs in the present. Wearing these tokens, members brought this power into the house and displayed it during the winter when religion was foremost in Tsimshian life. While many masks were clearly male or female (with a labret), the crucial point is that they were conveyed through men in mirror image to the crests, which were also passed to men and women, but through a line of females.

HALAIT BRANCH

In general, the term *halait* applied to shamans, chiefs as priestly or ceremonial leaders, cult dancers, and witches,[41] along with each and every item of paraphernalia they used.[42] Shamans had inherent power from their ancestors, acquired by personal questing; chiefs and dancers became halait via initiation

into the secret orders; and witches used malevolent intent and recipes involving noxious ingredients in secret. Each chief, nonetheless, was supposed to
have a sorcerer on his staff to vex opponents and tax the wealthy with expensive cures. "It was widely rumored that shamans collaborated with witches in
order to extort huge fees from the wealthy. Each shaman was supposed to have
a witch-associate whose job was to cause a wealthy individual to fall ill"
(McNeary 1976b:158). The cure consisted of the shaman having the witch remove the spell, after he or she had performed a curing rite—if they both
wanted the patient to live, that is.

The halait artifact that mediated between crest hats and wonder masks was
the wooden frontlet, a carved figure worn on the forehead of royalty during ritual displays. Located between the crown and the face, the forehead mediated
between the hat and mask. The frontlet was a hallmark of a complex outfit, including woven cedarbark hoops, which Guédon correctly describes as a mark
of rank, not of kinship: "the raven rattle, the *amhalait* [frontlet] headdress, and
the chilkat robe . . . [do] not carry connotation of crests or house membership but only indication of high rank and symbols of nobility, peace (eagle's
down), and sacred intent" (1984a:156). When a chief died, his or her halait
objects were burned with the body because they were personal, not corporate,
possessions.

## HALAIT

In her careful consideration, Marie-Françoise Guédon writes that halait refers
to the paranormal and extraordinary: "It means 'something special,' 'something different,' 'a gift, a wonderful ability, which sets you apart.' One woman
in Hazelton remarked that 'if you have a Ph.D., you are a *halait* of some
kind; if you are endowed with some musical gift, you are a *halait*. . . . The
original meaning of the term, however, has probably to do with twirling'"
(1984a:138).

In most cases, the abilities of shaman and chief were strongly contrasted as
ordinary and special. As Halpin observes,

> Two basic sources of power can be identified as *chiefly* and *shamanic*.
> The source of chiefly power is the "bright mirage" of heaven which is
> reached through a hole in the sky (= smoke hole in the house). It can be
> opened by certain chiefs who receive its power directly and "throw" it
> into others. Once strengthened by the mediated chiefly powers, ordinary

*11. Tsimshian Chief as* smhalait. *On his head is a frontlet, on his back a chilkat robe, in one hand a raven rattle, and in the other a staff. His seat is a wooden box. (Courtesy of the Museum of Northern British Columbia.)*

persons can themselves be thrown through the opening into heaven to acquire wisdom (= enlightenment) from its denizens and achieve full humanity (becoming human + divine) as "made persons" (chiefs are called *semoiget* or "real persons"). (1981:272)

On the other hand, "Shamanic power is acquired unsought and outside the ritual framework through possession by animals which causes 'temporary' death. Through the ancient medical formula that to cure one must be cured, the shaman reverses his own power encounter, moving back from illness to health, and death to life" (1981:274).

Chiefly power was of the sky, but that of shamans was closer to the earth. Potent images for the shaman included the whirlpool and canoe (Guédon 1984b:197, 186), but most particularly the mouth and eye (1984b:193, 206). All shamans were individualists, transcending the boundaries of society while at the same time marking them. All had "spirit helpers" who provided an alternative point of view (a different light) for looking at situations. A modern Gitksan shaman views herself as "a big rope of light going from way, way back to way, way in the future" (1984b:204).

The twisting and twirling of the shaman, as rope and as whirlpool, indicate that they are attuned to the potency of light, "looping" through a full pulsation or revolution of such illumination.

## SHAMANS

According to contemporary Tsimshian elders, of all forms of halait, that of the shaman (*swansk* 'blower') was the most powerful.[43] While many men and women acted as curers, only a few of them were believed to actually possess "real" halait, mostly through inheritance from a powerful relative, often a maternal uncle (mother's brother).

The power of a shaman resided in his or her hair, which was, therefore, never disturbed. More than any other insignia, long unkempt hair was the badge of a shaman.

While certain lineages had a propensity to produce shamans, the act of empowerment was always an "individual solitary vision quest" (Guédon 1984a: 143). While carvings, masks, and regalia transmitted this power into curing contexts, shamanism was most concerned with focusing the intent and mental abilities of the shaman to transform him- or herself into other states and dimensions. To be effective, a shaman had to enter periods of trance and ecstasy

*12. A Shaman. He wears a bear claw crown, apron, and hide cloak, while holding a
rattle and drum; this image was superimposed over a picture of a carved pole.
(Courtesy of the Museum of Northern British Columbia.)*

to marshall the power and ability necessary for a successful cure. To achieve these mental states, a shaman used songs, regalia, and "charms," evoking spirit helpers or various types of naxnox. These charms were intricately carved of bone, wood, teeth, or stone to represent a particular helper (Gitksan: *atiasxw*). In addition to a robe made from the hide of a mountain goat, or of a bear, lynx, or other predator, worn with a crown of bear or lynx claws or goat horns, a shaman donned necklaces and a decorated apron. A one-sided drum (*nahooł*) and carved rattle (*gakst*) were also essential. A special bag contained necessary charms and the rest of a medical kit, including red ocher, eagle down, bird skins, animal skulls, stuffed pelts, and crystals (Guédon 1984b: 196–97).

Since the power of the shaman was personal, ongoing, and inherent in certain family lines, shamanism provided the pattern for other forms of spiritual displays, such as the varieties of halait that characterized the Tsimshian elite. While the *smhalait* represented the chief in his religious, almost priestly, role during the winter, the *wutahalait* comprised the four secret orders adapted from the Bella Bella or Heiltsuk Kwakiutlans over a century before.

Virtually global in its distribution, shamanism was also ancient among the Tsimshian, as illustrated by several stories, summarized below, about famous shamans recorded by William Beynon for Marius Barbeau (1958: 39–55, 67–73; Barbeau and Beynon 1987a).[44] The first concerns a child of the nobility who achieves his full potential as a shaman; the second is an unusual story because the shaman, Only-One, was remarkable for his goodness; the third presents the career of a woman shaman; and the fourth describes that of Isaac Tens, a Gitksan curer and carver of the early 1900s.

### The Prince

A young man of noble family lived at Metlakatla with his four companions.[45] One day on the beach, he decided to play at being a shaman. He took a clam shell and put pebbles inside it to use as a rattle. He took pieces of cedar-bark matting to wear as a crown and an apron. (A real shaman wore a crown made of grizzly bear claws and an apron of skins.) His companions drew back because they knew that such simulation, bordering on mockery, was not allowed because powerful spirits (naxnox) were likely to be offended. Still, the teenager persisted and, as he was a prince, the companions could only acquiesce.

The young man made up a song and began to dance like he was starting a cure. Soon he fell down in an unconscious trance. The companions were very much afraid, but they could not go back to the town for help because they were

*13. "Soul Catcher." This hollow carved bone tube was a vital part of the kit of
a shaman, who used it to concentrate his breath while blowing or to hold an
ailment sucked from a patient. (Photo by Bill Holm, used by the courtesy of
John and Grace Putnam.)*

obliged to watch and guide the prince, and his present condition did not reflect
well on them.

Instead, they carried the prince to a small hut, stocked with food, in the
woods where they often camped. There they awaited the outcome. The prince
was delirious for a day. He spoke in a strange language to people the others
could not see.

The next day, the prince awoke and acted normal. He told his companions
that he was now changed forever. He was a halait with power from a Crane.
The others were amazed and asked for proof. The prince had a cut on his hand
and one of the young men suggested that he cure himself. The prince agreed
and sang his new songs from the vision while rubbing his cut finger. Then they
ate breakfast. When the meal was over, all saw that the cut was healed. Now
they believed.

They started to go home, and along the way, at the edge of the water, stood
a large crane, which rose into the air as they got closer. A shiny object dropped
from the crane and landed on the ground. The prince went there and found the
crystal he had been promised as an amulet to aid his work. He took it and they
went back to Metlakatla, but they said nothing to anyone.

The next day, the young men went for crabs. While the companions speared
them from the canoe, the prince looked up at a goose flying over the ocean. He
wondered how powerful his crystal was. So he took it out of the pouch where

he had hidden it and, addressing it as a naxnox, told it to kill the goose. Instantly, the amulet flew away and the goose fell dead. They paddled over to the goose and picked it up. The prince retrieved the crystal, immensely pleased with its power.

They resumed spearing crabs in the shallows until they saw a man walk down to the beach. He was a chief who was known to be mean. A companion asked the prince to make the chief sick so that they could earn fame and fortune by curing him. The prince agreed and sent the crystal to strike the foot of the chief, who screamed in pain and fell down.

The boys paddled the canoe to shore and helped the chief get back to his house. His own relatives and house mates who were halait tried to cure him but they could not. The chief got worse.

Finally, one of the companions went to his aunt who lived in the chief's house and mentioned his prince so she could tell the others. They sent a herald to invite the prince to try to cure the chief. The prince agreed, asking for time to assemble his helpers and to prepare his outfit. Now that he was known as a shaman, he wore a moose hide apron with a fringe of deer hooves and puffin bills, a crown of grizzly bear claws pointing up, and carried a rattle carved to look like a crane. The crystal was his great secret, kept hidden at all times and known only to the companions.

The men got into their canoe and went to visit the chief. When they got there, the prince asked his companions to cover the chief over with a woven cedar mat. He dressed in his insignia and began to dance and sing, calling on the Crane for help. He held the crystal in one hand and moved it over the foot of the chief, asking it to improve the foot but not cure it completely. The chief felt better. Then the young men left.

A few days later, they were called back to further cure the chief. This time, he asked the crystal to give the chief total relief. It did so. To signify this, the prince cupped his hands over the foot, appeared to take something out, went to the fireplace, and blew it out through the smokehole. The chief arose and felt so well that the young men received many gifts in payment.

The prince's fame increased and he performed many other cures, becoming wealthy, as did his companions. Soon he considered marrying. A strong chief in the next town had a beautiful daughter, but her father would never consent to her marriage with anyone.

The prince asked his mother to intercede for him since the strong chief belonged to their clan, the Blackfish. The mother gathered moose hides, fur robes, and much food as a dowry. She put it into a great carved box and had a slave carry it to the chief's house. The slave placed it in front of the chief and the mother asked for the daughter (who, like his wife, was a Raven), in marriage to her son. The chief listened and said that he would consider the request. The mother left, disheartened. Several days later, indeed, a slave of the chief returned the box of gifts, thereby rejecting the offer. The prince and his companions went into the hills to think. There, one of the men suggested that the prince make the princess ill so that only he could cure her and win her as a wife. He agreed.

They went to the woods near the strong chief's town and waited. The woman was never alone. Later in the day, the princess, accompanied by many women attendants, went down to the beach to relieve herself. The prince sent the crystal to hurt her foot. She cried out and was carried back home, growing increasingly weaker. All of the doctors in the house and the town were called to try to cure her, but none succeeded. The chief called halaits from the other tribes, but they too failed.

Finally, one of the councilors suggested to the chief that they call the young shaman known as Sge'nu, but the chief was embarrassed because he had rejected that man as a son-in-law. Still, the moans of his daughter grew worse and the chief relented.

The prince now had his chance because he himself was Sge'nu. The herald brought many gifts and placed them before the prince, asking him to cure the daughter. He only replied that he would think about it. The messengers left in despair. The chief sent them back a second time with more gifts, but still the prince was noncommittal. The men left, discouraged. The daughter was very weak and near death so the chief sent the herald back with more gifts and the promise that the prince could marry the daughter if he cured her. The prince consented.

The shaman and companions went to the home of the chief and covered the woman with a mat. The prince dressed, danced, and sang while he rubbed the foot with the crystal. Ordinarily, modesty required that the shaman not touch the patient, but he could rub her foot because he was expected to marry her. Soon she was cured and could walk around. The prince married her and moved into her home, as did his companions.

Everything went well until famine stalked the country. Food was very scarce and many died of starvation. One night the prince told his companions they would hunt seals in the morning. They borrowed his father-in-law's largest canoe and left at daybreak. The prince wore his crystal in a pouch about his neck. When they saw a seal, the prince asked his amulet to kill it. Soon the canoe was filled with seals. They went home and the prince told the slaves to pack the seals into the house.

The next day the men went for sea lions and returned with a large canoe full. Another day, they went for whales, towing each back to the beach in front of the town. Everyone was ecstatic because whale was a great delicacy.

The chief was very proud and held many feasts for the starving people in other towns. He became very famous and wealthy. He potlatched himself, his house, and his clan to greatness with the help of his son-in-law, who now moved back to his own town with his wife and companions so he could inherit the chiefship from his uncle. All went very well.

One night, the prince called his companions and said that strangers were coming to ask for help. They should be prepared to leave when these messengers came in the middle of the night.

Late that night, the strangers came and the men went with them to cure a chief who was near death. Their canoe moved of its own accord and took them to an island far out to sea, unknown to anyone. Inside the rocky outcrop was the home of the chief, who was the leader of the hairy spirits called Bagwas.[46] Many halaits, spirit and human, had tried to cure the chief, but without success. Hearing of the fame of the prince, the Bagwas chief sent for him. To protect themselves from the insanity that contact with the Bagwas usually caused, the prince and his men bathed in urine daily while away from home.

When they arrived, the prince went to the patient and dressed in his outfit. As he sang and danced, he asked the crystal to diagnose the problem. In a trance, the Crane came to him and explained that a rival chief had made an effigy of the sick chief and was poking a stone arrowhead into its back, slowly killing the patient. When the point severed the backbone, the chief would die.

The Crane told the shaman to have kinsmen of the chief go to the rival and tell him to stop annoying the sick man. The other chief would then know he had been found out and risked having his power turned back upon him.

Later, the shaman danced again and sent the crystal at night to retrieve the effigy. The next day, the shaman danced around the figure and asked the crystal to remove the arrowpoint, which it did. To simulate this, the prince acted as though he removed something from the chief's back, took it to the smokehole, and blew it into the sky. Something was heard to fall onto the roof. A slave was sent to fetch it. He brought back a stone arrow point. The chief was completely cured. The rival chief immediately took sick and died because he could not hold off the rebounding of his own power.

The curers were paid with many gifts of furs, hides, coppers, and foods. The chief himself gave the prince the ability to prophesize the future to protect his people. Then the men were sent back in a canoe that was actually a whale. All of their gifts were crammed inside. When they got home, it took the slaves a whole day to pack all of these treasures into the house.

While the prince thought they had been away six days, it had been six years of human time. Many things had changed, but the town now prospered. The prince gave a great potlatch and made the name Sge'nu famous all over the world.

*Only-One*

One of the greatest of the Tsimshian shamans had the halait name of Only-One because he was uniquely known among his colleagues for great kindness. Indeed, shamans were expected to be mean and selfish, as their reactions to Only-One make clear.

Among the Gyilodzau [Giluts'aaẅ], three men decided to become halaits. Since their families were unblemished, they expected success. They went to a *spahalait* that was a pit in a rock from which strange noises sometimes emerged. Most people avoided it. Instead, these men went with a rope, which was tied around the waist of each man as he was lowered into the hole. The first and second men only got a short way before they pleaded to be pulled up because they were being badly stung by insects. The third man made it to the bottom, where it was very dark. There he waited.

Soon he was deafened by a sound like thunder as a door opened in the side of the pit. A shining youth came out and asked what he wanted. The human asked for shamanic powers and was led through the door to the being's father, an old chief sitting in the rear of a large house, wearing a crown of grizzly claws, and holding a living rattle in each hand. The man was seated beside him.

Another door opened, and a bright youth came out dressed as a shaman. From another door, cedar planks, clubs, and a drum came out to play themselves for the shaman. When the man had seen and heard all of this, the chief rubbed his eyes and made him blind. He called out and his companions pulled him up.

Outside of the hole, the man could see again. The men got back into the canoe and headed home. As they approached, the man in the bow fell over unconscious, and later the man in the middle did the same. Both vomited blood, which was proof that they had become shamans, but, of course, they were never as powerful as the man who met the owner of the house in that place. He never lost consciousness and poled the canoe into the town.

The other men were carried home and lay in a trance for some time. The third man also remained confined to his sleeping cubicle. When they recovered, the men began to cure the sick. Their fame increased and they became rich.

A year later the third man disappeared. No one could find him. Late one night, everyone heard a crash and found the man face down in the mud behind the town. He appeared dead, but was carried to his bed. The other two men covered him with a cedar mat and left him alone. Later, everyone heard singing and went to where the man was. He had recovered and said only that he was called back to the hole in the rock to be given more power, including the ability to restore the dead to life. He was given the name of Only-One (*gamk'ool*). The other two men became his aides. They did great things together.

Soon the other shamans were jealous and repeatedly tried to kill him. He saw all of their traps and snares with his inner eyes and avoided them. The other shamans got angry and more desperate. Only-One cured all who asked for help, whether rich or poor. He never refused anyone, unlike the other shamans who only cured the wealthy to get richer.

They arranged to have a prince pretend to be sick so they could lure Only-One to his death, but he was warned and allowed the prince to die.

One night the leader of the Bagwas sent for him. His aides and two nephews went along with him, carefully washing themselves in urine as protection. The Bagwas chief's nephew was ill because a witch had made an effigy of him and was piercing it with a thorn. When the point reached the heart, the prince would die. In constant agony, the boy shrieked with pain. The chief went to the home of the witch, who was a powerful halait, and confronted him. He took away the witchbox and burned the effigy after removing the thorn. Only-One then finished the cure by removing a stone arrowpoint from between the ribs of the prince, who became well. Only-One was paid many pelts and treasures for the cure. He was sent home very rich.

One of the halait of Kitkatla sent for Only-One. He was wasting away because the other halaits were using him as a lure to kill Only-One. When he arrived, Only-One saw the nets and pits that were placed in his way and avoided them. Only-One told the patient that some of his waste had been put into the corpse of a recently deceased shaman. The old man knew the location of the remote cave where the shaman's body had been deposited and sent his nephew to remove the feces. Once the nephew did so, the man was cured.

A great feast was held to celebrate, with Only-One as the guest of honor. The other shamans planned to feed Only-One cooked human flesh. Since it was an insult to refuse food, Only-One was told by his naxnox to make a hole in his stomach so the food could pass through his body without poisoning him. Only-One did this, then gave the food to the other shamans, who ate it and died in great agony.

Only-One was now the most famous of all the halaits, wealthy, kind, and much loved. He grew very old. One spring, while everyone was preparing salmon, a strange man came into the town and went to Only-One, saying that his master wanted him. Then the stranger left. Only-One prepared to depart. He gave all of his powers away, assigning a few to each helper and nephew, so no one was ever as powerful again. When Only-One sat in his canoe, it went swiftly away of its own accord to the pit where his first powers had come to him. There he vanished. He did not die, but became the chief of all the halaits and the leader of the naxnox. He now gives out powers to those who fast and quest. He is still kind.

*A Woman Shaman*

While there were fewer female than male shamans, some of them were quite powerful. Beynon heard the story of one such woman, who belonged to the house of Sats'aan of the Ginadoiks.[47] Once, while with her father hunting mountain goats, she awoke to find her legs charred and useless because the goats had gifted her with power. When her father returned to camp to discover her condition, he went for help. She was wrapped in an elkskin and lowered down a cliff using ropes made from cedar bark and caribou skin. Halfway down, the rope broke, but the girl showed her power by suspending herself in the air and floating to the ground. After she recovered the use of her legs, she began to cure. If the patient would survive, her own legs darkened. If her legs remained the same, the patient died or remained ill.

She also was able to save her people from hardships. During a drought, the rivers dried up and no salmon came. She asked her father to show her how high the water needed to be for salmon to spawn. He put a stick in the river and marked the necessary height. She sat on the bank and sang a halait song until the river filled to that height and the salmon came. After her people had enough fish to survive, she stopped singing and the water receded.

During a wet spell, her people were unable to collect nettles and fireweed to extract the fibers to make nets. Her mother kept making loud comments about the great needs of the people and the woman relented. She went outside, sat down, and pointed at the sun. All day long, men took turns holding up her arm so that it would continue to point. As the land dried, women went out to gather the plants. When they had enough, the woman lowered her arm and the rain resumed.

Her last act was to predict her own death. She composed herself and waited until mountain goats appeared across from the town. Her legs darkened to their charred appearance, and she died.

### Isaac Tens

When he was thirty, Isaac had his first brush with his shamanic familiar. He was alone in the hills cutting firewood when a loud noise startled him. An owl appeared and tried to lift him up by the face. He became unconscious and fell into a snowbank. When he revived, ice coated his head and blood ran from his mouth. He rushed home, but the trees loomed over him and seemed to be crawling like snakes. He finally reached his father's house and collapsed. Two shamans came to work him over. He was delirious, thinking there were flies all over his face and he was swirling in a whirlpool. When he recovered, the halaits who worked on him said it was time to become a halait himself, but he ignored the incident entirely.[48]

Later, while hunting on his own territory, he saw an owl, shot it, but never found the body. It vanished in a very strange way. Then he heard a noise like a crowd chasing him and rushed home. Along the way, he fell unconscious and revived with his head covered with ice and buried in a snowbank. He walked home along the frozen Skeena River until his father found him and brought him home. His heart raced and his body trembled. He was put to bed while halaits were called.

As the cure began, a song rose from Isaac's lips unbidden, while visions of huge birds, a bullhead, and other animals appeared to him. He memorized the songs and knew it was time to become a halait.

For the next year, he trained and meditated, learning new songs. Four men, cousins in the Wolf clan, looked after him constantly. After a year, other halaits were called in by his father to hold a public ceremony to strengthen Isaac. His father paid them well because thereafter Isaac was a *swansk*.[49] He worked with other halaits and learned to perfect his abilities. He began to diagnose through dreams, and he acquired charms, amulets, and talismans. One of the most important of these was a model of a canoe, which appeared in a dream as an Otter floating either on the water or in the clouds. In the beginning, he was paid ten blankets for a cure. Any request to perform a healing had to be met, as long as enough goods were offered. Otherwise the shaman would be suspected of willing the death of the patient and might be killed by the grieving relatives if the person died. "This was the hard law of the country."

Every shaman had about twenty songs to choose from during a cure. Isaac had twenty-three songs. Most had texts featuring a simple sentence that evoked some naxnox or event with significance to the shaman, his predecessors, or his house and clan.

Songs included references to the spirit who did the actual work. One song contained these verses:

The Salmon spirit (naxnox) weakens when I do,
The town shall be cured when my Salmon spirit floats in,
The chief of the Salmon is floating in the canyon underneath me,
The Woman Robin has flown away with me.

A second song has two verses, based on a vision of two uncles, who were famous shamans, and their spirits:

The Grizzly shall go a long way from here behind the sky,
The halait envisions the fires of the commoners through the ground.

A third song also had two verses about a vision of a large pool of water:

My feet are held fast in a large spring,
A Mussel Shell is holding my feet.

A fourth song mentioned:

Bee Hive spirit stings my body,
Grandmother is making me grow.

A fifth one described:

Mountains were talking to each other as I walked about,
I went into the river where it makes a loud noise in the canyon,
My trail leads down a steep incline.

In the vision, Isaac went by canoe across the river and into the mountains, which rang out as though engaged in speech. Finally, he walked to the bottom of the peaks.

A sixth song's verses concerned a trip in the canoe through several terrains and dimensions:

Whose canoe is it where I stand with the stranger,
It floats about among whirlpools.

For the worst cases, Isaac wore a bearskin robe and bear-claw crown and put a snare around his neck with the end held by one of his helpers. There were four of these, one in each corner. Another threw water over his head so that all of them could stand around the pool on the floor to prepare a diagnosis.

The patient was covered with a mat to protect the spirit or soul of the person. If the spirit were very weak, a hot stone rubbed with melted fat was used to strengthen it.

Other shamans were particularly difficult to cure because they were so involved with spirits. Since they were not truly human, they were expected to suffer a very hard death.

After becoming a Christian, however, Isaac used standards like the Lord's Prayer in his treatments and avoided any contacts with the naxnox and the old ways. As a convert, his body changed and he became human. When his children became sick, if physicians could not cure them, he had to pay a *swansk halait* to make them well.

By mid-century, however, the Gitksan had devised a Christianized version of shamanism that enabled members of families to inherit these powers and practice them on people who suffered from traditional maladies not susceptible to allopathic or hospital medicine.

## PRIVILEGES

Unlike the shaman, whose power was acquired personally, with a tendency for the ability to pass through family lines after members of each generation were "tested" by curing personal illness, the abilities of the halait were acquired through initiation. In the past, shamanism was ascribed, while halait was achieved. Since both relied on the use of potency to cure and influence others, they have become fused over time, particularly after the adoption of Christianity when both were proscribed.

According to Marie-Françoise Guédon (1984a:140), halait was and is the manifestation of potency, with naxnox as its source. Therefore, *halait* (*halaayt*), sometimes translated as "power," referred explicitly to the privileged position of a "shaman dancer, shaman's dance," an initiated member of a secret order borrowed from the neighboring Wakashans.

The several degrees of halait were added at different times. *Halait* itself usually meant "shamans" and was ancient; *smhalait* 'real halait' referred to the chief in his priestly winter aspect; *wihalait* 'great halait' were the four orders of secret societies diffusing north from the Northern Wakashans, especially the Bella Bellas. Both Garfield (1939:293) and Guédon (1984a:143) regarded these cults as the most recent additions to a system of spirit quests and naxnox displays.

Among Tsimshians, these four secret societies or orders were, by name, the *miła* (Dancers), *nuṭim* (Dog Eaters), *ludzista* (Destroyers), and *xgyedmhalait* (Cannibals). The first two orders functioned as secret societies with initiated members. The last two orders seem to have been the personal privileges of high chiefs and, as such, had no cult associations. In all cases, however, membership in these orders was an indication of the nobility and the royalty of a clan and town. Unlike the more open naxnox displays, the halait were truly a badge of the elite.[50]

Royal children, during winter, were initiated into these orders, with the Cannibals reserved for the greatest chiefs, who bore halait names linking them with Heaven, the eminent being of the Tsimshian cosmos (Boas 1916:543).

While little has been published about these orders, Beynon's manuscript materials distinguish some of their stances: "A person belonging to *mitla* [Dancers] would hold right hand over heart and left hand extended as far as elbow with forearm raised. A person belonging to the *xgedem* [Cannibals] would have right hand over heart and left hand fully extended. *Nuhlim:* a person belonging to this group [Dog Eaters] would extend both hands upraised" (Cove 1987:255).

In his comparative study of these secret orders, Drucker (1940:223) reported that Gitksan Dog Eaters wore a bearskin robe, dance apron, and rings for the head and neck woven of mixed red and white cedar bark, while Dancers wore only red for rings, eagle down, and paint. The patron spirit of each order was a particular naxnox who was sent away at the end of the initiation. The highest ranking member, a chief, danced around the fire, made a grasping motion at the sound of a whistle to grab the spirit, and finished his circuit. Then he threw the spirit to the next ranking member who did the same and passed it down to the next lower-ranked member. The last member threw it back to the chief, who danced around the fire four times and hurled it through the smoke-

*14. Two Men as* smhalait. *Their insignia are complete with frontlets, chilkat robes, aprons, anklets, and raven rattles. (Courtesy of the Museum of Northern British Columbia.)*

hole into the sky, closing the full loop. The diminishing sound of a whistle indicated that the spirit was returning to the "cave of the spirits."

For Guédon,

Halait refers to any shamanic or ritual manifestation of power. It is both the dance and the dancer, the person manifesting power as well as the ritual event within which the manifestation occurs. Naxnox is a personification of power, or that which is manifested in Halait. While it can be inferred from mythological contexts and ritual action that power in its pure or generalized aspect is the light (heat) or potency of Heaven (which is personified as the Chief of Heaven or Sun Chief), it seldom appears in this form, but is refracted into numerous concrete personifications—animals, monsters, shining youths, crystals, and the myriad humanoid beings . . . who were impersonated by means of masks. (1984a: 138)

*Beynon Text*

In careful fieldnotes on a halait initiation, William Beynon, Tsimshian ethnographer and Wolf chief (Halpin 1978), was told by Julia White and Mrs. R. Tate how an initiate vanished at the sound of naxnox secret whistles and went to Heaven to "become elevated" (Beynon mss.).[51] Later, the child returned to town riding on a representation of a family crest. While this crest was inherited through the mother, the display itself was arranged by the father. Thus, the halait made use of both crest and wonder, mother and father, to create a new identity. Throughout his writings, Beynon described halait initiation as "elevation" and initiates as "elevated," calling attention to its celestial aspects.

These events were noteworthy because they involved Ligeex, the high chief of the Tsimshian during the historic period. During the first stage of initiation, called *tsiik,* the father of the child arranged for him or her to be elevated up (*m-nya*).

At the halait house of the Gispaxlo'ots, there were five children, cared for by paternal aunts, until Ligeex arrived and threw his great halait power into them. Instantaneously, they disappeared, supposedly ascending to heaven, but actually quickly hidden away by their aunts. Their parents then distributed much wealth to the guests, particularly to Ligeex.

On another occasion, as whistles sounded, a girl was led by her father's sister into the house of Ligeex and seated with formality. Ligeex came toward her singing and dancing, but, as he reached her, she disappeared. (Her aunt took her outside and hid her in the back of her own house, where she was dressed in a small dancing garment [*ts'uu gwishalait*] with cedar bark rings around her neck and head.)

Previously, craftsmen (*gitsontk*) had made a big swan that could open its wings and had mounted it on a small canoe. The Swan was one of the foremost crests of her father. Ligeex found a young girl to double for the initiate. The night before the girl came back from Heaven, the double was taken out in the canoe with the swan. Early in the morning, warned by blasts of naxnox whistles, people rushed to the beach to watch the girl's return from heaven. Off shore, a huge swan appeared with the girl (her double) on its back. The swan floated toward shore, opening its wings, and then suddenly sank out of sight. As the canoe vanished, the girl and the paddlers swam underwater and hid behind boulders near the shore.

Then, as the sound of whistles came from the hills, Ligeex, wearing a chilkat robe (*gwishalait*), went into the forest and came back with the now naked girl. Dancing and singing, they visited all the homes in the village, before going to the halait house of Ligeex, where she dressed. Her parents gave away wealth there, and the girl went into seclusion. Eventually, the whistles were heard outside of her father's house. Ligeex went inside, took the cedar bark rings off the girl, and received many gifts from her father. The girl went back into seclusion, until this removal of the woven rings was done a second and a third time, after which the girl was free to resume a normal life and play with her friends.

### Luxon

Chief Luxon, a Gitksan Frog of Kitwankool, displayed several named naxnox during his halait demonstrations (Adams 1973:44–46).[52]

For *Deyget* (Capturing People), a masked dancer entered the house at night and made motions to capture all the people there. The man in charge then rushed forward and appeared to kill the spirit, in revenge for his "torture" of the guests. The body was placed at the rear of the house upon a mat. Chiefs were called in turn to revive him from the dead. This was the most powerful of all the halaits and was called *sedulsa*. First to try were all the Wolf chiefs of Kitwankool, then the Eagles, Wolves, and Frogs of Gitwangak. Each acted as a shaman but had no results. The Kitwankool Wolf chief named Gwooslam had been left out of the series, and he was called last. He placed an offering in the fire while the house became very quiet. The sound of a naxnox could be heard coming from the hills across from Kitwankool, increasing in volume as the spirit got nearer to the house. The man in charge welcomed it into the house in the form of a man with a bow and arrows in his hands. While people sang the songs of this spirit, the man shot at the rear of the house. Each time his arrows magically returned to him. Then he went to the rear of the house and shot forward, with the arrows again returning to him. When he finished, the dead spirit revived and left the house with him.

For *Gwisgalgals,* the man possessed by this naxnox would circle the house from east to north to west to south before entering it and rummaging through all the boxes left along the sides. He took what he wanted and then slowly regained his human identity. When aware of his actions, he lavishly compensated the owners for whatever he had damaged or taken.

*Tsegx* had protruding eardrums that looked like long tubes hanging from the sides of his head. As songs were sung, these tubes sunk into his head and his hearing became normal, allowing him to pay attention and act decently, like a normal human.

*Axgotluluq* (Reckless Corpse) came into the house dressed as a bear. He removed his robe and, with reckless gestures, smothered the fire, plunging the house into darkness.

*Biliist* (Stars) then appeared brightly at the rear of the house and became a shooting star whose sparks fell on some of the guests, burning their clothes. Proper guests ignored these burns because any reaction would be used to tease or embarrass them. Later, they were well compensated with gifts.

*Semgik* was a woodpecker that flew around the back of the house and left.

*Gimilaxa* (Higher Heaven) was a carving of a dog with pointed ears and an upturned tail shown to the audience while a special song was sung. Since European dogs were once a novelty among the Tsimshian, this effigy may derive from historical experiences.

*Gilax Naxnox* was a spirit who came into the town during the day and put out everyone's fires. People gathered in the feast house, and when all the chiefs were there, this spirit came in and poured water on the fire, the last in the town. Everyone began to sing a sad song about their suffering from cold and famine. Soon whistles and other noises of naxnox would be heard coming from the hills toward the house. The house master invited them in, singing to welcome them. Suddenly, the fire blazed up and the house was filled with light while the naxnox sang, "I have been to the bottom of the sea and now I come out through the center of the fire." Everyone took some of this fire home to rekindle their hearths.

For *Hamom,* a toy top[53] was spun along the floor and whoever it touched had to rise immediately and sing his or her halait song. Of course, only nobles could do this and others were embarrassed by the unwanted attention.

*Ksemso'q* (Woman Robin) was shown as a mask with a long recurved beak. It was worn by a man. It is significant that, although the spirit was clearly female, her embodiment was by a man, indicating again the masculine quality of the naxnox.

*Gwilkshanaqs* (Pretending To Be A Lady) was portrayed by a woman who went to each chief by rank and offered herself. All remained absolutely still and silent, showing their high morals. Her name is intended to be ironic and, because of the overtly sexual nature of the dramatization, it was necessary for a woman to play this role.

# 4. Reflections

In addition to the major branches of Tsimshian culture, there were and are other facets or aspects that reflect on the life of individuals—as categories, historical figures, and images—and that were significant in traditional and historical Tsimshian society. Beginning with the concept of Tsimshian personhood, which was another intermeshing of the major branchings, like that of the house and the cosmos, the discussion will then consider the effects of European intrusion, as treated in *adawx,* in historical documents, and in long-term consequences, such as the rise of the Tsimshian chiefdom under Ligeex, the missionary work of William Duncan and others, and scholarly understanding of the ethnography, the cosmology, and the artistic tradition.

## PERSONHOOD

Long before birth, a Tsimshian baby was exposed to the cultural reality in which he or she would be raised. The mother, father, and other relatives observed a variety of food, behavioral, and other restrictions in hopes that the baby would develop in certain ways. Among the Tsimshian and other native communities (cf. Kan 1989) along the northern coast of British Columbia, the father's sister assisted at the delivery so that all family lines were represented, although the baby belonged to the kinship group of the mother.

Often the birth was also accompanied by the expectation that certain cycles of death and rebirth would continue. Women would dream that a deceased relative was coming for a visit and thus know that the baby was a reincarnation of that person. As proof of such claims, the baby would have birthmarks, attitudes, behaviors, and bodily features like those of the deceased. Dents in the earlobes indicated former ear piercings, and experiences of déjà vu later in life added further confirmation.

Without exaggeration, therefore, among the peoples of the north Pacific coast, belief in reincarnation was and is vital to their existence, both as individuals and as communities.[1] Among the Tsimshian, from the moment when light first flashed throughout the world, an eternal reality was created and perpetuated by succeeding generations of named humans.

While children inherited their primary identity from the mother, the father had a supportive role throughout life. His sisters assisted during the births of his children and brought them gifts. The relatives of the father announced the birth and made the first public bestowals of wealth on behalf of the baby. The house of the mother provided marmot skins as gifts to the community. When a child was born to the nobility, a chief announced the birth.

The name bestowed on a child by the mother's clan often cross-referenced the father's clan. For example, a child with a father who was a member of the Orca crest might have "glistening" as part of the name, as in "Eagle Glistening in the Sunlight."

The family of the father supplied the cradleboard for the child. A strong belief in reincarnation meant that the child was considered an ancestor returning to the mother's house. This circularity of life was indicated by vocabulary. Both the cradleboard of a baby and the grave box of a corpse were called by the same term (*wo*). Similarly, a special house song could serve as both lullaby and dirge (Halpin and Seguin 1990:279).

Among the Nishga, at least, parents formerly did not sleep together for a year if their first child was a son, or for six months if a daughter (McNeary 1976b:171).

Ceremonies were held when ears were pierced. Nobles also pierced the nasal septum, and highborn girls had a labret placed in the lower lip. Throughout her life, other celebrations were held as larger labrets were assumed.

When a noble child was about seven, dramatic winter initiations were held to bestow privileges. A father made arrangements for his child, often together with related children of the same age, to be hidden under a mat while chiefs threw power into them. This infusion began the process of "elevating" a child to membership in halait orders.[2]

*15. Woman Wearing a Labret. Buttoned through in her lower lip, this ornament was an insignia of all adult freeborn women. The larger its size, the more high ranking the woman. This woman holds her dog while sitting for a portrait at Port Simpson. (Courtesy of the Museum of Northern British Columbia.)*

At puberty, a child was given the first of a series of adult names. These were selected from the roster of names belonging to the mother's house, usually with cross-reference to the father's crest. Girls were secluded at menstruation, with the duration and elaboration commensurate with the rank of the family. Afterwards, high-ranking girls slept in cubicles set above the sleeping area of their parents and accessible only by a ladder. Among royal families, a slave sometimes slept at the foot of the ladder as further protection of the girl's virtue.[3]

Marriages were arranged by families and houses to create alliances with lasting political and social consequences. The mother and uncle (mother's brother) of the groom initiated the bond by presenting gifts to the mother of the bride, who reciprocated. The actual wedding was celebrated with a potlatch, the elaboration of which depended on the rank of the houses involved. Spouses were expected to be social equals; otherwise, the child took the status of the lesser-ranked parent.

Various strategies were called into play in arranging marriages. According to Dunn (1984c:53), marriage of a man to a woman in the category of mother's brother's daughter assured that treasures and privileges remained within the household after death and the memorial potlatch. Marriage of a man to a father's sister's daughter, however, was a more daring strategy because it distributed goods more widely at the memorial and created a wider sense of obligation within the community.

After marriage, a couple lived where they had the most advantages and opportunities. If the groom were heir to a title, they lived with his mother's brother so he could be trained to assume the office of a chief. Prominent men had more than one wife to better meet the obligations of hospitality and generosity. Slaves also contributed to these duties.

Throughout life, success depended on good relations with the spirits and with one's own and father's crests. Any undertaking required a rigid discipline that involved sexual continence, fasting, and the taking of purgatives brewed from hellebore. These rituals merely made a person appealing to the spirits, who valued cleanliness, but they did not guarantee success. Skill and luck were also required for a proper outcome. Other rituals, such as those of witchcraft and sorcery, however, seem to have been mechanical or automatic in their results. Only by reversing the ritual or rebounding the harm could a cure be effective.

At death, the house and clan distributed marmot skins and paid for the funeral. The actual labor of preparing the body and conducting the ceremony was a final obligation of the father and his house. Traditionally, the body was cremated at a location unique to each town, and, ideally, it was burned on a clear day when the smoke could rise to Heaven in an uninterrupted flow. Chiefs in particular were cremated so their heirs could assume the full authority of the title. Alternatively, the chief's heart might be buried and his body cremated, or his corpse eviscerated, placed in a box that was secured high in a tree, and his internal organs burned. Afterward, the deceased's house held a black feast, where they wore black paint as a sign of mourning, to compensate the father's house.

Other social ranks received other forms of burial. Shamans were taken to isolated places, often caves, with all of their paraphernalia. Only family members would know the location, and they would use it to quest for the return of these powers to kin. Slaves were often disposed of without regard or ceremony.

A memorial potlatch was held about a year after the death to commemorate the deceased and to confirm the heir in the office. This was known as the "red feast," and participants wore red paint to mark the end of their mourning.

For the Tsimshian, human descendants circulated through a series of fixed identities, based in a household, whose pedigrees and characteristics were described in hereditary chronicles where these names engaged in specific tasks at specific locations. By virtue of these sacred histories, people, events, and places were interlinked through successive reincarnations (*nabahon,* Cove 1987:74; *nabelgot,* Beynon mss.: Text 238) within a household.

At the center of each household was a communal fire representing its corporate nature. In the same way that this hearth was lit and relit successively, so the names of the house were repeatedly "held" by human generations. Indeed, in its recurrent flaming up and dying down, fire provided an apt metaphor for reincarnation, like the light that was the symbol for Tsimshian culture as a whole.

In terms of its constituents, a person had three spiritual aspects: a *baa'lx,* a *haayuk,* and an *oo'tsn* (Dunn 1978). The first, glossed as 'corpse, ghost' (but better expressed as "remains") is the essence that reincarnates into the matrilines, as new generations substitute for older ones through renewal. Modern stories tell of older women, angry with their families, threatening to be reborn into other clans, or, if really upset, into white babies (Adams 1973:32). A *baa'lx* implies an aspect that is inert, fixed, closed, and exclusive. The word *haayuk,* glossed as 'soul, spirit', derives from a term meaning "to stand or stand up" (Dunn 1978:36, 659). The third aspect, *oo'tsn,* glossed as 'spirit, nothingness', seems to represent expansive aspects of the Tsimshian cosmos, which was regarded as a void framed as an enormous gabled house.

Relying on the materials William Beynon sent to Marius Barbeau, now in Ottawa, John Cove, in his phenomenological study of "what does it mean to be human" for the Tsimshian (Cove 1987:10), discusses modalities that are totemic, shamanic, and privileged (i.e., related to the secret societies). For the totemic, factors of social class play an important role in defining "real people," that is, nobles, as distinct from commoners and slaves. To the human form, which is common to all humans, are added souls, names, crests, wonders, and powers which make individuals increasingly more "real," with initiated chiefly royalty being the most real of all.

For humans, the body is fragile because Elderberry gave birth first. "As food, humans are like leaves and berries. Their fixity represents another kind of vulnerability. They are prey to those who are mobile" (Cove 1987:80). Accordingly, "Stone represents potential," according to Cove (1987:64), as one is reminded by the teeth and hard nails of fingers and toes still borne by humans.

In his study of the neighboring Tlingits, however, Sergei Kan (1989:55–58) notes that, in this wet coastal climate, stone represented admirable qualities of nature such as dryness, hardness, heaviness, and longevity. It is, therefore, the opposition of dry stone to wet wood which is being symbolized at creation, and adopted by native nobility. For example, noble women wore labrets, often of stone or inlaid wood, in the lower lip, with the labrets of royal women the biggest and most elaborate of all.[4]

Pervading the universe and all else were the important concepts of *ptex, naxnox,* and *halait,* relating respectively to crests, shamans, and rank orders. In his analysis, however, Cove (1987) does not distinguish naxnox from halait, using the latter for both shamans and secret society members. While this slights the importance of naxnox, it is suggestive that he emphasizes the most expansive of the terms, halait, despite a murky discussion.

Cove recognizes shamans as mediators between varieties of people and species, but misconstrues the significance whereby "The term *naxnox* itself is ambiguous, referring as it does to a type of being, powers, names, rituals and objects. For *naxnox* to be in the world, they must have physical embodiment, for example, crests or souls" (1987:135). While crests ultimately derived from the encounter of naxnox and ancestor, it was masks and other winter ceremonial items which provided their direct representation, particularly during a *sedulsa* dramatization when the most powerful chief at a gathering revived or cured another chief who appeared to be dead.

Mediation by the halait orders is lacking in Cove's analysis, although he provides significant information on the political and dramatic ramifications of membership in the four secret societies for transcending crest and wonder distinctions. For example, two important chiefs, "Gunaxnuk and Tsibasa receive, respectively, the first seals and sea otters of any canoe going out from Kitkatla, irrespective of House; although in this instance, secret society powers are associated with the ability to demand such tribute" (Cove 1987:247). Through these deferences and other symbols, Tsimshian affirm their world because "Native people use symbols to make sense of multiple realities. Symbols can be thought of as existing at the boundaries between realities. Not only do they serve to make those realities intelligible, they provide a bridging mechanism. Symbols facilitate movement across these boundaries, and provide for a meaningful integration of realities. They are both a means of facilitating non-ordinary experiences, and of making sense of the entirety of experiences" (1987:23).

Ultimately, for Tsimshian, therefore, "Existence is based on subsistence and thus life is predicated on the death of others. In lacking the powers of non-humans, whose physical needs are the same, humans are highly vulnerable" (1987:287). But, in compensation, "The answer posed is reciprocity, that each category of being can do something for others by virtue of either specific powers and/or dominance over domains. Yet, each category requires bodies and souls. This makes death inevitable in spite of powers" (1987:291).

## CONTACT

Tsimshian recount several versions of their first encounters with Europeans arriving by ship. Many of these are now part of the *adawx* of houses, used to explain their claims to various novelty items used as crests, such as the image of a picket fence, iron kettles, and, most curious of all, "Mr. Ross's Dog," claimed at Kisgegas about 1827 (Halpin 1973:142). Dunn has provided a sensitive and poetic translation of one such incident.

### Driftwood

Saaban, "Leaps Out Of The Water," was a chief at Kitkatla when he led a group to a fall camp called "on the outside edge of the spawning sockeye salmon."[5]

While there, a sea monster approached, covered with hairy beings, who came ashore inside a large spider (for so they viewed the long boat with oars). The Kitkatlas could not escape because a high cliff blocked them from leaving the beach. Greatly distressed, the warriors calmed themselves with the traditional remedy of urine rubbed into the hair.

Confronted, the Kitkatlas watched as the beings made a fire, larger than needed and in the wrong way, using flint and steel. Ancient Tsimshian made fire with hemlock sticks coated with ear wax to create friction to ignite cedar bark cotton. The strangers cooked in an iron pot, a novelty that indicated their strong powers.

They spoke, but no one could understand them, and most offensive of all, they brought their own food, a shameless arrogance. The strangers offered food to the Tsimshian, who regarded it as maggots, coagulated corpse blood, and a lichen called ghost bread. (The sailors were offering rice, molasses, and biscuits.)

Saaban ordered the people to eat the disgusting foods, and they complied so as not to give offense to the beings or their chief. In return, the ship captain gave gifts to the chief, including bars of "soap." Hearing the word, Saaban took the name to be his own, indicating that he was famous even in other worlds. As proof of the encounter, Saaban added the long bars of soap and a butcher knife to his crests.

In details and context, the encounter of Europeans and Tsimshian was phrased in terms of a meeting with a naxnox, albeit an immensely alien and powerful one. Unlike other naxnox, however, these beings were shiftless drifters associated with ghosts, whose bones were bleached driftwood. Still and all, cannibal power was one of the greatest, and Saaban benefited from the common knowledge that he had eaten the strange foods shared at the meeting.

At another meeting with a ship captain, Ts'ibasaa, the great chief of Kitkatla, exchanged names so that, today, his heirs are known as Hale.

Over time, these offshore visits led to the land-based posts of the fur trade, such as that at Fort Simpson, which forever changed the world of the Tsimshian.

CHIEFS

Among early published accounts by Europeans, a surprising amount of recognizably Tsimshian material was provided by the month-long stay in 1792 of Jacinto Caamaño and his ship, the *Aranzazu,* near a town on Pitt Island. Seguin (1985:28–37) has examined the account and noted that one of the two chief names, Githawn, remains in use.[6] The other, Xamisit, cannot be further identified.[7] Yet, after a month of contacts, this latter chief greeted the ship from a stage made by lashing two canoes together. He danced with a variety of masks, which he changed behind a white skin curtain. In this way, he invited the captain to an elaborate feast, which strongly resembled modern ones. To prevent hostilities, eagle down was scattered over the heads of sailors and natives alike. During the early events, a crest hat of a bird head, which the captain called a seagull, and a puppet were displayed.[8] Unfortunately, the guests left early, and the final displays and gift giving were missed.

The next year, in July, George Vancouver sailed up what is now Portland Canal into Nishga territory, where he found many groups fishing for salmon. Three American sailors had been killed by natives there in 1791, so relations were strained.

Tsimshian life was forever altered when Fort Simpson was founded on the Nass River in 1831, then moved to its present location in 1834. There, members of all the tribes settled together, often in neighborhoods. But the discrete boundaries provided by separate towns did not exist in the new community, and many new solutions to rank, rivalry, and respect had to be negotiated and confirmed by potlatches.

William Duncan arrived at the fort in 1857 and began learning the Tsimshianic language. His active lay missionary work and the delivery of sermons in Tsimshianic started in June of 1858. In 1862, just before a devastating smallpox outbreak, he led converts back to the central winter site of Metlakatla to found a Christian community. In 1887, religious differences with the Anglican church and bishop caused Duncan to accept land in Alaska and move most of the community to New Metlakatla.

Clergy who had served at Metlakatla founded missions elsewhere. Rev. Robert Doolan settled Nishga at Kincolith in 1864, and Rev. William Collison went to Hazelton among the Gitksan. Robert Tomlinson moved a Nishga mission at Greenville to Aiyansh in 1878 and, the next year, began another Gitksan mission at Kispiox.

Thomas Crosby founded a Methodist mission at Port Simpson in 1874, at the invitation of Alfred and Kate Dudoward, nobles who had been converted in Victoria the year before (Bolt 1992).

The first salmon cannery in the region was built on the Skeena in 1875, relying heavily on native labor, with others built on the Nass shortly after. After World War II, these canneries moved to Prince Rupert, where they still function during the summer fish runs.

Many of the most successful fishermen continue to be ranking chiefs, owning expensive boats and equipment and supporting large crews. Sometimes, a

*16. Good Templars. After Thomas Crosby established Methodism at Port Simpson, church groups like this one with distinctive and attractive insignia were introduced. (Photo courtesy of the Prince Rupert City and Regional Archives.)*

chief will take his boat out and bring in a load of salmon, which he then distributes free to members of his community. Thus, the tradition of chiefly generosity continues.

The Tsimshian had this well-developed sense of elites, as the archaeological record shows, and it is phrased in very human terms. For example, James McCullagh, resident Nass missionary, had difficulty explaining the concept of an abstract God because his converts continued to regard the Christian God as they did Heaven, as a divine person who acted like a human chief.

Indeed, Tsimshian earthly chiefs had been gaining in power and dignity. Ligeex was the most famous of these high chiefs. Boas (1916:510) reported that by 1888 six men had held this name over a period of 150 years. The first Ligeex memorialized his fame by having a portrait painted above a row of coppers on a cliff across from Port Essington on the Skeena River.[9] The location was significant, of course, for many of the tribes frequented this locale in the fall.

The mother, K̲'amdmax̱ł ("Ascending The Mountain With A Costly Copper") of the first Ligeex eloped with a man from Kitamat, whose family belonged to the highest ranked of the Wakashan secret societies. This privilege passed through her to her Eagle crest.

Ligeex had many halait privileges uniquely his own. One naxnox was manifested as two enormous hands that reached down from the roof and lifted a man toward Heaven (Barnett 1940 [book 2]:2), while another, called Crack Of Heaven, was a mask that made the house divide in two, move apart, and rejoin (Boas 1916:556). His halait names included *txagaxsm laxha, hanatana,* and *gaguiksgaax* (Boas 1916:513).

When the previous Eagle great name of Nisbalas was discredited because its holder was beheaded by members of the Raven crest (Boas 1916:357), the name of Ligeex was substituted and potlatched into prominence.[10]

The man called Ligeex always married into the Blackfish crest to a woman named Ksmgamk. The high chief of the Blackfish, who resides in Kitkatla, in turned married the sister of Ligeex named for their mother. As a boy, the inheritor of the Ligeex name is called Hadziksnee'x.

The basis for the prestige of Ligeex was his exclusive claim to trade with the Gitksan, after the Kitselas began the yearly enterprise. Among the populous coastal tribes, he dictated the trade along the Skeena River and thus had a boundless source of revenue.

Ligeex protected these prerogatives in various ways. He provided the land for the second Hudson's Bay Company post at Fort Simpson, and his daughter married the chief factor. Yet when the company built a trading post at Lake Babine, Ligeex led a thousand warriors upriver and destroyed it. The company only began to trade effectively with the inland tribes after it purchased the privilege to do so from Ligeex in 1866, providing the funds that were probably used for the elaborate potlatch described in chapter 3.

Homer Barnett collected information on the later history of the Ligeex line and the reasons behind the conversion of one of the last holders, who joined the Duncan community at Metlakatla after being compromised by a rival for the title. The name Ligeex has not been used since the mid-1900s.

Ts'ibasaa, chief of Kitkatla and, by extension, the Southern Tsimshian, eventually traded names with one of the first ship captains to visit his territory, taking the name of Hale (Hail), which still reigns in the town. Early chiefs of this line were haughty, as Mitchell (1981) shows in his reconstruction of the Kitkatla seasonal round for 1835, based on three diaries kept by employees of the Hudson's Bay Company.[11] At least two Haida crests, Grizzly and Moon (discussed below), were given to their chiefs by Ts'ibasaa, a powerful means of forging an alliance with foreigners.

Nekt was also known for his belligerence and success (MacDonald 1979, 1984a). From his ingenious fort among the Gitksan, he raided and terrorized widely. His mother was a Frog (Raven) from the Nass, captured and married to a Haida chief. Later, she killed and beheaded her husband, escaping with her son, who was quieted by suckling on the tongue that protruded from his father's head. Reckless and cunning, Nekt controlled trade over a large region. His fort was attacked and destroyed about the time the first Ligeex took over the Skeena River trade, probably as part of a deliberate strategy of control. Coastal towns also had such forts where people took refuge from attackers. Often they were the cones of extinct volcanos (Dunn 1978:97), whose rich soil was later used to grow potatoes, introduced by traders, for lucrative sale to the Haida and the trading post.

Sagewan (Mountain) arose among the chiefs of the lower Nass River during the 1860s. He was an Eagle and lived at Gitiks near the mouth of the Nass beside the commercial routes. He eventually controlled the trade along the Nass to the interior Athapaskans, particularly the Tsetsaut. Among Nass chiefs, rivalry focused on the height of their poles. The Wolf and Killerwhale chiefs were in such fierce competition that the Killerwhale man was shot and killed. For protection, the Wolf chief allied himself with the leader of the Laxluutkst branch of the Eagles, whose chief was Sagewan. To mark his ascendancy, Sagewan commissioned the tallest pole on the coast, now at the Royal Ontario Museum in Toronto (McNeary 1976b:52, 141).

Later, one of Sagewan's wives deserted him to marry William McNeill, chief trader of the Hudson's Bay Company. To shame her, he sent her a gift of marten skins, accompanied by a taunting song. Not to be outdone, she sent him a Haida canoe. To recover his prestige, Sagewan held a potlatch to renounce his wife, but she countered by erecting a memorial pole for her deceased brother, elevating herself to the status of a Wolf chief beyond the pettiness of her former spouse (McNeary 1976b:188).[12]

The human qualities of these great men and women are lost in the available literature. The highest ranking Nishga chiefs were left out of Sapir (1915), while Boas (1902) merely noted that Chief Mountain (Sagewan) provided him with some Nishga texts.[13]

WILLIAM DUNCAN

Duncan was born near Beverly, England, in April of 1832 to an unwed, working-class mother (Murray 1985). Intent on making a success of himself in Victorian terms, he finished basic schooling at thirteen and was employed by a leather company, becoming a drummer (traveling salesman) in his late teenage years. He devoted much time to reading self-help and improvement books, intended to dissipate radicalism by exhorting laborers to "find joy in work, to persevere, to be thrifty, dutiful and of strong character; to change himself rather than society" (Usher 1974:6). He made every effort to place himself in a state of grace and became committed to the aims of Evangelical Anglicanism. He attended church twice on Sunday and also taught a Sunday school class.

At the age of twenty-two Duncan offered himself to the Church Missionary Society, intending to work in Africa. In London from 1854 to 1857, he trained as an elementary school teacher and made efforts among the poor because this "was considered good preparation for work among the heathen, for the same moral depravity that kept the heathen in a state of barbarism was seen as the cause of the social condition of the working class" (Usher 1974:10).

For Victorians, Christianity and civilization were identical, so any converts were expected to adopt British conventions. The Church Missionary Society, under the inspired leadership of Henry Venn, sought the development of a native church through the efforts of its missionaries, who were intended to replace themselves with native clergy. Many of the changes which Duncan brought among the Tsimshian actually followed the plans developed by Venn for the missions in West Africa and New Zealand.

Missionaries were to learn to speak the native language fluently and to translate Christian texts. They were to prompt and promote native development without dictating a particular course. Trade, commerce, and sources of revenue for native churches were to be encouraged. Health, industry, and decent home life were also encouraged by the mission. Native leaders continued to be respected and supported until missions, on their own, found other forms of government.

As graduation approached, Duncan was selected to begin the Protestant mission to the natives of the north Pacific coast. Roman Catholics had been active along the coast since 1838, and Russian Orthodoxy was in Alaska from the late 1700s. As a quick decision had to be made in order to accept an offer of free boat passage to Port Simpson, Duncan was selected because he already stood out among his classmates. He went as a lay schoolmaster, and so he remained throughout his entire career. Though there were times when he was urged to accept ordination, he refused.

By the 1830s, the fur trade had shifted to coastal forts, instead of ships anchoring offshore to acquire sea-mammal pelts. Fort Simpson was built by representatives of the Hudson's Bay Company at the mouth of the Nass in 1831, then moved to a site just below Portland Canal in 1834. There furs were exchanged for muskets, ammunition, blankets, cloth, rice, molasses, tobacco, beads, buttons, chisels, needles, thread, knives, and scissors.

While natives were forbidden to enter Fort Simpson in large numbers, many of the traders had native wives, and other native women were employed inside the fort to do laundry and tend a garden. The Tsimshian quickly learned to plant potatoes and traded them widely along the coast.

In addition to trade goods, Europeans also introduced disease. Smallpox killed at least a third of the people at Fort Simpson in 1836. Alcohol and prostitution, transmitting venereal diseases, also took a toll. With the death of many chiefs and heirs, the Tsimshian were forced to make some adjustments in their leadership. A generation later, Duncan himself became involved in this shift.

After seven months in the fort, giving evening lectures to the men and teaching the métis children, while also studying the language with Clah,[14] a native speaker, Duncan began his mission by preparing a sermon in Tsimshian. He accepted the offer to use the house of Ligeex, the highest ranking Tsimshian chief, for a school until one could be built and, thereby, began with an auspicious sponsor.[15] His first pupils were the sons of chiefs, as was common during this period of colonialism. These heirs were expected to learn about changing conditions and use this knowledge to benefit their constituents.

The schoolhouse was ready in November of 1859, and had two hundred students divided into three classes. Pupils were issued a colored ticket denoting their class, name, and number, in the style of Victorian schools.

In 1861, Rev. L. Tugwell, sent by the Church Missionary Society, arrived at Port Simpson to minister to the community. He baptized about sixty converts, mostly young people. Among the few adults were men whose personalities made them congenial with a Christian outlook. The first convert, Sugunaats, was baptized as Samuel Marsden in honor of a famed evangelical missionary among the Maori of New Zealand. Later, his son, Edward Marsden, caused dissension at New Metlakatla.

Many of the new converts were orphans, at least in some sense, with one or both parents dead. Many had no fathers, the person who did the most to advance the position of a child in Tsimshian society. Christianity, therefore, gave them another spiritual connection in what seemed to be a hopeless situation.

Ligeex himself became a convert for political reasons (Barnett 1942). The previous titleholder had died before Duncan arrived, and a younger brother and a nephew vied for the name. Since Haidas had killed several members of the Gispaxlo'ots, the nephew succeeded to the title with a promise to avenge these deaths. A house was built to stage an elaborate feast for the Haida, during which they were to be killed. The house was built but never used because another chief found an opportunity to spread eagle down, a pledge of peace, over the head of Ligeex. His plans thwarted, his uncle, who took a lesser chiefly name in another tribe, lost no opportunity to deride his lack of bravery. Frustrated, Ligeex tried several means to regain prestige, including trying to kill Duncan and shooting at the chief trader. At a secret meeting of the elders of his tribe, they decided that Ligeex should leave Fort Simpson and join the converts at Metlakatla, where he died in 1869. The uncle, to better define his own position, became a foe of the Christian mission.

The majority of the Gitlaan tribe joined Duncan for similar reasons. Another Tsimshian tribe had killed several of their high-ranking members, but the Gitlaan mismanaged their revenge. Until they were successful, about three hundred members moved to Metlakatla. Eventually, at a Fort Simpson marriage feast where whiskey was served, two chiefs of the other tribe were killed. The Gitlaan chief was wounded and became an invalid. Several years later, he was taken to Metlakatla, where he converted and asked forgiveness.

Major changes were also occurring in Euro-Canadian society. British Columbia became a crown colony in 1858, in the aftermath of the Fraser River gold rush. In 1860, Bishop George Hills arrived in Victoria to institute the Diocese of Columbia. His episcopal prerogatives were soon under attack by the dean of the cathedral, Rev. Edward Cridge, a close friend of Duncan.

During 1860, Duncan visited the villages on the Nass, opening the way for conversions. Later missionaries achieved remarkable success through the use of their medical skills. Traditionally, for the Tsimshian, religion and medicine were one and the same, so it was logical for medical successes to be met with religious ones (McNeary 1976b:33).

In 1862, smallpox devastated the coastal tribes of British Columbia. Since Duncan was in the process of moving his converts to Metlakatla as the epidemic moved northward, many Tsimshian soon found haven with the converts.

From 1862 to 1887, Metlakatla was a much-praised utopian community sustained by the sales at its store, the labor of its members, donations from all over the world, and the support of the Church Missionary Society. Duncan's intention throughout his career was to awaken "the long slumbering offspring of Adam," as he called the Tsimshian. While not openly hostile to native traditions, he taught by word and example that Christianity and Victorian civility provided a better way to live in the modern world.

*17. Houses at Christian Metlakatla. Identical homes at Old Metlakatla,
William Duncan's cooperative Evangelical community, were built of milled
lumber so that all would be equal in the eyes of God. (Courtesy of the Museum
of Northern British Columbia.)*

Remarkably, he was willing to consider local conditions and native intent. He allowed spouses who converted to leave their heathen partners and join the Christian flock. Someone who needed to be expelled from the community was not confronted directly, since that was not the native way. Instead, a black flag was raised over the jail, precipitating gossip that identified the culprit. Tsimshian sense of personal shame did the rest, and the person left the town.

In 1863, Duncan was appointed justice of the peace, and, while there was considerable opposition to his prosecution of the liquor trade and domestic disputes, he kept half of all fines for use by Metlakatla. These funds were used at his discretion and were generally put to the public good for the purchase of supplies and lumber.

Housing was carefully planned in the new community. Tsimshian traditional houses had consisted of huge, open, rectangular buildings with families living along the sides, with the ranking families at the rear. At Metlakatla all the houses looked the same so all would be equal before God. During the 1860s, the new houses were forty feet long with a separate bedroom at either end and a communal room in the middle. There were shingled roofs, doors, and glass windows, which initially had been such exotic trade goods that they

*18. Saint Paul's Church at Metlakatla. Once it was the largest church north of San Francisco and west of Chicago. (Courtesy of the Museum of Northern British Columbia.)*

replaced painted house fronts as emblems of prestige. Only Ligeex, because of his rank, was allowed to have a house larger than the others.

After 1871, a new house plan was instituted by a native committee. Two houses were built side by side, thirty feet apart. While each had a separate second story, the first floors were connected, with the intervening space providing a communal room. Doors led into each house and into the shared room.

The community also constructed a church in the 1870s that was impressive for its time and place. St. Paul's, which could seat one thousand worshippers, was described as the largest church north of San Francisco and west of Chicago. Standing above its plain altar were two carved poles. One combined a

*19. Saint Paul's Interior. These poles were carved with images for each of the four
crests (Orca and Wolf on the right, Raven and Beaver on the left). Beaver is an
affiliate replacing Eagle; according to a still-current joke, Beaver was substituted
because Duncan and the Tsimshian, as good businessmen, were well aware
that beavers provided money during the fur trade era.
(Courtesy of the Museum of Northern British Columbia.)*

Wolf and a Blackfish and the other a Raven and Beaver, thus representing each
of the four crests.[16]

Other public buildings included a guest house, a courthouse, a jail, and a
school. In 1881, a town hall was added. Later, a four-story trading post, a public reading room, and a museum were built.

Local industries included a blacksmith, a carpenter, a sawmill, a soaphouse,
worksheds, and a salmon cannery. Wharfs and roads were build by community
labor. As much as possible, Duncan intended Metlakatla to benefit from the
sale of furs, lumber, and fish. Industry was often given preference to religion
by Duncan, for which he was later criticized. After 1872, boys were only
taught at night so they could work during the day. As Duncan wrote, "Let the
big boys earn their bread in daylight and come to school at night, that will be
my rule" (Usher 1974:76).

After 1870, the men were organized into ten companies, each with an identifying color, two of its members on the village council, and two others serving as constables. Women also had ten groups, with a responsible elder female in charge of each one. Ten years later, each company also included a chief, two native teachers, two constables, three councilmen, two musicians, and ten volunteer firemen and their captain.

The Metlakatla council consisted of Duncan, all convert chiefs, and ten councilors elected by the men of the village. The annual village tax was divided in half between Duncan, who used it for the village, and the chiefs, who used it to sustain their positions and supporters.

The tradition of forming teams to play games, characteristic of the fall settlements, was continued by Duncan, with the teams coming from the east and west sides of the mission.

New events included the celebration of Christmas, the New Year, and the Queen's Birthday. The latter had the additional consequence of reinforcing the prestige of the chiefs, since they too were royalty. Ranks and wealth were also displayed at the New Year. "The constables, fire-brigade and band all assembled in their uniforms; the chiefs and council members proudly displayed their badges of office; the companies were led to the flagpole by the elders, and speeches were given by all the leaders in order of importance, headed by Duncan and the chiefs" (Usher 1974:86).

On important concepts, Tsimshian religion and Duncan's evangelicalism were in close agreement, particularly in terms of the significance of light. Indeed, "The aim of the evangelical missionary, according to Duncan, was to open the eyes of the heathen and to turn them from dark to light" by appealing to the heart rather than the head (Usher 1974:95). This aim was nondenominational, however, and that created problems between Duncan and Anglican officials.

During the early 1880s, Duncan and the Church Missionary Society had a falling out because of "Duncan's inability to retain various helpers sent to him by the society, his refusal to take clerical orders, his quarrels with Bishop Hills, his support of the Reverend Edward Cridge in his dispute with the Anglican Church at Victoria, [and] his refusal to allow the celebration of the Holy Communion at Metlakatla" (Usher 1974:91).

In 1877, Rev. A. J. Hall, who began the mission at Alert Bay among the Kwakwaka'wakw (Kwakiutl), preached in Metlakatla while Duncan was away in Victoria. The result was an outburst of religious visions and fervor that

Duncan took pains to eradicate. By denying this religious frenzy, Duncan imposed his will upon the Tsimshian, although this dispute marked the first time that natives had challenged Duncan's religious authority.

In similar fashion, some clergy were themselves challenging the authority of the local bishop. In Victoria, the dispute between Cridge and the bishop resulted in Cridge joining the Reformed Episcopal Church of the United States and being consecrated a bishop in that denomination.

Bishop Hills lost the support of other evangelicals during this dispute with Cridge. Relations with Duncan remained tense. The bishop of Athabasca, the Right Reverend W. C. Bompas, visited Metlakatla and found that while trade and economy thrived, religious training was deficient. He urged more liturgical translations into the native language and a concerted effort to introduce the forms of Anglican Christianity. When Bompas and other clergy tried to celebrate communion, they were dissuaded by Duncan, who felt that the halait privileges of Tsimshian chiefs, which included the dramatization of cannibalism, were too recent in the native past for converts to properly understand that eating the body and blood of Christ was different.

As a further attempt to minister to Anglicans and supervise Duncan, a bishop of Caledonia was created for northern British Columbia. William Ridley, a former missionary in India, was selected for the office. He was not an ideal choice because he mismanaged and antagonized the situation until Duncan and his followers left their model town and moved to New Metlakatla on Annette Island just across the border in Alaska. The Tsimshian of Metlakatla gained American support for their move and received a donation of land because they were seen as fleeing religious persecution.

Interestingly, during the dispute between Duncan and Ridley, many of the chiefs from Metlakatla took the side of the bishop. Given the careful regard that Tsimshian have always accorded matters of rank and privilege, it is significant that the chiefs went with the man with more prestige within the religious hierarchy.

To a large extent, Duncan had replaced the name-title of Ligeex as the paramount leader among the Tsimshian. His oratorical fluency in the native language, his care for the welfare of the community, and his constant industry were all marks of chiefly status (cf. Usher 1974:109).

The introduction of a local bishop, however, extended the hierarchy to include another external dimension. In much the same way that the greatest of the halait chiefs were initiated among the northern Kwakiutl, particularly at

Bella Bella, so the presence of the bishop elevated the status of his supporters. To this day, a frequent Tsimshian response to Pentecostals who visit their towns is, "But who is your bishop?" (McNeary 1976b: 199).[17] Such an appeal to status and rank helps in interpreting the success of Duncan's mission and the subsequent development of factions once Bishop Ridley arrived. Further, the revised Indian Act of 1880 recognized only hereditary chiefs as authority in native communities, giving these traditional leaders the only legitimate voice in the government of Metlakatla, despite the general recognition of an elected council.

Much of the bishop's plan for establishing further missions, moreover, was an implicit rebuke of the work of Duncan. Instead of founding new communities of relocated converts, Ridley sent clergy to existing centers of native population, such as Alert Bay.

The religious controversy also had political ramifications because natives in British Columbia began agitating for their land rights during the same time. The advice and encouragement of Duncan and other missionaries made their protest all the more sophisticated, but the province has always insisted that the colony was Crown land, with native right of occupancy confirmed but ownership denied. Elsewhere in British America, such rights were asserted by the Royal Proclamation of 1763. When Duncan found the Church Missionary Society unwilling to consider the issue of native land rights, he gained the support of the Aborigines Protection Society of London. Among settlers, opinions about title were racist, in modern terms, in that natives were considered to be like animals whose natural right to the land was limited only to "what they could hold by force or cunning" (Usher 1974: 128). The issue remains alive, fueled by anachronistic decisions in the provincial and national courts of Canada.[18]

After making various attempts to find a solution to their difficulties in Canada and England, about six hundred Metlakatlas loaded their possessions into canoes and accepted the offer of refuge in Alaska. For some years thereafter, northern Canadian canneries and other industries dependent on native labor suffered economic hardship, estimated at $50,000 in lost trade revenue each year, because of the departure of Tsimshian imbued with the Protestant work ethic.

Eventually, a modified communion service was held at New Metlakatla, three times each year, "in the form of a memorial, the bread and wine being distributed among the congregation by lay elders, as Duncan read the Lord's commands from the Scriptures" (Usher 1974:158 n. 86). To this day, most Tsimshian communities begin their Christmas services with a special hymn composed in the native language by Duncan.

Duncan continued to lead the new community despite new controversy. Edward Marsden went to college in Ohio and became an ordained Presbyterian minister. The son of the first convert and Duncan's housekeeper, he was unusually hostile to Duncan. He founded a Presbyterian faction that tried to replace the government of New Metlakatla with a native chiefdom led by a Gitlaan and succeeded in destroying Duncan's property in 1914. From 1916 until 1932, when he died, Marsden was the appointed "secretary" of the town. Strong Presbyterian and Anglican factions developed and persist to this day at New Metlakatla.

Duncan died in 1918 at the age of eighty-five, leaving his own money in trust for the community. Since long life was a sign of spiritual power throughout the native Americas, this longevity was interpreted as another indication of the strength and appropriateness of Duncan's divine calling.

SCHOLARSHIP

Although Duncan maintained a correspondence about Tsimshian culture with Edward Tylor (Usher 1974:157 n. 66), the early British anthropologist, these materials have not been used by scholars.

After conversion, the Tsimshian developed a tradition of literacy in their own languages. Duncan's system of writing was used to publish a newspaper at Metlakatla. Bishop Ridley developed another orthography for translating liturgy and scripture. The most ambitious program was that of the Anglican Reverend James McCullagh among the Nishga. In 1893, he had a printing press shipped to Aiyansh, where he published a grammar, translations of the Gospels, a summary of Old Testament history, and a newspaper called *Hagaga* (McNeary 1976b:34).

Academic scholarship, it seems, was initiated by a Tsimshian. Henry W. Tate (Maud 1982, 1989; Miller 1995), a resident of Port Simpson, responded to Franz Boas and offered to record stories for pay. From 1902 to 1914, using the orthography of Bishop Ridley, Tate sent texts to Boas (1916), who then read them to Archie Dundas, a younger speaker from New Metlakatla attending Carlisle Indian School in Pennsylvania. These materials reflected Tate's Christian morals and status because they were general tales in the public domain, distinct from the sacred histories of houses and devoid of any of the standard motifs suggesting impropriety and immorality to a white reader-ship.[19] Tate would listen to old men telling stories on a bench and then retreat home to record them in English, later adding a Tsimshian version.

While not as extensive as his publications on the Kwakwaka'wakw (Kwa-kiutl), Boas published several important works on Tsimshian, beginning with his own collection of texts translated into German in 1895, others from the Nass in 1902, a grammar of Coast Tsimshian in 1911, retranscribed materials from Tate in 1912, and the monumental collection and analysis of 1916. There Boas suggested an interior origin for the Tsimshian, based in part on their tra-ditions of Prairie Town and some of the crests, but this has been disproved by the long record of habitation uncovered by recent archaeology (Matson and Coupland 1995).

In 1915, Marius Barbeau, a French Canadian trained at Oxford who long worked for the Canadian National Museum, began an extended period of re-search among the Tsimshian, specializing in mythology and art.[20] While he later developed untenable theories about the Asiatic origins of some crests and the European inspiration for other traditions, the quantity and quality of his primary data are impressive (Duff 1961, 1964a; Cove 1985; Riley 1988).

More significantly, Barbeau encouraged the personal research of William Beynon (1888–1958), a Tsimshian raised in Victoria. The son of a high-rank-ing Wolf crest mother and a Welsh steamer captain, William was the only one of six sons to become fluent in Tsimshianic (Halpin 1978). When his uncle, Albert Wellington, died in 1913, Beynon went to the funeral at Port Simpson and succeeded to the position of chief of the Wolf crest in the Gitlaan tribe by assuming the name-title of Gusgain. Of particular note, Beynon's maternal grandmother was from the Nass and his grandfather was Clah (Arthur Well-ington), the Tsimshian who taught William Duncan the native language during the months before Duncan's mission began.

Over his long life, from 1916 to 1955, Beynon sent materials to Barbeau (Barbeau and Beynon 1987a, 1987b), Boas, Edward Sapir, Philip Drucker, and others. He was a source of information on the traditional culture for Viola Garfield and on the language for Amelia Susman, who had been sent by Boas into the field in 1939 to improve Beynon's transcriptions and text recording.[21] Though unpublished, these notes revised much of the previous work by Boas on Tsimshian grammar. As with this linguistic work, most of Beynon's materi-als remain unpublished, mixed within the archives of Barbeau, Boas, and insti-tutions like Columbia University and the American Museum of National His-tory. Among his most significant work was a heroic account of eight days of potlatches and masked wonders at Gitsegukla in 1945, filling four volumes (200 pages) of notes.

Using mostly published liturgical materials in Tsimshian, Count A. C. Graf von der Schulenberg published a grammar and dictionary of Tsimshian in 1894 that has been translated into English (1982).

Collections of Tsimshian artifacts were assembled and sold to museums by Barbeau, with the help of Beynon. In 1876, James G. Swan, relying on local agents, collected the important house front from Port Simpson that is now in the Smithsonian. It represents the important Blackfish crest mentioned in the sacred history of Nagunaks, recounted in chapter 3. Other small collections were made along the Nass and Skeena during brief trips by George Emmons, between 1905 and 1913, and Louis Shotridge, in 1918. Shotridge (188?–1937) was a Tlingit Eagle chief from Klukwan who worked for the University Museum in Philadelphia from 1912 to 1932 (Milburn 1986).

Under the direction of Boas, Viola Edmundsen Garfield (Miller 1988) did her dissertation research among the Tsimshian at Port Simpson, analyzing features of politics, economics, and social organization.

Amelia Susman was sent by Boas to work with William Beynon on a retranscription and analysis of the grammar. These materials are now in the Boas collection at the American Philosophical Society in Philadelphia. Susman eventually settled in Seattle, where I met her, and had a long career in medical counseling.

In the summer of 1940, Homer Barnett (1942) collected information on acculturation and change at Port Simpson, providing keen insight into the personalities of Ligeex and other key figures of the previous century.

While employed by the British Columbia Provincial Museum, Wilson Duff arranged for the preservation or copying of totem poles along the coast. During this process, the Gitksan town of Kitwankool agreed to publish accounts of their poles and customs (Duff 1959), which remain the earliest and best of the community studies.[22] Later, when assembling stone artifacts for a famous exhibit in Victoria, Duff matched two stone masks that proved to nest together so that the outer one was blind and the inner one had holes bored for the eyes. These masks represent one of the most powerful statements of naxnox that exist.

More than anyone else, Claude Lévi-Strauss has called attention to the richness of Tsimshian materials and their significance for understanding features of regional and universal human societies. The publication of his study of Asdiwal, translated into English in 1967, sparked a renewed scholarly interest in the Tsimshian.

20. *William Beynon and Amelia Susman. The photo was taken in 1940 while these scholars were engaged in fieldwork at Hartley Bay. (Courtesy of the Museum of Northern British Columbia.)*

George MacDonald at the Canadian National Museum directed the major excavations in Prince Rupert harbor that established the millennia of Tsimshian presence there (1979). His work on the historic fort of Nekt among the Gitksan, the axial symbolism of shamans, and the redundancies of body, house, and cosmos have clarified basic principles of the culture (1981, 1984a–c).

John Dunn, following up on linguistic work among the Gitksan by Bruce Rigsby, has provided a range of linguistic and analytical materials on Tsimshian language and kinship (1979b, 1984a, 1984c). His grammar (1979a) and dictionary (1978) are now standard references for all types of research by scholars and for use in Tsimshian schools. His poetic translations of Tsimshian narratives have set a new standard for sensitivity and nuance (1984b).

Marjorie Halpin, after prodigious research among the Beynon and Barbeau papers and in museum collections, characterized dynamic and distinctive features of Tsimshian society and the crest system in her monumental dissertation (1973). Her articles have summarized these findings and discussed features of art and religion (1978, 1981, 1984, 1994). More recently, reflecting trends in academia, she has considered the importance of ambiguity and native hegemony in the system (n.d.).

Margaret Seguin Anderson, beginning with linguistic work, has edited and published monographs on generalized and spiritual aspects of the culture, being concerned primarily with feasts (1984a, 1985, n.d.). With her husband, a native speaker of Tsimshian, she has taught an intensive course on Tsimshian language and culture at the University of Western Ontario and more recently at the new University of Northern British Columbia.

From 1965 through 1967, John Adams and Alice Kasakoff worked among the Gitksan. Adams, stimulated by the work of Lévi-Strauss, was particularly interested in the relations between mythology and society. Together, they studied features of kinship and marriage. In addition to several articles on these topics (1974), Adams has done a useful if uneven treatment of the modern potlatch (1973), stressing his own insight that these events redistributed people as well as goods. By acting as a host or a guest in this public forum, a person could indicate shifts in allegiance and membership.

John Cove also worked through the extensive Beynon-Barbeau materials in Ottawa, producing a helpful guide (1985). In 1978, he worked for the Gitksan collecting materials relevant to their land claims on aboriginal relations with nature. Another result was his provocative phenomenological study of Tsimshian existence (1987), discussed above.

Marie-Françoise Guédon, working among the Gitksan and other First Nations, has assembled a file on shamanic traditions and done much to interpret Tsimshian concepts of power (1984a, 1984b). Andrea LaForet (1984) has looked at Tsimshian artifacts, especially basketry, to establish tribal characteristics. As a primary artistic outlet for women, basketry has much to say about the culture. Marie-Lucie Tarpent (1982, 1983) has concentrated on the Nishga language for use in their schools and produced a voluminous grammar as her dissertation. Jean Mulder (1987) specifically studied the grammatical feature of ergativity, which equates subjects of intransitives with objects of transitives and so contrasts with the accusative structures of English.[23] These scholars and others are featured in a pair of edited collections (Seguin 1984b; Miller and Eastman 1984).

Lastly, it is important to note that our greatest advances in understanding the Tsimshian came when researchers entered those towns occupied by a single tribe. While the earliest work was done in the populous but amalgamated communities of Port Simpson and Metlakatla, this work more often confused than clarified the record. As scholars working in other regions, such as the Southwest and Northeast, have learned only too well, the study of individual communities is the best way of establishing the basic ethnographic facts. Regional and comparative studies are also important, but these need to rely on focused studies of communities to establish the specific and generic patterns.

For the Tsimshian, however, we have such studies only for the Gitksan in the monographs on Kitwankool (Duff 1959), on artifacts from Gitwangak (G. MacDonald 1984c; J. MacDonald 1984), and the family epics of Walter Harris (1976). Scattered in the writings of Seguin, Dunn, Ken Campbell (1984), and myself are materials for an overview of Hartley Bay (Hartley Bay School 1985a–c, 1987a–b). Also, the Prince Rupert school district has published useful booklets about Hartley Bay presenting a historic overview of the town, the clans, and seasonal activities (Prince Rupert School District 52 1992a–g).

COSMIC EQUATIONS

As a person has skin and a house has walls, so the Tsimshian universe seems to have a rim, very much like the undulating formline of their famous art style, which images the cosmos as a bounded void.

For Tsimshian, crests and wonders were extreme modes for handling light. One caught and held it, the other flashed it around. In their unsympathetic critique of Asdiwal, Thomas, Kronenfeld, and Kronenfeld (1976:153) note that Lévi-Strauss has the hero turn to stone on the slope, rather than the "very top" of the mountain, as specified in the narrative. Such an apical location was not accidental. During his stay with various naxnox, Asdiwal was reminded of the importance of light by many lenses, including fire, water, and ice crystals. As the founder of an *adawx,* however, it is appropriate that he ends his career on the crest of a mountain. As the cap, lid, or vertex, he is a petrified reminder of the character of crests and their rigid position within a linkage of wonders and potency, naxnox and light.

The Tsimshian developed to a high degree two expressions of their echo. These are mythology (Spier 1931) and art (Holm 1965; Carlson 1983). In the former, Tsimshians trace the beginnings of their culture to the efforts, often selfish, of Raven, who came to earth as a "shining youth," but who was transformed into a glutton. In mythic times, everything had an owner: food, tides, and, especially, light.

Further, all of these events were given artistic portrayals in crests, wonders, and halait objects. Characterizing these decorations was the artistic convention of the formline style, which epitomized the Tsimshian universe. A formline aptly expresses a closed system for containing light since, as Holm describes it, a primary color, or more usually black, creates a continuous border: "A formline is the characteristic swelling and diminishing linelike figure delineating design units. These formlines merge and divide to make a continuous flowing grid over the whole decorated area, establishing the principal forms of the design. One of the most striking features of the primary design is its continuity. In a typical piece all primary units are connected, with the exception of the inner ovoids of joints and eye designs. It is possible to begin tracing the primary forms at any point and to touch them all, with the exception noted, without a break" (1965:29).

The origins of this continuous formline can be traced to the Arctic, where Eskimo and Inuit painted a "horizon line" around the inner lip of a decorated bowl. Within this border creatures will be shown from any and all perspectives, in keeping with the Arctic tradition of seeing things with the mind's eye rather than with the optic nerve. The horizon line defines the space and allows the viewer a context for the varied portrayals. In a much more elaborate manner, the formline does the same thing, allowing the inner ovoids to add their own light to aid the viewer.

Given the importance of eye as lens, it is significant that the ovoid motif is independent within the overall design, floating within the formline. As a conjoining element, blending line and curve, the ovoid was an independent lens expressing the control of light. As a vortex, the pivotal placement of the ovoid allows it to concentrate and refract the potency of creation.

In the language, the word for face, *ts'al,* also means 'eye', and that for whirlpool, *ts'alaks,* an important familiar for shamans, means 'eye of the water' (Dunn 1978:100). Like any lens, it too refracts light and so assures its eternal availability within a closed universe. Moreover, Tarpent derives the Nishga term for "three" from 'eye-face', interpreting it to mean "stiffening the eye . . . metaphorically, [a] triangular pattern" (1983:70). By connotation, the number association suggests stability, since a tripod provides basic support.

ART PROFILES

As analysis continues in the tradition of Wilson Duff (1975, 1981), the basic humanness of the universe is confirmed by the art forms of the north Pacific coast. For Duff, many of these forms were explicitly sexual, either phallic or vulvic, in meaning and intent. As one example, he discussed the totem pole, which sometimes included genital details before Christian missionaries arrived and, after condemning the art, banished the poles entirely. Only the great pride of native peoples in these links with their ancestors has sustained the tradition into the present, although with unsexed figures.

In their version of tribal history, the chiefs of Kitwankool mentioned the importance of totem poles in their migrations: "bringing their poles, and the power came with the poles and went into the land" (Duff 1959:27). Once they had settled at a new town, each crest and chief set up poles to claim territories. "They had a ceremony and put their power on that river and land, which meant that it belonged to them as they had found it first" (1959:23). "They marked this boundary by singing this song at the place where the two rivers meet" (1959:26). Accompanied with song and dance to please the spirits, these poles became "deeds" to the homeland.

In contrast to much of the artwork, which relates to tribal crests and houses, certain items belong to the specialized regional network of the elite. The halait frontlet, robe, and rattle are among these, and so too is the copper.

This object, often called a shield, has mystified generations of scholars. Some have tried to derive it from the abstraction of details from other pieces of art, but these efforts seem misguided. Rather, following the insights of Widerspach-Thor (1981), the copper is best understood as a special kind of person. Each one had a name and a character. Owned only by the great chiefs, coppers sometimes served as surrogates. When a pole was raised either a slave or a copper was placed in the hole to increase the animating power of the link between sky, earth, and sea.

While Duff called the copper a statement of pure form and relationship, its parts are named, decorated, and regarded as a face and torso. The upper curved surface often bore the design of a face. The lower rectangle was framed by a T-shape representing the backbone and shoulders of the figure. It is noteworthy that the figure has no lower body. Among people of high rank, such anatomical (especially genital) references were regarded as rude and impolite in public, where the copper most often appeared.

Furthermore, the designs on a copper were not those of a specific crest, at least for the Tsimshian, but rather were generic formline figures. Since coppers were sold, traded, and smashed to shame a rival, no crest design could be used. The manner in which they were displayed was also a factor since, in most instances, the head was up, but to indicate death, the copper was shown or attached upside down. This was a common convention throughout the Americas, where clan symbols were often painted on grave markers with the totem's feet sticking up.

The widest-ranging study of the copper (Jopling 1989) begins with a discussion of its cultural context. Hampered by an inadequate understanding of the regional ethnography, she develops an argument that coppers were an invention of the early fur trade period fusing ancient and European themes. Yet copper itself already had a symbolic value along the coast, fostered by an extensive prehistoric trade in ornaments. Moreover, the flared trapezoidal form, so distinctive of the object, also characterizes slate artifacts found archaeologically. Other possible antecedents include Chinese bronze axes and mirrors, various regional masks or shamanic paraphernalia, and the reinforcement provided by the appearance of European military insignia.

But because every museum copper that has been tested has proved to be made of European sheeting, Jopling holds that the impetus for the artifact itself was provided by the copper plates that sheathed the hulls of trading ships until they emerged as an item in the fur trade because their readily workable thin surfaces could be shaped and embossed. While her argument conforms to existing data, it is too facile in ignoring native attitudes concerning the antiquity and integrity of the copper as a badge of rank.

Natives agree that copper nuggets were traded aboriginally from the Copper River of Alaska and were hammered into smaller versions of modern coppers. Since they are regarded as alive, they are described in terms of smell and texture. Some will ring when struck, and this is called their voice. According to older beliefs, however, native copper made no sound and had to be coated with a black sealer to retard corrosion. This blackening served as the backdrop for etching and painting the design.

21. *A Copper. Considered a living, significant emblem of any house, it was decorated with a house crest unless it was intended for exchange, in which case it had a generic design. (Courtesy of the Museum of Northern British Columbia.)*

Regardless of the debate about the antiquity of the copper on the north Pacific coast, its associations are ancient for the continent. Copper artifacts of exquisite manufacture were characteristic of the chiefdoms of the Americas. Mississippian leaders prided themselves on embossed bird-figured plates, and several modern Creek towns still prize such links with their past. Often, the dull sheen of the copper was regarded as an aspect of the Sun, the most important deity. Northwestern coppers, therefore, partake in a continental pattern that has identical meanings in terms of the personification and concentration of powerful energies in a hard metal plaque. Such links between the Northwest Coast and the rest of Native America, as with frogs and fresh water, are all too rarely indicated.

While the copper image was ancient, the copper itself undoubtedly received elaboration after the devastation of the population and the changes in wealth brought about by the fur trade. The copper became a repository for one or more bodies that could not sicken or die. It literally hardened, held, and protected the traditions of the elite. Both membership in the halait and the ownership of coppers for use in the potlatch provided a durable constant in the transmission of Tsimshian traditions.

# 5. Conclusions

Ultimately, the Tsimshian echoing tension produced a semantic equation based on light such that crest = lid (*ptex* = *haap*), wonder = lens (*naxnox* = *ts'al*), and privilege = loop (*halait* = *lui*), expressed as matriclans, patri-wonders, and bilateral-*halait* orders. Also, a person has a fixed *baa'lx*, a stretching *haayuk*, and a luminous *oo'tsn*. In other words, these three-way relationships uniformly segregate into categories which are *exclusive*, marked, segregating; *inclusive*, unmarked, integrating; and *inclosive* (Miller 1979), mediating.

Accordingly woman is exclusive, man is inclusive, and mind, as illumination, is inclosive. As a consequence, women of high rank in this aristocracy present a paradox, which the Tsimshian solve by invoking hierarchy. Thus, a commoner woman, at least before menopause, had only her membership in a matriclan and moiety. Elite women, in contrast, gained naxnox through their fathers or other male relatives and might even hold the name of a deceased male of their matriline. At the highest strata, those few women who joined halait organizations received names indicative of their closeness to Heaven. In all, the Tsimshian solved the paradox of elite women by making them increasingly more inclosive. As a woman moved from marked to unmarked and then mediating categories, she rose in rank. Also, for the overall system to make sense, children were a neutral category, from which they developed into females and males as they grew older.

NORTHWEST COAST COMPARISONS

Over millennia, the matrilineal nations of the north Pacific coast have worked out a common set of understandings, with the Tsimshian, whose society was the most elaborated, inspiring the borrowing that made this overall complex possible. All of these societies were organized in terms of houses, clans, and moieties, and all of their art recognized a distinction between artifacts intended as crests and those intended for use by shamans. The Tsimshian, however, elaborated these categories and developed the threefold systems of crests, wonders, and privileges. In the historic period, that is, during the past three centuries, the privilege system diffused widely along the entire coast as a means for identifying members of the elite. Yet this dispersal was only the most recent example in an ancient environment of cultural exchange.

John Dunn (1984a), following Boas, Swanton, and others, reviewed the commonalities based on the international moieties that equated Tsimshian Killerwhale-Wolf with Haida Raven and Tlingit Wolf-Eagle or Tsimshian Raven-Eagle with Haida Eagle and Tlingit Raven. But in his analysis he went further to show systematic sound and meaning correspondences in the kinship terms of these three cultures that indicate overall symbolic associations. From the perspective of the Tsimshian, the Tlingit were viewed as metaphorically female, younger, and human, thus associated by analogy with children of a clan. The Haida, on the other hand, far removed on their island homes, were regarded as metaphorically male, older, and other worldly, very much like the fathers of the clan, who, in the sacred histories, often were naxnox.

These three cultures also emphasize the importance of mind and thoughts, conveyed as beams of light and ultimately attributable to an otiose heavenly deity. While this belief in the power of light was widespread, only the Tsimshian institutionalized it in their ancient wonder displays and then reemphasized it in the burgeoning halait system.

In their marvelous collection of Tlingit sacred histories, the Dauenhauers (1987) mention several points relevant for understanding cultural dynamics along the north coast.

Among the Tlingits, a crest (*at.oow*) represents a covenant with the spirit world and includes the right to own certain land, names, heraldic designs, and important prerogatives. In traditional law, this right was "paid for" with a life. If an animal killed an ancestor in a story, then the descendants of that person could use the image of that being as a crest (1987:21, 25). Sometimes, older humans sacrificed themselves to compensate for a breach committed by a younger person, often a woman who would then give birth to children who would carry on the privilege within a house (1987:408). Thus each successive generation rebuilds this structure, making allowances for fluctuations in the number and composition of the membership (1987:414).

While they do not have traditions of shining youths or Heaven, Tlingits do make an equation between light and thought. In the famous history of Kaats, the man who married a female bear, his dogs searched for him and their thoughts were like sunbeams (1987:225). In the complementary story of a woman who married a bear, her brother searched for her and his thoughts entered the den as beams of light that the bear flashed back outside so that the den could not be found until the bears were ready to die and create the covenant of a crest (1987:179).

In their notes, the Dauenhauers indicate that thoughts and feelings, whether spiritual or emotional, are both expressed with a "nominal prefix tu-, meaning mind" (1987:395), and that these are visible as beams of light by creatures, such as bears, living in other dimensions.

In her analysis of northern Tlingit art, Jonaitis (1986) emphasizes the distinction between crest and shamanic carvings, with masks of familiars being characteristic of the latter. While only the Tsimshian had the naxnox system, its derivation from a shamanic tradition like that of the Tlingit or Haida, where shamans also wore masks, seems plausible. Indeed, the significance of light as a manifestation of powerful thought was reinforced among the Tlingit, where a novice received the call to become a shaman when he had a vision in which the sky opened and beams of light radiated into his head (1986:52).

The most ambitious recent study of the Tlingit is Kan's (1989) study of the nineteenth-century potlatch. Like the work by Boelscher (1988) on the Haida, discussed below, Kan is concerned with how symbolic structures are negotiated, manipulated, and used by Tlingits for social purposes. He begins with the Tlingit concept of the person as a series of layerings around "the (ḵaa) toowu, (person's) 'mind', 'soul', 'inner being', 'feelings', or 'inside'. It was related to *tu,* a theme prefix indicting the inside of a closed container" (1989:52). When personified, this essence appeared as a chickadee or as a spider spinning its web near a person's head.[1]

Purity was important for well-being and for relations with the supernatural, so people routinely engaged in periodic fasting, sexual abstinence, bathing in the ocean, drinking salt water, scraping the skin with a special stone, and consuming purgatives (1989:55). The intention was to make the body drier, harder, and heavier, in contrast to the coastal environment which was wet, soft, and mushy. These qualities, along with wealth and longevity, were symbolized by the use of stones.

Individuals took their identity from membership in a house, much in the same sense as Tsimshian do. Houses in turn belonged to clans and to one of the moieties, Raven or Eagle. Each clan treasured its *shagoon,* which referred to ancestors, heritage, origin, and destiny. On a higher level, the word was also used for the supreme being.

For Tlingits, as for Tsimshians, the ideal person was a member of the nobility, particularly an elder who was thereby believed to be heavier and more pure. Chiefs themselves were regarded as "real" or "ripe." As a group these nobles exchanged their ritual expertise and esoteric knowledge in return for the labor and assistance of members of the lesser ranks. Noble status required constant attention to morality and behavior. An improper marriage, suspected witchcraft, cowardice, and inability to host a potlatch diminished one's rank. The negative example that all tried to avoid was characterization as an outcast, people seen as greedy, lazy, improvident, cowardly, and immodest. While actual outcasts were represented by only a few illegitimate children, criminals, marginals, and those unable or unwilling to collect their own food, the threat of being called an outcast kept most people on their best behavior.

At death, the layers and spirits of a body separated, beginning with the central mind. The body was painted with clan designs and lay in state in the rear of the house, surrounded by crests, if a noble. After burial, the body and its ghost resided in the cemetery, which was the first of a series of lands of the dead. Other aspects of the person were expected to reincarnate into a baby of the same house, lineage, or clan.

Since the moiety of the deceased was in mourning, the other moiety took over the funeral arrangements and prepared the body. In particular, these were the father's kin, who were called "my box, shell, container, womb, grave, coffin" (Kan 1989:152). A widow painted her face black until her husband's clan painted it red at the memorial potlatch and announced the name of her next husband.

Most bodies were cremated, which removed their polluting aspects and produced ashes that were dry, hard, and heavy. Cremation also gave the spirit of the person a place near the fire in the house of its dead clanspeople. Interestingly, the Tlingit term for cremation also meant to shine or burn a light. This ancestral house was in the second land of the dead beyond this world. The trail there led through the cemetery, into the forest, and up a mountainside. The dead lived much as the living, but they did no work, surviving on offerings placed into a fire by their kin.

Shamans were buried separately. The wake lasted four days with the unpainted body placed each night in one of the four corners of the house, then removed through the smokehole. It was taken to a gravehouse in a remote location and deposited through an opening in the roof. The body was believed to resist decay by drying up. Those who wished to become shamans visited the gravehouse, sleeping there, but otherwise the place was avoided by everyone.

Warriors were also not cremated, their spirit going to a special cold place in the sky where they were visible to the living as the Northern Lights.

Chiefs lay in state wearing or near the conical hat that was the primary crest of the house (Kan 1989:129). The chiefly emblem was a staff, a symbol of their *shagoon*. More recently, deceased nobles have worn a frontlet (*shakee.at*), which was adopted from the Tsimshian. "For the Tlingit, the Tsimshian were the master craftsmen, owners of valuable songs, dances, and regalia, and powerful shamans—in other words, the kind of powerful outsiders with whom one fought as well as traded and intermarried" (1989:244).[2]

"The tragic irony of the Tlingit funeral was that the individual reached the peak of his social career when he was no longer living and his body was in its most polluted state" (1989:163). The ambivalence of these mortal remains was not a factor, however, in the memorial potlatch held a year or more later to "raise" the dead by placing the bones and ashes in a new container, such as a box, gravehouse, or mortuary pole. During the potlatch, the guests served as intermediaries between the living and the dead, who were a strong presence throughout the events. Such potlatches were held at night because that was the time when the dead were most active.

While most guests received gifts of food, skins, and blankets, only members of the elite were given the most prestigious offerings of slaves, coppers, chilkat robes, and abalone shells. Tlingit coppers had both generic designs, which could be given and traded to other nobles, and crest figures, which belonged to the *shagoon* and remained within the house. Like a noble, a copper was hard, heavy, and had a sheen. Unlike a noble, it did not die and, thus, represented the most permanent and valuable relations among the elite.

In conclusion, Kan (1989) shows how the Tlingit potlatch was used to negotiate social and power relations among the living, while simultaneously expressing feelings and attitudes toward the living, the dead, and all other aspects of the world.

Similarly, in her work on Haida society and discourse, Boelscher (1988) is particularly concerned with how the Haidas use formal and logical aspects of their culture to negotiate and legitimate claims to prestige and positions and with how symbols and categories are manipulated for personal and social advantage.

For Haidas, a person has several components, including a mind (*guudaang*, also meaning 'respect') and a soul. The skin, as the outer wrapping, receives considerable attention in terms of decoration and hygiene because it is the boundary between the inside and the outside of the person, as well as the zone of contact with the larger world.

Haidas were organized into houses, lineages, clans, and the overall moieties of Raven and Eagle. Each house owned property (*skil*), especially a hat woven of spruce roots worn by chiefs at potlatches. After hosting a potlatch, the chief was entitled to add another canister-like woven segment to the column that adorned the center of the hat (1988:139). The slightest movement of the head caused this shaft to jiggle, silently calling attention to the successes of that house. In addition, a chief had, as an emblem of his position, a carved staff or talking stick.[3] As MacDonald (1981:228) has noted, the segmented hat resembled an articulated backbone, a symbol of the ancestors. The staff, moreover, also invoked the vertical dimension that elevated the chief above the people.

The Haidas attribute several of their important crests to the Tsimshian (Boelscher 1988:141). Relations between the chiefs of Kitkatla and those of Skidegate were particularly close. In recent times, Ts'ibasaa "gave" the Grizzly Bear, in the form of a war coat, and the Moon, in the shape of a doorway, to particular Haida chiefs, whose houses and lineages passed them on. Some of these borrowings may be quite ancient, since archaeology suggests that Tsimshian have been influencing Haida ancestors for 2,500 years.

The Haida equivalent of the naxnox was called *sagaana,* which referred to killer whales, supernatural beings, and power in general (1988:160, 172, 183). The foremost killer whale was the chief of the Ocean People and received offerings and prayers addressed to "my chief" by members of the Raven moiety, for whom killer whales were a primary crest, or to "my father" by those of the Eagle moiety. In addition, there were also Forest People, comprised of numerous species who lived as humans in homes of their own. The ultimate source of all power was *sins sagaana,* Power of the Shining Heavens (1988:173).

Furthermore, the word in Haida for shaman is *sgaaga,* meaning someone permanently attuned to power. During their cures, shamans wore masks to better represent their supernatural helpers. Again, such evidence suggests a derivation of the Tsimshian naxnox from a more ancient system of shamanic practices.

Finally, as Mary Helms (1988) has shown so brilliantly, elites in all societies valued the exotic. The greater the distances involved in making these contacts, the more treasured they became. In this way, elites distributed across great geographical spaces found common ground and acquired substantial knowledge about a variety of topics, which they used for the benefit of themselves, their families, and their communities.

The virtue of the Tsimshian is that they provide a particularly vivid example of this larger pattern. While their crests meshed with others along the coast, their naxnox remained uniquely their own until, with the development of the frontlet, robe, and rattle of the *smhalait,* all the chiefs along the coast could don the same regalia of rank, facilitating even greater communication. With the development of the copper, a shared commodity connoting status was introduced to maintain a chiefly equilibrium during the dark and deadly days of European settlement.

Christianity has now assumed many of the aspects of the traditional religion, but except for the loss of masking and certain other artistic expressions of spirituality, the fundamentals remain. Today, crests persist as expressions of ancestral traditions partly encouraged by Canadian regard for English royalty and heraldry. Naxnox and halait have been superseded in public by Christianity, enthusiastically embraced by the Tsimshian for over a century. Still, ancient logic stands firm when Tsimshian raise their voices to sing "Jesus is the light of the world."[4]

# Appendix: Tribes and Towns

Tsimshian winter village names, given below, are usually prefixed by *git-* or *kit-* meaning 'People of'. Following the < the referent or translation (? if unknown) for the tribal name is given. Enclosed within brackets are the spellings approved for use in the excellent books prepared for the Prince Rupert School district, which are now the standard.

SOUTHERN TSIMSHIAN, SOUTH TO NORTH:

Gitisu (Gidestsu, kitasoo) < ? now at Klemtu or China Hat
Gitḵa'ata (gitḵ'a'ata) < 'staff, cane' [now at Hartley Bay]
Kitkatla (gitḵxaała) < 'channel', on Dolphin Island

COAST TSIMSHIAN, MOVING UPRIVER:

Gitwilgyots (gitwilgyoots) < 'kelp'
Gitzaklalth (gitzaxłaał) < 'berries' (?)
Gitsees (gits'iis) < 'salmon trap'
Ginakangeek (ginaxangiik) < 'mosquitos'
Ginadoiks (ginadoiks) < 'swift water'
Gitandau (gitando) < 'weirs'
Gispaxlawts (gispaxlo'ots) < 'elderberries'
Gitwilkseba < 'where water runs out'

Gilutsau (giluts'aaẅ) < 'inside'

Gitlan (gitlaan) < 'two passing canoes'

AT THE CANYON OF THE SKEENA:

Kitsumkalum (gitsmgeelm) < 'plateau'

Kitselas (gits'ilaasü) < 'canyon', two villages at this canyon

ABOVE THE CANYON OF THE SKEENA:

*Gitksan*

Kitwanga (kitwangax) < 'rabbits'

Kitwankool (gitanyow) < 'narrow valley', along the Grease Trail

Gitsegukla < Sagukhla Mountains

Gitanmaaks < 'torchlight fishing', now Hazelton

Kispiox (gispaaayeks) < 'hiding place'

Kisgegas < 'seagulls', joined about 1880 by the Anlagasamdak

Kuldo < 'camp'

NASS RIVER: NIS<u>G</u>A'A (NISHKA)

DOWNRIVER WERE THE GITKATEEN < 'FISHTRAPS' AT:

Laxgaldzap (lakalzap) < 'town', modern Greenville

Gitiks < 'canoe poles'

Kwunwoq (gwinok) < 'sleep over'

Angidaa < 'to rake candlefish'

Kincolith (gingolx) < 'scalps'

AND THE GITGIGENIK AT:

Andegulay (andegwalee) < 'happy place'

Gitlakaus (gitlaxaws) < 'sand bar'

UPRIVER WERE:

Gitwunksiłkw (gitwinksihlkw) < 'lizards' at Canyon City

AND THE GIT'ANWILIKS AT:

Laxwilmogwunt < 'strawberries'
Gitlakdamiks (gitlaxt'amiks) < 'ponds' at New Aiyansh
Aiyansh < 'early leaves'

# Notes

1. Tsimshian relish the geographical details of these stories, but they are only for insiders. Native place names must be used with great care and selectively published, if at all. Even now, coastal names are used by native fishermen over their radios to gain an advantage over other competitors. At various times, I have been specifically asked not to print place names (Miller 1981a:28).

Throughout, my presentation of these epics does not follow the convention that has recently developed in response to the court cases and land claims that are consuming much of Tsimshian attention. In these documents, each text is identified by its narrator(s), date, location, and general context of authority—such as the right by which that person provided that history at that time and place. In such matters, usually, house leadership and clan chiefship are invoked.

2. The letter inviting me was signed by Daphne Anderson, who died tragically a few years later.

3. Both de Laguna and Charles Borden noted an Eskimoan presence in early Northwest Coast artifacts, but recent archaeologists deny this (Matson and Coupland 1995: 147). Yet, from a cultural standpoint, many Northwest Coast features seem to be elaborations of Inuit ones, as with the "formline" developing from the "horizon line" around Eskimo paintings.

4. Ligeex, also spelled Legaic or Ligeak, is the subject of disagreement among scholars and natives. Scholars, thinking and writing in terms of European notions of politics, deny that Ligeex was anything like a high chief (Mitchell 1983; Dean n.d.). Yet he did have economic, social, and ritual precedence, if not paramountcy. Politics, as such, were not elaborately developed on the coast. After long consultation with Tsimshian chiefs and elders, along with scholars, the first book produced by Prince

Rupert School District 52 says, "The Gispaxlo'ots were led by several chiefs of different housegroups of different clans, but, of them all, the Eagle housegroup of Ligeex was considered the most powerful. Because of this, the House of Ligeex was considered the leading House of all the Maxłak̲xaała Tsimshian" (1992d:70).

Tsimshian themselves report that Ligeex had "first say" among chiefs, indicating that he was foremost. Yet, because he was so "high," people criticized him and his line of heirs because chiefs should not become too haughty. For the same reason, rival traders delighted in thwarting his claim to the Skeena River trade.

Thus far, I have not treated Ligeex as "the" Tsimshian leader; I will continue to refer to him as a "high chief" in discussing further his role in the Tsimshian response to European pressures. Ligeex may not have been as famous as Seattle, Tecumthah (Tecumsah), or Pontiac, but he too might have mobilized a chiefdom, if not an eventual international confederacy. Certainly, like them, the holders of the Ligeex name rose to preeminence as war leaders during times of threat from outsiders. His military successes offered protection to others. Moreover, the rise of the name to replace one that had been shamed certainly bespeaks a native, not a European, context for its beginnings. Those who doubt the historical existence of a Tsimshian confederation should be reminded of the thousands of years the Coast Tsimshian shared on Metlakatla Pass.

5. William Beynon thought that the first Bini was trying to introduce Catholicism as a new form of halait.

6. In an early response to this book, Margaret Seguin Anderson (personal communication) argued that if she had to "choose" five terms to represent the Tsimshian, these would be story, crest, name, territory, and feast—which are indeed very important concepts for contemporary Tsimshian—but they all reflect the only branch, that of the semi-moieties, to survive into the present. Both the naxnox and halait did not continue after William Duncan and Christianity took hold. Thus, the important tension between the maternal (substantial) and the paternal (spiritual) was redirected into existing clans and new beliefs, albeit continuing the all-pervasive recognition of coming into the light.

7. Naxnox are beings, supernaturals in their own right, the foundation of the other institutions. To distinguish the naxnox themselves from their primary expression, manifestation, or "instanciation" in masks and displays, the dramatizations themselves are here called "wonders." In the Tsimshian language, they are all included together in the term *naxnox*. For clarity of analysis, however, *naxnox* will refer to the immortal beings and *wonder* will refer to a cultural recognition of it.

8. While this garment is best known by the name of this Tlingit tribe, according to Tlingit tradition this artistry was brought to the town of Klukwan among the Chilkat by Hayuwaas Tlaa, an in-marrying Tsimshian woman. She brought with her a dancing apron, which the women of the Gaanaxteidi clan unraveled and studied so that they could begin to make the Chilkat weaving for which they became famous (Dauenhauer and Dauenhauer 1990:205, 353).

9. The spread of this elite halait from the Nass might coincide with the Nishga takeover of the lower river from the Tlingit.

10. The Haida, who had at least six privileged orders, traced them either to the Bella Bella or the Southern Tsimshian.

11. Renouncing the halait led the list of commandments that Duncan insisted all converts follow. Today, Tsimshian still concur on its banishment, recognizing that these orders sought to intimidate the laity and to cower commoners.

In full, these commandments were:

1. To give up their "Ahlied," or Indian devilry.
2. To cease calling on "Shamans," or medicine-men, when sick.
3. To cease gambling.
4. To cease giving away their property for display.
5. To cease painting their faces.
6. To cease indulging in intoxicating drinks.
7. To rest on the Sabbath.
8. To attend religious instruction.
9. To send their children to school.
10. To be cleanly.
11. To be industrious.
12. To be peaceful.
13. To be liberal and honest in trade.
14. To build neat houses.
15. To pay the village tax.

## 1. BACKGROUND

1. These five salmon species can be confusing because of the variety of local common names. They belong to the genus called *Oncorhynchus* and are designated by species.

1. *O. tshawytscha* (chinook, king, spring, quinnat), up to eighty pounds, spawns in large streams or rivers, sometimes with spring and fall subspecies.
2. *O. kisutch* (silver), usually six to twelve pounds, up to thirty pounds, runs in early fall but may not spawn until late fall, in smaller streams far from the sea.
3. *O. gorbuscha* (pink), three to ten pounds, spawns early fall, smaller streams near the sea.
4. *O. keta* (chum, dog), eight to eighteen pounds, spawns late fall, smaller streams near the sea, lean and smokes well.
5. *O. nerka* (sockeye), usually a few pounds, fattest species, spawns upriver in lakes; when landlocked, known as kokanee.

In addition, steelhead (*Salmo gairdneri*) is a sea-run rainbow trout, up to thirty-six pounds, that, like Atlantic salmon, spawns and returns to the sea. Pacific salmon, on the other hand, spawn and die, nourishing local carnivores and poor soils (Suttles 1990: 24–25).

2. Little is known about a tenth tribe called the Gitwilkseba. William Beynon (mss.) translated the name as "people where the water runs out" and collected a long text that justifies their extinction as a tribe, although descendants still live along the Nass just below Fishery Bay, Quinamass River, and Portland Canal.

By all accounts they were "thoughtless." Once, at a wake, they played, joked, and were noisy. A tall ghost wrapped in a blanket entered the house and waved his hands. After he left, many members of this tribe died. The survivors were quiet for some time. When their numbers increased, they again became thoughtless. Once, they were abusing village dogs when one of the animals scolded them. Many of the tribe died as a result. The survivors were Blackfish but their chiefs were demoted in their new towns because of the way this tribe had acted.

3. At the Kitselas town of Gitlaxdzooks ('fortress'), the house of Gaum (#7), the largest at the site, had a small door in the northeast corner leading to a rocky promontory facing upriver. Observers watched the sun's movement with regard to Kitselas Mountain from this fixed location, establishing the timing of certain events. For example, the end of the salmon run was marked by the sun setting inside a particular notch in the mountain (Allaire, MacDonald, and Inglis 1979:95–96, plate 26).

4. The Gispaxlo'ots claim to begin the annual trade derived from their rights to the location of an ancestral Blackfish town at the eastern limits of Coast Tsimshian territory, and, therefore, nearest the Gitksan.

5. This was and is not a simple exchange, as I learned by sweat and toil when I helped during the May 1993 seaweed harvest at Hartley Bay. Pulling the seaweed off rocks took most of a morning, then the rest of the week was spent drying, chopping, and seasoning the harvest. In the same way that much labor goes into the tanning of hides for trade, equally intensive effort was needed to prepare the seaweed.

6. This downriver fishery was once occupied by the Tlingit, but they were replaced by Nishga moving downriver.

7. When William Duncan visited the Nass in 1860, he was horrified to see "The [cooked] fish put on a board or table and the poor women pressed out the oil by leaning on the hot fish with their bare breasts." He immediately designed a mechanical press that was soon adopted after natives determined that the fish "were not insulted by using my style of press" (Murray 1985:54). Only women could process the fish, so this pressing was a gesture of respect to the savior candlefish. Also, the first olachen of the season was ceremonial roasted on elderberry sticks (Boas 1916:450).

8. While such "ceremonial chastity" (cf. McIlwraith 1948:110 for procedures among the Nuxalk) was a requirement for hunters and others about to undertake a dangerous task, abstinence alternated with license. Among the Nishga and other Tsimshian, after a set number of days, usually four, this purification was ended by a night with a "lucky woman." Then the fasting, prayer, and chastity were resumed for another four days. Often the "lucky woman" was the man's wife, but not always. Similarly, a woman who undertook purification before hunting had to sleep with a "lucky man" to end her days of chastity.

9. Cf. Boas (1916:192–206). A shorter version of this story, found throughout the north Pacific coast, describes how an ordinary boy refused to eat a piece of salmon that was moldy. For this disrespect, he was taken by the Salmon people for a year and taught proper respect for their generosity.

10. Beynon (mss.: text 190) said the shaman was named Niaswa-ye, and that the stone held in the mouth was actually a crystal.

11. Such raptor trapping from pits was also an important religious activity for warriors among tribes of the Plains.

## 2. BEAMING

1. Comparable texts make up the majority of Boas (1916). My account here, emphasizing miraculous aspects of the origins of Raven as a naxnox sent down from Heaven, is more in keeping with Raven's traditional career.

A version from the Nass River (Boas 1902:7–24) combines several otherwise distinct sagas. It begins with an unfaithful wife pretending to die so that her lover can visit in her grave box set high in a tree. When her husband comes to mourn below, she scrapes slivers from a horn spoon so they fall to the ground like maggots. Eventually, the lovers are found out and killed, but not before the woman becomes pregnant, unbeknownst to everyone. Her son is born and lives off her intestines. When children play archery nearby, he steals their arrows and so is discovered. Captured, he is taken to the chief and raised as his son. Donning a raven skin, he embarks on his adventures with the help of a brother called Woodpecker (*lagabuula*).

2. The Nishga say the exact place where this birth occurred is below the modern town of Greenville on the Nass River (McNeary 1976b:60).

In the 1980s, construction at Greenville unfortunately exposed a burial area with an amazing association. Of the fifty-seven indications from A.D. 566 to 1290, thirty-two were intact, with sixteen of these buried with elderberry seeds, including eight in heavy concentrations. While Cybulski (1992:73) suggests that these seeds might indicate brushy overgrowth, reused food-storage boxes, or food for the dead, referring to the Elderberry-Stone epic, he did not specify that the location of that event was this very same site. Clearly a site, where burials ceased seven hundred years ago, with such a strong link to elderberries, suggests the antiquity of this usage among Tsimshianic peoples.

In a less dignified, more earthy version, Elderberry (*lo'ots*) and Rock (*lo'op*) are euphemisms for vulva and testes (*lo'op*) (Seguin quoted in Cove 1987:105), further explaining why Elderberry gave birth more easily. These puns add to the common enjoyment of the epic.

3. Compare with the word for Rainbow, *maaxay* (Dunn 1978:71). Perhaps, *maax* is the Raven baby-talk version of *goypax*.

4. By implication from this event, Tsimshian shamans used frog images in their cures and rituals because frogs were "closer" to the beginning of things and had special reserves of primordial power.

5. Cf. Boas (1916:125–30).

6. Brian Compton has identified sloe wood as black hawthorn for me.

7. The Haw-haw was a dangerous supernatural being in the Tsimshian bestiary. When William Duncan translated a bible school song about Daniel in the Lions' Den, How-how became the term for the lion of the Old Testament. Thus the monster continues to exist for Tsimshian in a Christian context.

8. 'Loon' is *gool* (Dunn 1978:26), also called *'am'taa,* and 'empty, space, hole' is *gal* (1978:19–20), which appears in compound words for 'nose ring' (*galksiłoosk,* the shell loop formerly worn in a hole in the nasal septum to signal elite status), for 'town' (*galdzap,* meaning 'space to lay down'), for 'stomach' (*gal'oos*), for 'pail' (*galdm'aks,* meaning 'space for water'), and for 'empty box' or 'coffin' (*galgal'üüng*).

9. A term given for the cedar bark ring worn by halait initiates is *lui.*

10. Throughout the Pacific Northwest, salmon bones were returned to the water to permit the beings to be reborn and return the next year. By burning the bones, the Tsimshian again emphasized the importance of light.

11. As these actions by the living toward the dead indicate prestige, so do beliefs about soul transmutation. Among the Haida, and probably some Tsimshian, people who drowned or were lost at sea had their souls reincarnated as killer whales, the most awesome of the "Ocean-people," whose name in Haida is synonymous with power itself (Boelscher 1988:153, 182–86). According to related beliefs, native people who narrowly escape drowning become land otters or other hairy beings. In each case, of course, these other species are equally "real," and thus appropriate vehicles for souls during successive existences.

## 3. BRANCHING LIMBS

1. Throughout the north Pacific coast, a clan house could add to its fame by commissioning international artists to produce items of crest art. Therefore, Tsimshian artists were in demand by the Haida and Tlingit chiefs, and this has led to some confusion.

The famous painted rainwall screen and carved posts in the Whale House at Klukwan are sometimes attributed to a Tsimshian artist (G. MacDonald 1984b), whom Emmons (1991:54) said was paid ten slaves, fifty dressed moose skins, and many blankets. All evidence, however, indicates that these were the work of a Tlingit named Kadjisdu.axtc. Final clarification was provided by Steve Brown, of the Seattle Art Museum (personal communication), who noted that there are two Whale Houses in Klukwan, and that the screen of the Killerwhale house was the work of a Tsimshian artist, as shown by illustration 6 in Jonaitis (1986).

2. Since the classic matrilineal peoples, such as Hopi and Iroquois, were also matrilocal (kinswomen lived together), McNeary (1976b) argues that Tsimshian traced descent through women as a means of fostering alliances between houses, clans, and semi-moieties. Thus, a man who lived with his mother's brother had other ties with the houses of his own father, of his wife or wives, and of his sons when they married. Such widely ramified kinship ties were indeed important aspects of chiefly rank throughout the region.

3. Some Tsimshian families now give ancestral canoe names to their motor boats.

4. The mother of the first Ligeex was such an example; she may have been captured and married twice, the last time at Kitamaat.

5. This was an idealized image because, of course, all Tsimshian houses faced the beach or riverbank rather than a specific direction.

6. Garfield's generally inaccessible publications on the carving of a raven rattle and the making of a box design (1955a, 1955b) also provide significant information on the spiritual and practical training of an artist.

7. In more technical language, the vertical axis of the crest was syntagmatic, while the horizontal one was paradigmatic.

8. As Dunn (1984:107) brilliantly indicates through study of sound correspondences and kin-term usages, the Tsimshian, Haida, and Tlingit nobility shared an expanded matrilineal kinship system in which Tsimshians viewed Haidas as symbolically male, older, foreign, and supernatural "fathers," while Tlingits were female, younger, known, and human "little sisters."

9. Cf. Cove (1987:177–226).

10. Along the coast, close observation of nature, coupled with cultural beliefs, led natives to equate killer whales and wolves as social carnivores joined together into a pod or pack. Often, these two species were regarded as dual aspects of the same supernatural being, who became an orca in the sea or a wolf in the forest, depending on the circumstances of the moment.

11. Cf. Boas (1916:297).

12. Cf. Boas (1916:131–35). By common knowledge, the site of this massacre was the mountain called Stegawdun or Rocher de Boule that looms behind Hazelton, British Columbia.

13. In some versions, this goat has only one horn.

14. Cf. Boas (1916:346–50).

15. The site of Nagunaks is claimed jointly by the people at Klemtu, Hartley Bay, and Kitkatla, clearly indicating its Southern Tsimshian affiliation and importance. People go there for abalone and bufflehead, a waterfowl.

16. In some versions, a group of people survive, led by three brothers: Ts'ibasaa, who settled at Kitkatla, joining 'Wiiseeks, who was already there; Saxsa'axt, who went to Metlakatla; and 'Wamoodmłk, who founded both Ksnga'at and Gitḵa'ata.

17. Sometimes, it is a blue jay carrying the elderberries.

18. According to Beynon (mss.: text 228), the woman had four children at a time because ducks lay and hatch four eggs at a time.

19. Beynon (mss.: text 228) also provides a version referring to the sensitive issue of Lowe Inlet (Kmodo). Though the Gitḵa'ata fought for and settled this inlet, a strong-willed Kitkatla chief with the name of 'Wiiseeks drowned there. Though the Gitḵa'ata had repeatedly warned him of the dangers, this chief nevertheless chose to risk his own life. Still, he died on their territory as their guest and, in compensation, the Gitḵa'ata gave Lowe Inlet to the Kitkatla heirs as temporary compensation. Its eventual return was expected and marriages were arranged to ease the transition, but the matter remains contested. Campbell, long familiar with the situation, says, however, that Lowe Inlet "has long been the major salmon camp for the head chief of Kitkatla" (1993:67).

20. Cf. Boas (1916:285–91). For Haida, the Nagunaks epic explained the origin of the secret orders among the Tsimshian, who transmitted some of them to Haida chiefs about 1700 (Swanton 1909:155–60). Others of the six to nine orders among the Haida are attributed to a Bella Bella source.

21. Cf. Boas (1916:260–69).

22. Beynon (mss.: text 125) reported that the village was named Dzik-way, the son was Astihlta, and the daughter was Diiks.

23. Throughout at least western Native America, Frog was regarded as the "owner" of fresh water (Miller 1983a, 1983b:349).

24. Cf. Boas (1916:186–92).

25. According to a nearly universal human belief, "life comes from between the legs of a woman," so when a young woman stepped or jumped over someone, he or she was revived.

26. For the Tlingit, these complexities are superbly described by the Dauenhauers (Dauenhauer 1995; Dauenhauer and Dauenhauer 1990).

27. While marmot skins were the minimal unit of value, they also had an important symbolic aspect. Standing in front of the burrow, a marmot appeared to be watching the sky from a fixed location, just like the astronomers who served the chiefs. Thus, marmots knew the environment and could predict the weather, adding further to the well-being of the recipient.

The Gitsegukla History (1979) notes that while groundhog skins were used before money, rabbit skins had highest prestige when given at feasts.

28. The inability to reject offered food was, of course, the mechanism for changing the shining youth into Raven.

29. Among the Nu-chah-nuulth and other nations, these greeting ceremonies simulate the throwing of a crystal back and forth to show that the powers of host and guest were equal, at least for the duration of the potlatch.

30. Garfield (1939:204) gives, in her spelling, this ranking as Kitkatla, Gitzaklalth, Ginakangeek, Gitsees, Gilutsau, Gitwilgyots, Ginadoiks, Gitandau, and Gitlan.

31. The author was specifically invited and attended the week of events. As a joker noted at the time, "What would a potlatch be without an anthropologist?" A certain sense of the cosmopolitan was conveyed with the gifts I received, as suggested by the manufactured items: a Canadian-made towel, from the Ravens; a heavy red flannel shirt made in the People's Republic of China, from the Blackfish; heavy socks and handkerchiefs, from the chief; and a large towel made in Poland, from the Eagles. In the past, such gifts would have included items that were similarly exotic and foreign in origin.

32. Since I have since compensated for this mistake at another feast, it would be inappropriate to bring it up again. The "sordid" details are in Miller (1984b).

Seguin (1985:88) mentions the feast when I was named but treats the incident as passing banter. The chief and others have assured me that the term that became my name was carefully chosen from a song text during discussion among older women of the Blackfish and Eagles. I remain grateful for their kindness.

33. The resonances of the naxnox along the coast include the aboriginal rituals of the Kwakwaka'wakw, which Boas thought represented the inherited crest or privileges "of the animal [ancestor] from which they descended" (1966:258).

34. Recently, Gitksan have used the term *naxnox* as the name of one of their legal corporations.

35. Though not developed here, Tsimshian agree with most of humanity in associating men with the right and women with the left (Needham 1973). Presumably, the main difference between these masks was that those of women had labrets on the lower lip.

36. Cf. Boas (1916:285). According to Edmund Patalas (Waemawdemłk), the story of Gunaxnesemgyet occurred among the Gitisu (Barbeau 1950:276–82).

37. Here the naxnox does in fact what the wonder and halait dramatizations did in emulation.

38. Sending a slave to learn information was a common motif in the epics, also appearing in the account of Prairie Town.

39. As MacDonald remarked, the story of Asdiwal "has received more attention, as a testing ground for structuralist theory, than has any other myth in the world. Several dozen articles spanning the last decades in anthropological and linguistic journals have concerned the Azdiwal myth" (1984a:67). Important among these are Lévi-Strauss (1967), Adams (1974), Ackerman (1975), Barbeau (1961), and Leach (1967).

As recorded by Duff (1959:12, 43), As-de-wal (Accidentally) is the fifth ranking man's name in the house of Neas-la-ga-naws, the second Wolf chief at Kitwankool. Other houses in other towns also have valid claim to this name and its history.

According to Dunn, *asdiwaal* is a verb meaning "to have an accident; to make a mistake" (1978:7) and derives from *asdi-* "from the front to the middle of the house; to make a mistake" (1978:6). As the front and middle was the most public part of the house, where slaves and commoners lived, mistakes there were particularly obvious. The name is appropriate because all important names indicate something that was "overcome," to the credit of the titleholder and house. The Nishga name Asi-hwil has been translated "Going Across The Mountains" (Boas 1902:226). While this may be another form, it is more likely another interpretation. Among the Tsimshian, the more important the name, the more interpretative translations it has to encourage attention, commentary, and increased prestige.

My summary of the narrative, therefore, will stress a native interpretation of the events, relying on the overall account by Boas (1916:792–825), along with additions from the most detailed one (Boas 1912:71–146).

40. On the coast, a version of the Asdiwal name is used in Kitkatla (Dunn and Dunn 1972), an island town mentioned in the story. Further, Southern Tsimshian say that the marks of Asdiwal's snowshoes can still be seen on the rocky face of one of the offshore Gander Islands. Presumably, this is the exact place where he hunted sea lions. Intrigued, I asked how he died (since in this version he kept his snowshoes) and was told that his child asked what he ate when he lived with the sea lions. He had been told never to reveal this. Caught off guard, he said, "Red snapper," and died. A similar ending is reported by Boas: "Asi'wa didn't want to tell him at first but when his son pressed him, he said, 'They gave me rock cod and eulachon oil which tasted very nice.' As soon as he had said this, he fell down dead and fish bones grew from his stomach" (1974:286). As Lévi-Strauss notes, red cod, red snapper, and rock cod are in the same taxonomic family. They are "frightening creatures because of the sharp fins and spines that cover their body" (1982:50). Their meat is lean and dry, benefiting from a dipping in oil.

More importantly, "It is known that an internal organ of these fish comes up to their mouth and swells when they are pulled out of the water" (1982:214). In his own comments on this indiscretion, however, Lévi-Strauss says, "In the present state of our ethnographical knowledge of the Tsimshian, we do not know why this revelation constitutes a lapse" (1983:190).

By living with the sea lions, Asdiwal took on some of the characteristics of a sea creature. By calling out the name of the cod in his especially charged state, it was as though he called the fish out of the water, rupturing its swim bladder and pushing its stomach out (Iglauer 1988:28). Thus, the fish regurgitated into Asdiwal's throat and its prickly spines killed him. In contrast, Ackerman (1982) interprets this death as the result of tension between paternal and maternal stresses among the Tsimshian, but he fails to note that sons have the right to hunt on the lands of their father's clans.

The Story of Asdiwal, hence, is "about" how a semi-divine man encountered naxnox and gained potency that became crests within a house. The name of Asdiwal was that of the "boy" founder, the first in a series. Throughout his life, via matrilineal inheritance from his human relatives, he acquired rights to other, more important names. "Potlatch Giver" and "Stone Slayer" are specifically mentioned (Boas 1912), but there may have been others. Each marriage and name potlatch brought him into another kinship web. Among ranking Tsimshian, there are indications that the same important names intermarried every generation, so his succeeding wives may have also been associated with his later names.

41. Witches were probably not included among the halait in pre-contact times. With the adoption of Christianity and the condemnation of the halait, however, witchcraft became combined into this forbidden category.

42. Beynon (mss.: text 193) specified that *guhalait* referred to the Nodding or Chief's Dance itself, and that *hakhalait* was the plural that referred to any performance. The artists who made special devices for this branch were called *dlhalait*.

43. Though data are lacking, the multiple terms for shamans suggest there may have been four primary types of shamans among the prehistoric Tsimshian, before conversion, which would be consistent with the other branchings. Certainly, based on where they were encountered, shamanic familiars "lived" in four different locations, i.e., in the sea, forest, caves, and mountains.

44. Text 63 (Beynon mss.) from William Smith to William Beynon describes how two shamans, one on the coast and one in the interior, presented gifts to each other. The coastal shaman placed shellfish into his fire, which materialized through the smokehole of the interior shaman. In return, chokecherries were sent back from the upriver fire to the coastal smokehole.

45. This prince specifically lived at the important town of Gadu, across from Metlakatla, on Digby Island where Prince Rupert airport is now located. In ancient times it was a Raven town where many momentous events took place, including the story of the Revenge of Heaven.

46. These hairy supernaturals were an aspect of the bestiary throughout the region, where they have become known by the Fraser Salishan term of Sasquatch. While they

were powerful, and thus closely associated with shamans, many modern people assume that they were some kind of North American ape, regardless of what biologists say about the distribution of primates.

47. William Smith to Beynon (Beynon mss. [reel 2]: text 61, 78–91).

48. Most of the powerful allies of a shaman are mentioned in this text, including Owl, Ice, and Whirlpool.

49. *Swansk* means 'blower' and refers to the shaman's ability to remove illness by blowing with his lips or using a "soul catcher" tube when curing.

50. Halait dramatizations represented the chief in his or her most powerful priestly guise. As such, halait enactments by chiefs were used to seal trade alliances and dynastic marriages. After Hale had returned to Kitkatla, he performed a halait in which he appeared from behind a curtain wearing a top hat and formal attire, while his people shouted, "hail, hail." Similarly, when Duncan visited the Nishga in 1860, he was forced to attend the halait of a chief, who, contrary to expectations, appeared from behind a curtain wearing a suit and tie and proclaiming his willingness to hear the Word of God, examine the Book, and ask pity from Heaven (Arctander 1909: 146).

51. Beynon (text 179, 1937). Microfilm. Interview with Julia White and Mrs. R. Tate, reel 3, volume 12, 74–106 (Halait of Legaix).

52. These portrayals have been slightly expanded and clarified on the basis of my own understanding of this system. Susan Marsden (n.d.) has stressed the antisocial aspects of many of the naxnox among the Gitksan, describing how a chief will show a tight control over the performer representing one of his naxnox, sometimes holding up his own arms to shield the audience from the masked dancer.

53. The word for top is *halhal* (Dunn 1978: 38), sharing the root of *hal*ait, and indicating a shared meaning of spinning, twisting.

## 4. REFLECTIONS

1. Reincarnation beliefs play a vital role among the nations of the north coast. The Tlingits performed rituals to assure the return of a soul to a particular woman, sometimes by placing bits of the corpse in that woman's belt, and sometimes by leading her eight times around the funeral pyre, sketching a path away from it, and having her urinate at the end while praying for a revival of the spirit (Kan 1989: 109).

In my own experience, reincarnation has been taken for granted in several other native communities where time is considered cyclical.

Delawares believe that some babies are reincarnations of former relatives. After a baby is born, old women will visit to determine if he or she has dented ear lobes, particular scars, or the quiet disposition of an ancestor. They will look for indications that the soul has lived before by noting that the baby keeps his or her body relaxed and hands unclenched, is quiet and watchful, or reacts favorably to places and things associated with a deceased person. Neither formal nor institutionalized, this belief remains vague among Delawares now in Oklahoma.

Among Colville Interior Salishans of north central Washington State, some elders assumed that because I knew the names and character of individuals long dead, I had somehow lived with them and had recently come back to find out about their subsequent lives. Since there is no firm barrier between living and dead, who often visit back and forth at Colville, I am not sure to this day if elders thought I was a reincarnate or a ghost, but those still alive definitely treated me as a mortal.

Among other communities, however, such as the Navajo, Apache, and other Athapaskans, negative attitudes toward the dead proscribe any possibility of reincarnation.

2. Barnett (1940: [book 3]: 20) listed the stages of elevation as *tsiaks, halait, hilaxa,* and *kawunaxnox.* All sources report the first, often translated as "dentalia" or tuskshells, while the next two also make sense as degrees of halait and elite associations with Heaven. The last, translated as "grasping naxnox," would represent a supreme degree of privilege, given how carefully and respectfully the naxnox were supposed to be treated by one and all.

3. Fiske (1991) argues that male dominance in the colonial era eroded the high status of Tsimshian women, as indicated by their prehistoric control of critical resources, dispensing of patronage, and involvement in decision making. By relying on the published record, however, she has confused different aspects of Tsimshian society. Many of the features she attributes to high female status are common attributes of matrilineal kinship and social ranking defined in terms of a noble house.

Nor does she realize the significance of the roster of eternal names that were and are passed through succeeding generations. Some of these elite names are male and others female, but the names of men always outrank those of women. Regardless of gender, however, such names define membership in the nobility and leadership of a house. Indeed, at important initiations, both boys and girls were inducted at the same time. Thus, if there was or is no male heir to assume a vacant name, a family will confer it on a woman so as to retain control of the privileges associated with that name. In this regard, a woman holding a man's name is always treated as a male at potlatches.

Despite the denigration and criticism documented in nineteenth-century sources, women remained the backbone of Tsimshian society. Their "triple burden" of labor, cooking, and child care sustained their importance. While modern Canadians and government officials have tried to curtail their involvement in the public arenas of church, council, and commerce, their voices remain strong. As one woman said to me, "Because the whites tried to silence us in the hall, we had to speak louder in the house." And, indeed, they do.

4. The pebble (crystal) passed around in the Salmon epic served a similar function.

5. Dorothy Brown of Kitkatla told this vivid history to John Dunn in 1968, and a revised version for use in the Tsimshian curriculum was published in 1992 (Prince Rupert School District 52 1992g).

6. Githawn remains an important name among Tsimshian and Haida towns, where it belongs to the Eagles. In Txałgiu, the current holder is the school principal and heir to the Eagle chiefship.

7. A possibility is that the name Xamisit is related to Humchitt, the foremost name among the historic Bella Bella (Campbell 1993:36, 133).

8. Since Githawn is an Eagle crest name, the hat probably depicted an eagle.

9. A Beynon text (mss. [reel 2]: 111–128) places this painting on the Nass River, but

it still exists and is on the Skeena. The original artist's name was Dzumks, although Gaya of Gitlaan later refurbished it. The basket Dzumks stood in and the rope used to suspend the basket were purchased from a Skidegate Haida chief for five coppers and five slaves. It took eight days for the chief to go home and return with the basket and rope.

10. Beynon (mss.: text 222) recorded this prior name as Niswamak̲ and reported that a chief of that name returned the body of a Heiltsuk chief, who died of natural causes while visiting the Tsimshian, to Bella Bella. In gratitude, he was initiated in the secret orders and his nephews became the first *gitsontk,* bringing the *wihalait* to the Tsimshian.

11. While Mitchell (1983) and others have made extensive use of Hudson Bay Company records, mostly to deny the status of Ligeex or of Tsimshian cohesion, they have not addressed the bias in these accounts or their own ethnocentric notions of how they think the Tsimshian confederacy should have functioned (cf. Dean 1993, n.d.; Alexcee n.d.).

12. This Nishga woman chief was Neshaki, whose sister was married to Clah or T'amuks, baptized as Arthur Wellington, the man who taught Tsimshian to William Duncan. Her Christian name was Martha, but it was seldom used. Usually, she is called "Mrs. McNeill" in the records. After her marriage, she maintained her own trading network on the Nass River, extending the reach of Fort Simpson into the interior.

Barbeau (1951:124, song 27), who purchased Sagewan's pole after his death, records the song used to shame Neshaki, although Barbeau gives her name as Weeyae and that of her brother as Neeskinwaetk.

13. Maud (1982:55–59) summarizes these involvements of Chief Mountain, including scattered details such as his conversion to Christianity after his privileged ability to handle fire and red hot iron failed him.

14. Matthew Johnson told Homer Barnett (1940:[book 1]:12) that Clah, his mother's brother, was from Klemtu, a brother to Lans and Lag̲ax'niits, ranking chiefs there. Clah was called Laadex (?) as a boy and T'amuks as a man. Other sources report that, just before Duncan arrived, Clah killed a woman suspected of sorcery and had to go into hiding. This gave him an incentive to affiliate with powerful and protective outsiders and to teach Duncan the language.

15. Throughout recent history, the holders of the Ligeex name have initially allied themselves with Europeans. As earlier chiefs of this name aided the Hudson's Bay Company, so later ones helped Duncan and other foreigners, at least for a time.

16. Duncan substituted the Beaver for the Eagle because, as modern Tsimshian joke, he was a businessman who understood what beaver pelts did for the people.

17. At Kitkatla, an Anglican town, Hale, the high chief, was installed by the local bishop.

18. Court decisions are anachronistic in that they rely on white (or at least British) supremacy beliefs about notions of "discovery," thus denying aboriginal rights. Despite rather humane programs for First Nations initiated by James Douglas, the province continues the arrogance of Joseph Trutch.

Mobilizing to fight for their land claims, Nishga Christians produced the famous "Nishga Petition" of 1913, affirming their sovereignty within British Columbia and Canada (LaViolette 1973; Tennant 1990). In the 1973 Calder Decision, six of the seven justices of the Supreme Court of Canada ruled that the Nishga had had aboriginal title, and three further concluded that the nation retained land title. A draw, this split judgment meant "the Land Question was an issue to be negotiated between us [Nisga'a] and the governments of Canada and BC" (Nisga'a Tribal Council 1992:20). In 1975, the Nishga reaffirmed this position in the Nishga Declaration, and on 12 January 1976 began negotiations with other governments. In further support of their claims, they raised the Unity Pole at New Aiyansh in 1977, which was carved with emblems of the major crests.

In 1991, the Gitksan and Wet'suwet'en (Carrier) of the upper Skeena lost their case for the recognition of their sovereign authority and land claims in the provincial court, which showed little sympathy for or understanding of the profound cultural differences that the natives brought to the case (Bruce Miller 1992; Cassidy 1992; Marsden and Monet 1992; Monet and Skanu'u 1992).

19. Barbeau called Tate a commoner, but given his relationship to Clah, that seems unlikely. Instead, Tate may have stood apart from the Coast Tsimshian nobility because of his links with the Southern Tsimshian. While not of the royalty, Tate certainly qualified as noble.

20. For the record, Barbeau actually arrived at the very end of 1914.

21. Beynon and Susman were briefly engaged.

22. Kitwankool recently returned to their prior name of Gitanyow. Among the motivations for recording their town traditions were the growing momentum of Nishga and Gitksan land claims, which conflict with their own.

23. While ergativity is a common feature of Australian languages, it has a more limited distribution elsewhere in the world, with Tsimshian being one of its prime American examples.

5. CONCLUSIONS

1. This association of spider, web, and thought (from the heart) is nearly universal (Miller 1980a, 1980b).

2. Indeed, according to this logic, the Tsimshian are to the Tlingit as the Haida are to the Tsimshian, in terms of creativity and magical power.

3. It may prove significant that in the southern Tsimshian town of Hartley Bay, where epics of the Eagle crest have ties with the Haida, this tribe is known as "people of the cane."

4. Similarly, the epitaph on William Duncan's tombstone is "He Brought Us Light."

# References

Abbott, Donald, ed.

    1981    The World Is As Sharp As a Knife: An Anthology in Honor of Wilson Duff. Victoria: British Columbia Provincial Museum.

Ackerman, Charles

    1975    A Tsimshian Oedipus. Proceedings of the Second Congress of the Canadian Ethnology Society, vol. 1, 65–85. National Museums of Canada, Mercury Series, Ethnology Service Papers 28. Ottawa.

    1982    A Small Problem of Fish Bones. In The Logic of Culture: Advances in Structural Theory and Methods, edited by Ino Rossi, 113–26. South Hadley, Mass.: J. F. Bergin.

Adams, John

    1973    The Gitksan Potlatch: Population Flux, Resource Ownership, and Reciprocity. Toronto: Holt, Rinehart, and Winston of Canada.

    1974    Dialectics and Contingency in "The Story of Asdiwal": An Ethnographic Note. In The Unconscious in Culture: The Structuralism of Claude Lévi-Strauss in Perspective, edited by Ino Rossi, 170–78. New York: E. P. Dutton and Co.

Alexcee, Fred

    n.d.    Drawings. Calgary: Glenbow Alberta Museum.

Allaire, Louis, George MacDonald, and Richard Inglis

    1979    Gitlaxdzawk: Ethnohistory and Archaeology. In Skeena River Prehistory, edited by Richard Inglis and George MacDonald, 53–166. National Museums of Canada, Mercury Series, Archaeological Survey of Canada 87. Ottawa.

Arctander, John

1909    Apostle of Alaska: The Story of William Duncan of Metlakahtla. New York: Fleming H. Revell Co.

Arima, Eugene

1983    The West Coast People: The Nootka of Vancouver Island and Cape Flattery. British Columbia Provincial Museum, Special Publication 6. Victoria.

Barbeau, Marius

1928    The Downfall of Temlaham. Toronto: Macmillan Company of Canada.

1929    Totem Poles of the Gitksan, Upper Skeena River, British Columbia. National Museums of Canada, Bulletin 61, Anthropological Series 12. Ottawa.

1950    Totem Poles. 2 vols. National Museums of Canada, Bulletin 119, Anthropological Series 30. Ottawa.

1951    Tsimshian Songs. *In* The Tsimshian: Their Arts and Music, 97–280. Proceedings of the American Ethnological Society 18. New York: J. J. Augustin.

1958    Medicine-Men of the North Pacific Coast. National Museums of Canada, Bulletin 152, Anthropology Series 42. Ottawa.

1961    Tsimsyan Myths. National Museums of Canada, Bulletin 174, Anthropological Series 51. Ottawa.

Barbeau, Marius, and William Beynon

1987a    Tsimshian Narratives 1: Tricksters, Shamans and Heroes. Edited by John J. Cove and George F. MacDonald. Canadian Museum of Civilization, Mercury Series, Directorate Paper 3. Ottawa.

1987b    Tsimshian Narratives 2: Trade and Warfare. Edited by George F. MacDonald and John J. Cove. Canadian Museum of Civilization, Mercury Series, Directorate Paper 3. Ottawa.

Barnett, Homer G.

1940    Tsimshian fieldnotes. Special Collections, University of British Columbia Library, Vancouver.

1942    Applied Anthropology in 1860. Applied Anthropology 1(3):19–32.

Beynon, William

1941    Tsimshians of Metlakatla, Alaska. American Anthropologist 43:83–88.

mss.    Beynon manuscripts. Special Collections, Butler Library, Columbia University, New York. Microform in four reels by Microfilming Corporation of America, 1980.

Boas, Franz

1895    Indianische Sagen von der nord-pacifischen Kuste Amerikas. Berlin: A. Asher and Co.

1902    Tsimshian Texts, Nass River Dialect. Smithsonian Institution, Bureau of American Ethnology Bulletin 27. Washington, D.C.

1911    Tsimshian. *In* Handbook of American Indian Languages, edited by Franz Boas, vol. 1, 283–422. Smithsonian Institution, Bureau of American Ethnology Bulletin 40. Washington, D.C.

1912    Tsimshian Texts, New Series. Publications of the American Ethnological Society 3. Leyden, The Netherlands: E. J. Brill.

1916    Tsimshian Mythology, Based on Texts Recorded by Henry Tate. Smithsonian Institution, Thirty-First Annual Report of the Bureau of American Ethnology for the Years 1909–1910. Washington, D.C.

1966    Kwakiutl Ethnography. Edited by Helen Codere. Chicago: University of Chicago Press.

1974    Indian Legends of the North Pacific Coast of America. Translated by Dietrich Bertz. Victoria: British Columbia Indian Language Project.

Boelscher, Marianne

1988    The Curtain Within: Haida Social and Mythical Discourse. Vancouver: University of British Columbia Press.

Bolt, Clarence

1992    Thomas Crosby and the Tsimshian: Small Shoes for Feet Too Large. Vancouver: University of British Columbia Press.

Campbell, Kenneth

1984    Hartley Bay, British Columbia: A History. *In* The Tsimshian: Images of the Past, Views for the Present, edited by Margaret Seguin, 3–26. Vancouver: University of British Columbia Press.

1993    North Coast Odyssey: The Inside Passage from Port Hardy to Prince Rupert. Victoria: Sono Nis Press.

Carlson, Roy, ed.

1983    Indian Art Traditions of the Northwest Coast. Burnaby, B.C.: Simon Fraser University, Archaeology Press.

Cassidy, Frank

1992    Aboriginal Title in British Columbia: Delgamuukw v. The Queen. Lantzville, B.C.: Oolican Books.

Clayton, Daniel Wright

1989    Geographies of the Lower Skeena, 1830–1920. Master's thesis, University of British Columbia, Vancouver.

Compton, Brian

1993    'Real Trees' and 'Real Berries': Knowledge and Usage of Plants and Fungi among the Southern Tsimshian (Kitasoo). Unpublished manuscript.

Compton, Brian, and Marie-Lucie Tarpent

1994    Tsimshianic Animal Names, with Notes on Their Referents, Distributions, and Origins. Papers for the 29th International Conference on Salish and Neighboring Languages, 11–13 August. Pablo, Mont.: Salish Kootenai College.

Coupland, Gary

1988    Prehistoric Cultural Change at Kitselas Canyon. Ottawa: Canadian Museum of Civilization.

Cove, John

1976    Back to Square One: A Re-Examination of Tsimshian Cross-Cousin Marriage. Anthropologica 18:153–78.

1985    A Detailed Inventory of the Barbeau Northwest Coast Files. National Museum of Man, Mercury Series, Canadian Centre for Folk Studies Paper 54. Ottawa.

1987    Shattered Images: Dialogues and Meditations on Tsimshian Narratives. Carleton University Library Series 139. Ottawa.

Crumrine, N. Ross, and Marjorie Halpin, eds.

1983    The Power of Symbols: Masks and Masquerade in the Americas. Vancouver: University of British Columbia Press.

Cybulski, Jerome

1992    A Greenville Burial Ground: Human Remains and Mortuary Elements in British Columbia Coast Prehistory. Canadian Museum of Civilization, Mercury Series, Archaeological Survey of Canada 146. Ottawa.

Dauenhauer, Nora Marks

1995    Tlingit *At.oow:* Traditions and Concepts. *In* The Spirit Within: Northwest Coast Native Art from the John H. Hauberg Collection, 21–29, 30–90. New York: Rizzoli and Seattle Art Museum.

Dauenhauer, Nora Marks, and Richard Dauenhauer

1987    Haa Shuka, Our Ancestors: Tlingit Oral Narratives. Classics in Tlingit Oral Literature 1. Seattle: University of Washington Press.

1990    Haa Tuwunaagu Yis, For Healing Our Spirit: Tlingit Oratory. Classics in Tlingit Oral Literature 2. Seattle: University of Washington Press.

Dean, Jonathan

1993    'Rich Men', 'Big Powers', and Wastelands—The Tlingit-Tsimshian Border of the Northern Pacific Littoral, 1779 to 1867. Ph.D. diss., University of Chicago.

n.d.    "Those Rascally Spackaloids": The Rise of Gispaxlot Hegemony at Fort Simpson, 1832 to 1840, and "My Canoe Was Full of People—but It Capsized—and all the People Lost but Myself": The Rise and Fall of Legaic, 1840 to 1865. Unpublished manuscripts.

Dorsey, George A.

1897    The Geography of the Tsimshian Indians. American Antiquarian 19: 276–82.

Drucker, Philip

1940    Kwakiutl Dancing Societies. University of California Anthropological Records 2(6). Berkeley.

Duff, Wilson

1959    Histories, Territories, and Laws of the Kitwankool. Anthropology in British Columbia, Memoir 4. Victoria.

1961    Problems in the Interpretations of Marius Barbeau's Tsimshian Materials. Paper given at the 14th Annual Northwest Anthropological Conference, Vancouver.

1964a   Contributions of Marius Barbeau to West Coast Ethnology. Anthropologica 6:63–96.

1964b    The Indian History of British Columbia, vol. 1: Impact of the White Man. Anthropology in British Columbia, Memoir 5. Victoria.

1975    Images, Stone, B.C.: Thirty Centuries of Northwest Coast Indian Sculpture. Saanichton, B.C.: Hancock House.

1981    The World Is As Sharp As A Knife: Meaning in Northern Northwest Coast Art. *In* The World Is As Sharp As a Knife: An Anthology in Honor of Wilson Duff, edited by Donald Abbot, 209–24. Victoria: British Columbia Provincial Museum.

Dunn, John A.

1978    A Practical Dictionary of the Coast Tsimshian Language. National Museums of Canada, Mercury Series, Canadian Ethnology Service Paper 42. Ottawa.

1979a    A Reference Grammar for the Coast Tsimshian Language. Ottawa: National Museums of Canada, Mercury Series, Canadian Ethnology Service Paper 55. Ottawa.

1979b    Tsimshian Internal Relations Reconsidered: Southern Tsimshian. *In* The Victoria Conference on Northwestern Languages (4–5 November 1976), Heritage Record 4, edited by Barbara S. Efrat, 62–82. Victoria: British Columbia Provincial Museum.

1984a    International Matri-moieties: The North Maritime Province of the North Pacific Coast. *In* The Tsimshian: Images of the Past, Views for the Present, edited by Margaret Seguin, 99–109. Vancouver: University of British Columbia Press.

1984b    Some Ethnopoetic Features of Dorothy Brown's Soaban. *In* Mid-America Linguistic Conference Papers, edited by David Rood. Boulder: Department of Linguistics, University of Colorado.

1984c    Tsimshian Grandchildren: Redistributive Mechanism in Personal Property Inheritance. *In* The Tsimshian and Their Neighbors of the North Pacific Coast, edited by Jay Miller and Carol Eastman, 36–57. Seattle: University of Washington Press.

1995    Sm'algyax. A Reference Dictionary and Grammar of the Coast Tsimshian Language. Seattle: University of Washington Press for the Sealaska Heritage Foundation.

Dunn, John A., and Luceen Dunn

1972    An Equivalence Cycle for Kitkatla Kin-Status Terms. Anthropological Linguistics 14:240–54.

Emmons, George T.

1921    Slate Mirrors of the Tsimshian. Museum of the American Indian, Indian Notes and Monographs, n.s. 15. New York.

1991    The Tlingit Indians. Edited with additions by Frederica de Laguna. Seattle: University of Washington Press.

Farber, Carol

1984    Afterword: Time in a Box. *In* The Tsimshian: Images of the Past, Views for the Present, edited by Margaret Seguin, 309–18. Vancouver: University of British Columbia Press.

Fenton, William N.
1987    The False Faces of the Iroquois. Norman: University of Oklahoma Press.

Fisher, Robin
1977    Contact and Conflict: Indian-European Relations in British Columbia, 1774–1890. Vancouver: University of British Columbia Press.

Fiske, Jo-Anne
1991    Colonization and the Decline of Women's Status: The Tsimshian Case. Feminist Studies 17:309–33.

Fitzhugh, William H., and Aron Crowell
1988    Crossroads of Continents: Cultures of Siberia and Alaska. Washington, D.C.: Smithsonian Institution Press.

Fogelson, Raymond, and Amelia Bell
1983    Cherokee Booger Mask Tradition. *In* The Power of Symbols: Masks and Masquerade in the Americas, edited by N. Ross Crumrine and Marjorie Halpin, 48–69. Vancouver: University of British Columbia Press.

Garfield, Viola E.
1939    Tsimshian Clan and Society. University of Washington Publications in Anthropology 7 (3). Seattle.

1955a   Making a Bird or Chief's Rattle. Davidson Journal of Anthropology 1:155–64.

1955b   Making a Box Design. Davidson Journal of Anthropology 1:165–68.

1966    The Tsimshian and Their Neighbors. *In* The Tsimshian and Their Arts, edited by Viola E. Garfield and Paul S. Wingert, 1–70. Seattle: University of Washington Press.

Gisday Wa and Delgam Uukw
1989    The Spirit in the Land: The Opening Statement of the Gitksan and Wet'suwet'en Hereditary Chiefs in the Supreme Court of British Columbia, 11 May 1987. Gabriola, B.C.: Reflections.

Gitsegukla History
1979    Gitsegukla History (Anawkhl Gitsegukla). Privately printed.

Grumet, Robert
1975    Changes in Coast Tsimshian Redistributive Activities in the Fort Simpson Region of British Columbia, 1788–1862. Ethnohistory 22:295–318.

1982    Managing the Fur Trade: The Coast Tsimshian to 1862. *In* Affluence and Cultural Survival, edited by Richard Salisbury and Elisabeth Tooker, 26–39. Proceedings of the American Ethnological Society, 1981. St. Paul: West Publishing Co.

Guédon, Marie-Françoise
1984a   An Introduction to Tsimshian Worldview and Its Practitioners. *In* The Tsimshian: Images of the Past, Views for the Present, edited by Margaret Seguin, 137–59. Vancouver: University of British Columbia Press.

1984b    Tsimshian Shamanic Images. *In* The Tsimshian: Images of the Past, Views for the Present, edited by Margaret Seguin, 174–211. Vancouver: University of British Columbia Press.

Halpin, Marjorie

1973    The Tsimshian Crest System: A Study Based on Museum Specimens and the Marius Barbeau and William Beynon Field Notes. Ph.D. diss., University of British Columbia, Vancouver.

1978    William Beynon, Ethnographer: Tsimshian, 1888–1958. *In* American Indian Intellectuals, edited by Margot Liberty, 242–56. Proceedings of the American Ethnological Society, 1976. St. Paul: West Publishing Co.

1981    Seeing in Stone: Tsimshian Masking and the Twin Stone Masks. *In* The World Is As Sharp As a Knife: An Anthology in Honor of Wilson Duff, edited by Donald Abbot, 269–88. Victoria: British Columbia Provincial Museum.

1984    The Structure of Tsimshian Totemism. *In* The Tsimshian and Their Neighbors of the North Pacific Coast, edited by Jay Miller and Carol Eastman, 16–35. Seattle: University of Washington Press.

1994    A Critique of the Boasian Paradigm for Northwest Coast Art. Culture 14:5–16.

n.d.    Masks As Metaphors of Anti-Structure. Unpublished manuscript.

Halpin, Marjorie, and Margaret Seguin

1990    Tsimshian Peoples: Southern Tsimshian, Coast Tsimshian, Nishga, and Gitksan. *In* Northwest Coast, edited by Wayne Suttles. Handbook of North American Indians, vol. 7:267–84. Washington, D.C.: Smithsonian Institution.

Harris, E. A.

1990    Spokeshute: Skeena River Memory. Victoria, B.C.: Orca Book Publishers.

Harris, Walter

1976    Visitors Who Never Left: The Origin of the People of Damelahamid. Vancouver: University of British Columbia Press.

Hartley Bay School

1985a    Gitḵa'ata Crests: A Coloring Book. Prince Rupert: School District 52.

1985b    Hartley Bay, 100 Years: A Photo Album Published for the Centennial of the Village. Prince Rupert School District 52.

1985c    Hartley Bay Clans. Prince Rupert School District 52.

1987a    The People of the Cane. Prince Rupert School District 52.

1987b    The People of the Cane: Teacher's Guide. Prince Rupert School District 52.

Hawthorn, Harry, Cyril Belshaw, and S. Jamieson

1958    The Indians of British Columbia: A Study of Contemporary Social Adjustment. Berkeley: University of California Press.

Helms, Mary

1988    Ulysses' Sail: An Ethnographic Odyssey of Power, Knowledge, and Geographical Distance. Princeton: Princeton University Press.

Hindle, Lonnie, and Bruce Rigsby
  1973   A Short Practical Dictionary of the Gitksan Language. Northwest Anthropological Research Notes 7. Moscow, Idaho.

Holm, Bill
  1965   Northwest Coast Indian Art: An Analysis of Form. Seattle: University of Washington Press.
  1987   Spirit and Ancestor: A Century of Northwest Coast Indian Art at the Burke Museum. Seattle: University of Washington Press.

Iglauer, Edith
  1988   Fishing with John. Madiera Park, B.C.: Harbour Publishing.

Inglis, Richard, and George MacDonald
  1979   Skeena River Prehistory. National Museum of Canada, Mercury Series, Archaeological Survey of Canada 87. Ottawa.

Jensen, Allan
  1980   A Structural Approach to the Tsimshian Raven Myths: Lévi-Strauss on the Beach. Anthropologica 22 : 159–86.

Jensen, Vickie
  1992   Where the People Gather. Vancouver: University of British Columbia Press.

Jonaitis, Aldona
  1986   Art of the Northern Tlingit. Seattle: University of Washington Press.

Jopling, Carol
  1989   The Coppers of the Northwest Coast Indians: Their Origin, Development, and Possible Antecedents. Transactions of the American Philosophical Society 79(1). Philadelphia.

Kan, Sergei
  1989   Symbolic Immortality: The Tlingit Potlatch of the Nineteenth Century. Washington, D.C.: Smithsonian Institution Press.

Knight, Rolf
  1978   Indians at Work: An Informal History of Native American Labour in British Columbia, 1858–1930. Vancouver: New Star Books.

Laforet, Andrea
  1984   Tsimshian Basketry. *In* The Tsimshian: Images of the Past, Views for the Present, edited by Margaret Seguin, 215–80. Vancouver: University of British Columbia Press.

Large, R. G.
  1981   Skeena: River of Destiny. Sidney, B.C.: Gray's Publishing Ltd.

LaViolette, Forrest
  1973   The Struggle for Survival: Indian Cultures and the Protestant Ethic in British Columbia. Toronto: University of Toronto Press.

Leach, Edmund, ed.
  1967   The Structural Study of Myth and Totemism. London: Tavistock Publications.

Levi, Jerome

1978    Wii'pay: The Living Rocks—Ethnographic Notes on Crystal Magic among Some California Yumans. Journal of California Anthropology 5:42–52.

Lévi-Strauss, Claude

1967    The Story of Asdiwal. Translated by Nicholas Mann. *In* The Structural Study of Myth and Totemism, edited by Edmund Leach, 1–47. London: Tavistock Publications.

1982    The Way of the Masks. Translated by Sylvia Modelski. Seattle: University of Washington Press.

1983    Structural Anthropology, vol. 2. Translated by Monique Layton. Chicago: University of Chicago Press.

McClaren, Carol

1978    Moment of Death: Gift of Life. A Reinterpretation of the Northwest Coast Image "Hawk." Anthropologica 20:65–90.

n.d.    After Our Eyes Close: Seeing and Contemplating the Chief's Rattle; Towards a Hermeneutic of Visual Images. Unpublished manuscript.

MacDonald, George

1979    Kitwanga Fort National Historic Site, Skeena River, British Columbia: Historical Research and Analysis of Structural Remains. Ottawa: National Museum of Man.

1981    Cosmic Equations in Northwest Coast Indian Art. *In* The World Is As Sharp As a Knife: An Anthology in Honor of Wilson Duff, edited by Donald Abbot, 225–38. Victoria: British Columbia Provincial Museum.

1984a   The Epic of Nekt: The Archaeology of Metaphor. *In* The Tsimshian: Images of the Past, Views for the Present, edited by Margaret Seguin, 65–81. Vancouver: University of British Columbia Press.

1984b   Painted Houses and Woven Blankets: Symbols of Wealth in Tsimshian Art and Myth. *In* The Tsimshian and Their Neighbors of the North Pacific Coast, edited by Jay Miller and Carol Eastman, 109–36. Seattle: University of Washington Press.

1984c   The Totem Poles and Monuments of Gitwangak Village. Parks Canada, Studies in Archaeology, Architecture, and History. Ottawa.

MacDonald, Joanne

1984    Gitwangak Village Life: A Museum Collection. Parks Canada, Studies in Archaeology, Architecture, and History. Ottawa.

McIlwraith, T. F.

1948    The Bella Coola Indians. 2 vols. Toronto: University of Toronto Press.

McNeary, Stephen

1976a   Tsimshian Matriliny As an Instrument of Alliance. Paper presented at the Northwest Coast Studies Conference, Simon Fraser University, 12–16 May 1976.

1976b   Where Fire Came Down. Social and Economic Life of the Niska. Ph.D. diss., Bryn Mawr College, Bryn Mawr, Pa.

Makarius, Laura

1983    The Mask and the Violation of Taboo. *In* The Power of Symbols: Masks and Masquerade in the Americas, edited by N. Ross Crumrine and Marjorie Halpin, 191–203. Vancouver: University of British Columbia Press.

Marsden, Susan

n.d.    Controlling the Flow of Furs: Northcoast Nations and the Maritime Fur Trade. Unpublished manuscript.

Marsden, Namaste, and Don Monet

1992    Daxgyet. Smithers, B.C.: See-More Print.

Matson, Richard, and Gary Coupland

1995    The Prehistory of the Northwest Coast. San Diego: Academic Press.

Maud, Ralph

1982    A Guide to B.C. Indian Myth and Legend: A Short History of Myth-Collecting and A Survey of Published Texts. Vancouver: Talonbooks.

1989    The Henry Tate–Franz Boas Collaboration on Tsimshian Mythology. American Ethnologist 16:158–62.

1993    The Porcupine Hunter and Other Stories: The Original Tsimshian Texts of Henry Tate. Vancouver: Talonbooks.

Meilleur, Helen

1980    A Pour of Rain: Stories from a West Coast Fort. Victoria, B.C.: Sono Nis Press.

Milburn, Maureen

1986    Louis Shotridge and the Objects of Everlasting Esteem. *In* Raven's Journey: The World of Alaska's Native People, edited by Susan Kaplan and Kristin Barsness, 54–77. Philadelphia: University Museum of the University of Pennsylvania.

Miller, Bruce, ed.

1992    Anthropology and History in the Courts. BC Studies (special issue 95).

Miller, Jay

1978    Moiety Birth. Northwest Anthropological Research Notes 13:45–50.

1979    A Struckon Model of Delaware Culture and the Positioning of Mediators. American Ethnologist 6:791–802.

1980a   High-Minded High Gods in Native North America. Anthropos 75:916–19.

1980b   The Matter of the (Thoughtful) Heart: Centrality, Focality, or Overlap. Journal of Anthropological Research 36:338–42.

1981a   Moieties and Cultural Amnesia: Manipulations of Knowledge in a Pacific Northwest Coast Native Community. Arctic Anthropology 18:23–32.

1981b   Tsimshian Moieties and Other Clarifications. Northwest Anthropological Research Notes 16(2):148–64. Moscow, Idaho.

1983a   Basin Religion and Theology: A Comparative Study of Power (*Puha*). Journal of California and Great Basin Anthropology 5:66–86.

1983b   Numic Religion: An Overview of Power in the Great Basin of Native North America. Anthropos 78:337–54.

1984a    Feasting with the Southern Tsimshian. *In* the Tsimshian: Images of the Past, Views for the Present, edited by Margaret Seguin, 27–39. Vancouver: University of British Columbia Press.

1984b    Introduction. *In* The Tsimshian and Their Neighbors of the North Pacific Coast, edited by Jay Miller and Carol Eastman, xi–xxii. Seattle: University of Washington Press.

1984c    Tsimshian Religion in Historical Perspective. *In* The Tsimshian and Their Neighbors of the North Pacific Coast, edited by Jay Miller and Carol Eastman, 137–47. Seattle: University of Washington Press.

1988    Viola Garfield. *In* Directory of Women Anthropologists: A Biographical Dictionary, edited by Ute Gacs, Aisha Khan, Jerrie McIntyre, and Ruth Weinbery, 109–14. Westport, Conn.: Greenwood Press.

1989    An Overview of Northwest Coast Mythology. Northwest Anthropological Research Notes 23(2): 125–41. Moscow, Idaho.

1992    North Pacific Ethnoastronomy. *In* Earth and Sky: Visions of the Cosmos in Native American Folklore, edited by Ray Williamson and Claire Farrer, 193–306. Albuquerque: University of New Mexico Press.

1995    Review of The Porcupine Hunter and Other Stories: The Original Tsimshian Texts of Henry Tate. Anthropological Linguistics 37: 114–16.

Miller, Jay, and Carol Eastman

1984    The Tsimshian and Their Neighbors of the North Pacific Coast. Seattle: University of Washington Press.

Mitchell, Donald

1981    Sebassa's Men. *In* The World Is As Sharp As a Knife: An Anthology in Honor of Wilson Duff, edited by Donald Abbot, 79–86. Victoria: British Columbia Provincial Museum.

1983    Tribes and Chiefdoms of the Northwest Coast: The Tsimshian Case. *In* The Evolution of Martime Cultures on the Northeast and Northwest Coasts of America, edited by Ronald Nash, 57–64. Simon Fraser University (British Columbia), Department of Archaeology Publications 11.

Monet, Don (Niis Biins), and Skanu'u (Ardythe Wilson)

1992    Colonialism on Trial: Indigenous Land Rights and the Gitksan and Wet'-suwet'en Sovereignty Case. Gabriola Island, B.C.: New Society Publishers.

Mulder, Jean

1987    Ergativity in Coast Tsimshian (Sm'algyax). Ph.D. diss., University of California at Los Angeles.

Munn, Nancy

1986    The Fame of Gawa: A Symbolic Study of Value Transformation in a Massim (Papua New Guinea) Society. Cambridge: Cambridge University Press.

Murray, Peter

1985    The Devil and Mr. Duncan: A History of the Two Metlakatlas. Victoria, B.C.: Sono Nis Press.

Needham, Rodney

   1973    Right and Left: Essays in Dual Symbolic Classification. Chicago: University of Chicago Press.

Niblack, Albert P.

   1890    The Coast Indians of Southern Alaska and Northern British Columbia. *In* Report of the U.S. National Museum, Annual Report of the Board of Regents of the Smithsonian Institution for 1888, 225–386. Washington, D.C.

Nisga'a Tribal Council

   1992    Nisga'a: People of the Mighty River. New Aiyansh, B.C.: Nisga'a Nation.

   1993    Nisga'a: People of the Nass River. Vancouver: Douglas and McIntyre.

Olson, Ronald L.

   1967    Social Structure and Social Life of the Tlingit in Alaska. University of California Anthropological Records 26(1). Berkeley.

Pierce, William H.

   1933    From Potlatch to Pulpit, Being the Autobiography of the Rev. William Henry Pierce. Edited by J. P. Hicks. Vancouver, B.C.: The Vancouver Bindery.

Prince Rupert School District 52

   1992a    Adawga Gant Wilaaytga Gyetga Suwildook: Rituals of Respect and the Sea Otter Trade. Told by Henry Reeves. Teachings of Our Grandfathers (Suwilaay'msga Na G̲a'niiyatgm) 2. Prince Rupert: Prince Rupert School District 52.

   1992b    Conflict at Gits'ilaasü. Teachings of Our Grandfathers (Suwilaay'msga Na G̲a'niiyatgm) 6. Prince Rupert: Prince Rupert School District 52.

   1992c    Fort Simpson, Fur Fort at Laxłgu'alaams. The Teachings of Our Grandfathers (Suwilaay'msga Na G̲a'niiyatgm) 4. Prince Rupert: Prince Rupert School District 52.

   1992d    Na Amwaaltga Ts'msiyeen: The Tsimshian, Trade, and the Northwest Coast Economy. Teachings of Our Grandfathers (Suwilaay'msga Na G̲a'niiyatgm) 1. Prince Rupert: Prince Rupert School District 52.

   1992e    Na maalsga Walps Nisłgümiik: The Story of the House of Nisłgumiik. Teachings of Our Grandfathers (Suwilaay'msga Na G̲a'niiyatgm) 7. Prince Rupert: Prince Rupert School District 52.

   1992f    Ndeh Wuwaal Kuudeex A Spaga Laxyuubm Ts'msiyeen: When the Aleuts Were on Tsimshian Territory. Teachings of Our Grandfathers (Suwilaay'msga Na G̲a'niiyatgm) 5. Prince Rupert: Prince Rupert School District 52.

   1992g    Saaban: The Tsimshian and Europeans Meet. Told by Dorothy Brown. Teachings of Our Grandfathers (Suwilaay'msga Na G̲a'niiyatgm) 3. Prince Rupert: Prince Rupert School District 52.

Riley, Linda

   1988    Marius Barbeau's Photographic Collection: The Nass River. Canadian Museum of Civilization, Mercury Series, Canadian Ethnology Service Paper 109. Ottawa.

Rosman, Abraham, and Paula Rubel
  1971    Feasting with Mine Enemy: Rank and Exchange among Northwest Coast
          Societies. New York: Columbia University Press.
Sapir, Edward
  1915    A Sketch of the Social Organization of the Nass River Tribes. Canadian
          Geological Survey, Museum Bulletin 19, Anthropological Series 7. Ottawa.
Schulenberg, A. C. Graf von der
  1982    Tsimshian Grammar. 2 vols. Translated by Virginia Flaherty. University of
          Northern Colorado, Museum of Anthropology, Occasional Papers, Linguis-
          tic Series 8. Greeley, Colo.
Seguin, Margaret
  1984a   Rich Foods and Real People: A Problem with Tsimshian Food Categories
          in Boas' *Tsimshian Mythology*. Paper presented at the Nineteenth Interna-
          tional Conference on Salish and Neighboring Languages, 16–18 August,
          Victoria, B.C.
  1985    Interpretive Contexts for Traditional and Current Coast Tsimshian Feasts.
          National Museum of Man, Mercury Series, Canadian Ethnology Service
          Paper 98. Ottawa.
  n.d.    Coast Tsimshian Cedar Bark Basketry and Mats. Report to the National
          Museum of Canada, Ottawa.
Seguin, Margaret, ed.
  1984b   The Tsimshian: Images of the Past, Views for the Present. Vancouver: Uni-
          versity of British Columbia Press.
Shane, Audrey
  1984    Power in Their Hands: The Gitsontk. *In* The Tsimshian: Images of the Past,
          Views for the Present, edited by Margaret Seguin, 160–73. Vancouver:
          University of British Columbia Press.
Simonsen, Bjorn
  1973    Archaeological Investigation in the Hecate Strait–Milbanke Sound Area of
          British Columbia. National Museums of Canada, Mercury Series, Archae-
          ological Survey of Canada 13. Ottawa.
Spier, Leslie
  1931    Historical Interrelation of Culture Traits: Franz Boas' Study of Tsimshian
          Mythology. *In* Methods in Social Science: A Case Book, edited by Stuart
          Rice, 449–57. Chicago: University of Chicago Press.
Stewart, Frances L.
  1975    The Seasonal Variability of Fish Species Used by the Coast Tsimshians of
          Northern British Columbia. Syesis 8:375–88.
Stewart, Hilary
  1977    Indian Fishing: Early Methods on the Northwest Coast. Seattle: University
          of Washington Press.
Suttles, Wayne
  1990    Environment. *In* Northwest Coast, edited by Wayne Suttles. Handbook of

North American Indians, 7:16–29. Washington, D.C.: Smithsonian Institution Press.

Swanton, John R.

1909   Contributions to the Ethnology of the Haida. New York: American Museum of Natural History Memoir 8(1).

Tarpent, Marie-Lucie

1982   Ergative and Accusative: A Single Representation of Grammatical Relations with Evidence from Nishga. Working Papers of the Linguistics Circle of the University of Victoria 2:50–106.

1983   The Evolution of the Nishga Counting System: A Window on Cultural Change. Working Papers of the Linguistics Circle of the University of Victoria 39:60–86.

Tennant, Paul

1990   Aboriginal Peoples and Politics: The Indian Land Question in British Columbia, 1849–1989. Vancouver: University of British Columbia Press.

Thomas, L. L., J. Z. Kronenfeld, and D. B. Kronenfeld

1976   Asdiwal Crumbles: A Critique of Lévi-Straussian Myth Analysis. American Ethnologist 3:147–73.

Tooker, Elizabeth

1968   Masking and Matrilineality in North America. American Anthropologist 70:1170–76.

Usher, Jean

1971   The Long Slumbering Offspring of Adam: The Evangelical Approach to the Tsimshian. Anthropologica 13:37–61.

1974   William Duncan of Metlakatla: A Victorian Missionary in British Columbia. National Museums of Canada, Publications in History 5. Ottawa.

Widerspach-Thor, Martine de

1981   The Equation of Copper. *In* The World Is As Sharp As a Knife: An Anthology in Honor of Wilson Duff, edited by Donald Abbott, 157–74. Victoria: British Columbia Provincial Museum.

Wingert, Paul

1966   Tsimshian Sculpture. *In* The Tsimshian and Their Arts, edited by Viola E. Garfield and Paul S. Wingert, 73–94. Seattle: University of Washington Press

# Index